A History of Music at
Christ Church Cathedral, Dublin

A History of Music at Christ Church Cathedral, Dublin

Barra Boydell

THE BOYDELL PRESS

First published 2004
The Boydell Press, Woodbridge

ISBN 1 84383 044 2

The Boydell Press is an imprint of Boydell & Brewer Ltd
PO Box 9, Woodbridge, Suffolk IP12 3DF, UK
and of Boydell & Brewer Inc.
PO Box 41026, Rochester, NY 14604–4126, USA
website: www.boydellandbrewer.com

A catalogue record for this book is available
from the British Library

Library of Congress Cataloging-in-Publication Data
Boydell, Barra.
  A history of music at Christ Church Cathedral, Dublin / Barra Boydell.
    p. cm.
Includes bibliographical references (p.) and index.
  ISBN 1–84383–044–2
1. Christ Church Cathedral (Dublin, Ireland) – History.   2. Church of
Ireland – Ireland – Dublin – Liturgy.   3. Church music – Ireland – Dublin.
4. Church music – Church of Ireland.   I. Title.
  ML3132.8.D83B69 2004
  781.71'3'00941835 – dc22   2003016908

This publication is printed on acid-free paper

Typeset by Pru Harrison, Woodbridge, Suffolk
Printed in Great Britain by
Antony Rowe Ltd, Chippenham, Wiltshire

Contents

Plates and Musical Examples

Foreword

'Not angels but Anglicans', the title of a 1970s book on Anglicanism, might be a fair summary of this splendid account of the music and musicians of Christ Church Cathedral. This writer has memories of angelic choirboys giving a deep bow to each member of the congregation on receiving back collection plates that were rather more valuable in themselves than in the amount of money that lay on them. He also has memories of organists and choirmen equally as grumpy as any of those listed in this history. Cathedrals may be houses of God but the people that run and serve them are only too human – with all the frailties to which humankind is prone.

Christ Church and St Patrick's, as Dr Boydell shows, are the only two Irish cathedrals that could ever compare with the great English cathedrals in the choral scale and the complex ordering of the liturgy, whether pre- or post-reformation. By skilfully combining their resources they managed to attract many of the best voices from the larger kingdom to Ireland's capital. Dublin in the eighteenth century was a musical city the equal of many in Europe.

Such peaks, we are shown, were usually short-lived. The Act of Union may have been intended to unite eternally the two kingdoms and the two churches but the church succumbed to disestablishment in 1870 and twenty-six of the counties became independent in 1922. The union deprived the city and the cathedral of the trappings of state, disestablishment removed its few remaining endowments and independence left it a tiny Anglican rump in an overwhelmingly catholic state. Yet against this must be remembered the mid-Victorian surge as the Roe restoration renewed the fabric and re-endowed the choir. So too must the vision of Dean Salmon never be forgotten in the reinvigoration of the music by the enforced change from boys and men to that of a mixed voice ensemble from 1975.

Through the vicissitudes of time and the anathemas of Ireland's turbulent history of bad religious tensions, Christ Church has moved to the relative serenity of the twenty-first century where choirs and church leaders move freely between each other's churches. Here music can bring together within the Anglican liturgy the ethereal sound of Palestrina, the rich magnificence of Haydn, the grand opulence of Stanford who learned his early musicianship in this place, or the modernisms of Tippett and Leighton.

Dr Boydell has already contributed significantly to the earlier volumes of the history of Christ Church, published to mark the second millennium. This volume puts us even further into his debt. As Anglicans, if not necessarily angels, the cathedral must aim to continue, not just what is best in church music, but what in any sphere will be counted superb.

John Paterson
Dean of Christ Church
Trinity Sunday, 15 June 2003

Preface

This history of music at Christ Church cathedral, Dublin, has evolved out of the chapters which I was invited to contribute to a history of the cathedral published in 2000.[1] As I began to research the cathedral's music history it soon became evident not only how extensive the documentary and musical sources were, but also how significant they were both for the history of music and society in Ireland, and also within the wider context of Anglican cathedral music. An edition of documents related to music and of selected anthems was published in 1999 as an ancillary volume to the Christ Church history project, and a CD recording of anthems was issued in the same year.[2] But a single-volume history with eight contributors also covering the history, liturgy, architecture, and archives meant that the space that could be devoted to the cathedral's musical history was necessarily limited. The subject demanded more extensive treatment. The present book answers this need, being very significantly expanded from what has appeared in the cathedral history and developing a number of aspects, some of which I have already explored in individual published papers.[3] This book not only does fuller justice to the musical history of an institution that has been in existence for nearly one thousand years, but it also acknowledges the unique role played by Christ Church cathedral within the religious, social and political history of Ireland and within the wider context of Anglican cathedrals. The greater emphasis accorded here to the period from the seventeenth to the nineteenth century reflects on the one hand the more extensive survival of records following the beginning of this period, and on the other hand that this is the period during which Christ Church cathedral was at the height of its status and influence. The institutional, administrative and architectural histories of the cathedral have been extensively covered in the recent cathedral history and associated volumes to which the interested reader is referred.[4] These aspects are only dealt with here inasmuch as is considered necessary to explain or provide an immediate context for the musical developments.

Since the pioneering works on English cathedral music by John Bumpus at the beginning of the twentieth century and later by Edmund Fellowes,[5] more recent publications have focused on specific periods or aspects, or on individual

---

[1] Milne, *Christ Church*.
[2] Barra Boydell, ed., *Music: Documents*; *Sing* (CD).
[3] See bibliography.
[4] Milne, *Christ Church*; ancillary volumes in the History of Christ Church, Dublin: Documents series: Gillespie, *Proctor's Accounts*; Mills, *Account Roll*; Gillespie, *First Chapter Act Book*; Refaussé & Lennon, *Registers*; Barra Boydell, ed., *Music: Documents*; *Sing* (CD); McEnery & Refaussé, *Deeds*; Stalley, *George Edmund Street*.
[5] Bumpus, *History*; Fellowes, *English Cathedral Music*.

cathedrals. In the latter case this has most commonly taken the form either of individual contributions to cathedral histories or of catalogues of music manuscripts.[6] In the specific area of Irish cathedral music the pioneer was again John Bumpus whose extended article appeared in two parts in 1900.[7] Virtually no further research was carried out in this field until the later twentieth century when Michael Hoeg published a brief history of music at Derry (Londonderry) cathedral and postgraduate work was carried out by Barbara McHugh and Joseph McKee on music at St Patrick's cathedral Dublin in the late nineteenth century and at Armagh cathedral respectively.[8] Harry Grindle's book published in 1988 outlined the history of music at Anglican cathedrals throughout Ireland at which a choral tradition has at some time flourished.[9] This, the first extended work on Irish cathedral music, has stimulated further research and provided a crucial reference for the present study, although the broad spread of its subject matter meant that no individual cathedral could be covered in great detail.[10]

The present book breaks new ground in providing a detailed history of music at an individual cathedral throughout its history while also linking this into the broader historical environment. The cathedral's music – its personnel, organisation, repertoire and instruments – forms the backbone of this study, but this musical activity was shaped by the social and historical contexts within which it took place. From the cathedral-priory of the Middle Ages, through the civic and state cathedral of the Protestant ascendancy, to being one of two cathedrals serving a dwindling Protestant minority in the capital city of an independent and overwhelmingly Catholic state, the cathedral's changing relationships with city and state will be seen to have had a direct bearing at different periods and in different ways on the cathedral's musical life. Christ Church has had a complex history, a cathedral neither wholly Irish nor wholly English, and unusual amongst Anglican cathedrals in being both a religious centre and, for much of its history, a focus for state and civic ceremony. This history of music at Christ Church cathedral, Dublin, is therefore far more than just a history of one relatively small cathedral within the larger Anglican tradition. As cathedral church to the capital city

---

6   Selected recent studies include Gatens, *Victorian Cathedral Music*; Payne, *Provision and Practice*; Spink, *Restoration*; Shaw, *Organists*. Contributions to cathedral histories include those by Roger Bowers and Nicholas Thistlethwaite in Owen, *Lincoln*, Bowers in Collinson *et al.*, *Canterbury*, and John Harper in Aylmer & Tiller, *Hereford*. Music catalogues of individual cathedrals include Crosby, *Catalogue* and Young, *Lichfield*. Selected articles on aspects of cathedral music are individually listed in the bibliography.

7   Bumpus, 'Irish Church Composers'.

8   Hoeg, *St Columb's*; McHugh, 'St Patrick's'; McKee, 'Armagh'.

9   Grindle, *Cathedral Music*.

10 Publications since Grindle which relate specifically or substantially to cathedral music in Ireland include (listed chronologically): Johnstone, 'Organ Music'; O'Keeffe, 'Sources', 'Score-Books'; Barra Boydell, *Music in Christ Church*, 'Archives', 'Prickers and Printers', *Music: Documents*; McCartney, *Organs*; Barra Boydell, 'Now that the Lord', chapters in Milne, *Christ Church*, 'Cathedral Music', 'A Bright Exception'; Gillen & Johnstone, *Anthology*; Barra Boydell, 'Manuscript Sources'. Malcomson, *Agar* includes important sections relating to music at Cashel and, to a lesser extent, Cloyne cathedrals in the eighteenth century. Postgraduate theses have included: O'Keeffe, 'Study'; Moran, 'Three Eighteenth Century Anthems'; Cunningham, 'Selected Eighteenth Century Anthems'; Donnelly, 'Woodward'; Sherwin, 'Stevenson'; Parker, 'Stewart'; Houston, 'Music Manuscripts'.

and the archdiocese of Dublin, Christ Church is central to the Anglican tradition in Ireland. This study also contributes to the broader history of cathedral music in Britain as well as Ireland, and to Irish musical, social and political history, illuminating aspects of the religious and political dynamics which have played such a major part in the historical relationship between Britain and Ireland.

Acknowledgements

First and foremost I am indebted to my fellow contributors to the Christ Church cathedral history published in 2000, without whom this present book would not have been written: Kenneth Milne who initiated the project and acted as general editor, Alan Fletcher, Raymond Gillespie, Stuart Kinsella, James Lydon, Raymond Refaussé, Roger Stalley, and also Geoffrey Hand, for their active support and encouragement. I also owe my particular thanks to the Very Revd John Paterson, dean of Christ Church (now retired), for his support and encouragement, to Raymond Refaussé and his staff at the Representative Church Body library, Susan Hood, Heather Smith and Mary Furlong, for patiently facilitating my research and handling my queries; and to Michael Adams and the staff of Four Courts Press who published the cathedral history and ancillary volumes. I would also like to acknowledge the assistance and support of Mark Duley, organist and choir master of Christ Church cathedral during the period of the writing of this book, and the individual members of the cathedral choir, and of Mark Bowyer and the administrative staff. The National University of Ireland, Maynooth, granted me a period of sabbatical leave which made the writing of this book possible. Unless otherwise acknowledged, I owe information relating to music at St Patrick's cathedral to Kerry Houston, and I am indebted to my colleagues in the music department at NUI Maynooth and to scholars and colleagues, postgraduate students, librarians and cathedral musicians past and present who provided information and comments, facilitated my research, and helped in so many other ways, none of whose names I hope I have omitted: Richard Andrewes, George Bannister, Billy Boucher, Roger Bowers, Marie Breen, Ann Buckley, Donald Burrows, Brian Crosby, Trevor Crowe, Carol Cunningham, Barbara Dagg, Julian Dawson, Eithne Donnelly, John Feeley, James Garratt, Gerard Gillen, Harry Grindle, Sue Hemmens, Nicola Horn, Jill Ivy and the staff of the Dean and Chapter library Durham, Roy Johnston, Andrew Johnstone, Dean Philip Knowles of Cashel and the staff of the Bolton library, Colm Lennon, Muriel McCarthy and the staff of Marsh's library, Denise Neary, Emer Nestor, Maere O'Brien, Triona O'Hanlon, Lisa Parker, Malcolm Proud, Helen Roycroft, Peter Scott, Elaine Sherwin, Keith Sidwell, Eric Sweeney, Peter Sweeney, Nicholas Temperley, Leslie Whiteside, and the librarian and staff of the Department of Manuscripts at Trinity College Dublin. Ann Buckley, Kenneth Milne and Denise Neary provided many helpful comments on the earlier drafts of individual chapters; Andrew Robinson and Kerry Houston generously gave of their time to read and make detailed comments on the final draft of the full text, and without John Feeley's help I could not have completed the musical examples. I also wish to thank the editorial staff at Boydell & Brewer (to which company I am in no way related) for so ably seeing this volume through the press. Last but by no means least, I would like to thank my wife Irena and sons Oisín and Fergus for their patience and forbearance.

Publication of this book was generously supported by grants from the Publications Committee of NUI Maynooth, the dean and board of Christ Church cathedral, and the Standing Committee of the General Synod of the Church of Ireland. Its completion would not have been possible without the help of the music department at NUI Maynooth.

Excerpts from *Christ Church Cathedral: A History*, edited by Kenneth Milne (Dublin, 2000) appear by permission of Four Courts Press; text and musical examples 3.2, 3.3, 3.4 and 3.5 which previously appeared in my article ' "Now that the Lord hath Readvanc'd the Crown": Richard Hosier, Durham MS B.1 and the Early Restoration Anthem Repertoire at the Dublin Cathedrals', *Early Music* xxviii/2 (2000), pp. 238–251, by permission of Oxford University Press; text previously published in 'Cathedral Music, City and State: Music in Reformation and Political Change at Christ Church Cathedral, Dublin', *Music and Musicians in Renaissance Cities and Towns*, edited by Fiona Kisby (Cambridge, 2001), pp. 131–142, by permission of Cambridge University Press; text and musical examples 4.6 and 4.7 previously published in ' "A Bright Exception to the General Rule"? Musical Standards at Christ Church Cathedral Dublin in the Early Nineteenth Century', *Nineteenth Century British Music Studies ii*, edited by Jeremy Dibble and Bennett Zon (Aldershot, 2002), pp. 46–58, by kind permission of Ashgate publishers.

Illustrations are reproduced by permission of the following: Board of Christ Church Cathedral, Dublin (plate 8); Bodleian Library, University of Oxford (plates 3 and 4); Durham Cathedral (plate 6); Four Courts Press (plates 1, 9, 10); National Library of Ireland (plates 5, 9, back cover); Roger Stalley (plates 1, 2, 9); V & A Picture Library (plate 7).

Editorial Conventions

Quotations in the text are given in the original spelling except that abbreviations and contractions have been expanded and punctuation modernised. Deletions and insertions are not distinguished. Dates before 1751 are given new style with the year commencing on 1 January (for example, a document bearing the date 16 March 1619, or 16 March 1619/20, is referred to as 16 March 1620). Prices before 1826 are cited in Irish pounds unless otherwise stated (in 1826 the Irish and English (sterling) currencies were united, prices thereafter being in sterling).[1]

The location of manuscript and other primary sources is indicated in the footnote references with a library siglum or other abbreviation except in the case of materials in the archives of Christ Church and of St Patrick's cathedrals, designated C6/ and C2/ respectively, which are held in the library of the Representative Church Body, Dublin. Abbreviations and library sigla are listed before the bibliography. In cases where primary sources such as chapter books or proctor's accounts are neither foliated nor paginated, relevant dates are provided. Where archival sources have been published in modern editions, reference is made to these rather than to the manuscript source. Sources listed in the bibliography are referred to in the footnotes by author and short title.

---

[1] Irish currency broke with sterling in 1979 when Ireland, but not Britain, joined the European Monetary System.

Introduction

Religious and historical background

Cathedrals have long held a special place not only in the religious but also in the social and cultural lives of the cities of which they have formed such prominent architectural features since medieval times. Since the Reformation English cathedrals have also symbolised secular authority and the political establishment through the intimate association established by Henry VIII between church and monarchy. This association would manifest itself in cathedral music particularly between the later sixteenth and eighteenth centuries when the Chapel Royal provided the musical model which cathedrals sought to emulate. The study of music within the Anglican cathedral tradition therefore not only embraces matters of musical concern, but also draws on the broader social, cultural, and political environments within which the cathedrals have developed and evolved. Irish cathedrals of the Anglican tradition however differ in significant respects from their British counterparts. Although sharing essentially the same traditions, liturgy and structures as the Church of England, the Church of Ireland has always occupied a very different position in terms of its relationship with Irish society. Whereas the Church of England is a national religion representing the majority of the population, the Church of Ireland has never embraced more than a small minority of the Irish people despite wielding a disproportionate influence throughout much of its history and having custodianship of all the country's surviving medieval cathedrals.[1] The reasons for this anomalous situation can be traced back to the sixteenth century.

The Reformation coincided in Ireland with a more aggressive policy of conquest and settlement by England than had previously been the case.[2] Protestantism became closely identified with English control and settlement, and instead of the country as a whole adopting the religion of its rulers, as was the case elsewhere in Europe after the Reformation, religion largely became a signifier of political and ethnic difference.[3] Churches and cathedrals were anglicised and the public practice of Catholicism prohibited. The majority Catholic population was subjected to increasing repression and expected to worship in the established

---

1 Even at the height of its power as the established church during the eighteenth century, when the Catholic majority was subject to the penal laws, the Church of Ireland did not claim the allegiance of more than 10 per cent of the entire population of Ireland (Barnard, 'Church of Ireland', p. 112).

2 On the Reformation in Ireland see especially Ford, *Reformation*.

3 The situation was not however clear cut: although Protestantism was the religion of Ireland's rulers and widely identified with the British presence in Ireland before 1922, many Protestants did not support British rule. Indeed, the earliest concerted efforts to gain independence during the late eighteenth century were initiated and led by Irish Protestants.

church. By the later seventeenth and early eighteenth centuries the penal laws had been enacted whereby Catholics were excluded from public office and prohibited from owning land and having a political voice, a situation which encouraged the pragmatic conversion to Protestantism of a number of Gaelic landowners. In the late eighteenth and early nineteenth centuries the restrictions on the practice of Catholicism were relaxed (leading to Catholic emancipation in 1829), the first Catholic churches since the Reformation were built and the great majority of the Irish population could begin to practice its religion freely. The Protestant minority however continued to control the country's landed wealth and political power well into the later nineteenth century, by which time nationalist politics, increasingly identified with the resurgence of Catholicism, was beginning to change the political and religious climate. Following the independence in 1922 of the twenty-six counties which would comprise the later Republic of Ireland, the Church of Ireland represented little more than 5 per cent of the population of the new state.[4] However, within the six counties of Northern Ireland which have remained within the United Kingdom the Anglican community accounts for approximately 22 per cent of the population.[5] Any study of Irish cathedral music must therefore be understood within a very different historical environment from that which pertained in Britain. Even at the height of their wealth and influence from the seventeenth to the early nineteenth centuries it was only in the larger cities, most notably in Dublin, that cathedrals and their music could begin to approach the levels found in Britain. Elsewhere, rural Irish Protestant cathedrals are for the most part small and unassuming and, with occasional exceptions, have seldom managed to maintain more than a semblance of cathedral music traditions.[6] Outside the two Dublin cathedrals choral services today are only celebrated in a small number of the country's cathedrals (north and south), and in these for the most part only on Sundays.[7]

While the seat of the primate of all Ireland is in Armagh, the cathedral church of the Holy Trinity, Dublin, commonly called Christ Church, has traditionally held a pre-eminent position amongst Irish cathedrals.[8] Not only is it the cathedral of the capital city and archdiocese of Dublin, but from the sixteenth to the nineteenth centuries it served as the place of worship of the lords deputy and lords lieutenant, the representatives of the English crown who resided in Dublin Castle.[9] One of the more idiosyncratic features of Dublin's religious landscape is the existence of two cathedrals, Christ Church and St Patrick's, both belonging since the Reformation to the minority Protestant tradition. The origins of this

---

[4] In the 1926 census in the Irish Free State (subsequently the Republic of Ireland) there were 164,215 members of the Church of Ireland out of a total population of 2,971,992.

[5] 1971 census figure.

[6] See Grindle, *Cathedral Music* and Barra Boydell, 'Manuscript Sources'.

[7] Cathedrals outside Dublin with regular choral services, at least on Sundays, include Armagh, Belfast, Cork, [London]Derry, Kilkenny, Limerick and Waterford.

[8] Although most often referred to before the Reformation as Holy Trinity and thereafter increasingly but not exclusively as Christ Church, the latter name (by which it is generally known today) will be used throughout this book, irrespective of period.

[9] The chief governor of Ireland was referred to either as the lord deputy or lord lieutenant, the former title being more usual in the sixteenth and early seventeenth centuries, the latter from the later seventeenth century.

anomaly go back to the late twelfth century when John Cumin, archbishop of Dublin from 1182 to 1212, raised the church of St Patrick to the status of a collegiate church of secular canons. In itself this was not unusual and Cumin may not have had any thought in mind that St Patrick's should subsequently be raised to cathedral status. By the early thirteenth century monastic cathedrals like Christ Church were beginning to be considered as old fashioned, and Cumin may have wished to counteract the relative independence of the monastic chapter of Christ Church which was less susceptible to episcopal influence than a secular chapter would be. Whatever Cumin's reasons, it was his successor Henry of London who in c.1220 reconstituted St Patrick's as a full secular cathedral.[10]

Although Christ Church enjoyed preeminence as the diocesan cathedral and would later become recognised as the state cathedral, St Patrick's was more generously endowed. While the salary available to choirmen at either cathedral in later centuries was in itself generous by the standards of most English cathedrals, a system of pluralism developed from at least the earlier seventeenth century up to the late nineteenth century, it becoming customary for choirmen joining either one of the Dublin cathedral choirs to be granted a position at the other as well. The two cathedrals thus largely shared the one choir (the choral foundation at St Patrick's was however larger than that of Christ Church), choral services being organised in such a way that singers could serve in both cathedrals without a duplication of duties. With the possibility of earning two generous salaries it is not surprising that some of the finest singers were attracted from England. But although organists and masters of the choirboys did indeed often serve both cathedrals, the fact that this was not always the case reflects the degree of independence that existed between the two establishments notwithstanding the sharing of so many singers. Despite the two cathedrals being (and remaining) distinct institutions, each responding to its own dean and chapter, a history of music at Christ Church between the seventeenth and the nineteenth centuries is therefore to some extent also a history of music at St Patrick's.[11]

Following the introduction of Christianity into Ireland by St Patrick in the fifth century the Irish church developed as a system defined by monasticism rather than by diocesan bishoprics. The so-called 'Celtic' rite associated with this early Irish church persisted throughout most of the country until the later twelfth century.[12] Dublin however, founded by the Vikings as a trading base in the mid-ninth century, was essentially independent of the native Gaelic population.[13] Subsequently expelled by the local Irish kings of Brega and Leinster, the Vikings (or Hiberno-Norse) returned in 917 and re-established Dublin as a fortified trading port central to their domain of influence embracing the Irish Sea and the

---

10 Kinsella, 'Hiberno-Norse', pp. 49–50. On the origins of St Patrick's and the rivalries between the two cathedrals during the Middle Ages see Gwynn & Hadcock, *Religious Houses*, pp. 71–5; Hand, 'Two Cathedrals', 'Medieval Chapter of St Patrick's', 'Rivalry'.

11 For a period during the nineteenth century both cathedrals were united under one dean (see ch. 5). On music at St Patrick's see Grindle, *Cathedral Music*.

12 The traditional view of the early Irish church as purely monastic is however beginning to be questioned. See *OCIH*, pp. 382–3. On the music of the 'Celtic' rite see Buckley, 'Celtic Chant'.

13 On the early history and topography of Dublin, see especially Clarke, *Medieval Dublin* and Clarke, *Dublin*.

north of England including York. King Olaf (Amlaíb) Cuarán of Dublin converted to Christianity in 943. His son Sitriuc undertook a pilgrimage to Rome in 1028. Following his return he founded Christ Church in c.1030 close to the highest point of the medieval city, with Dúnán (Donatus) being created the first bishop of Dublin. Dúnán appears to have been consecrated by the archbishop of Canterbury, from whom subsequent bishops of Dublin during the eleventh and early twelfth centuries took their authority,[14] and the dedication of the new cathedral of Christ Church to the Holy Trinity (rather than to any local Irish saint) emphasised its links with Canterbury. Dúnán's successors as bishops of Dublin were trained as Benedictine monks in England: Bishop Pátraic (Patrick), who succeeded Dúnán in 1074, at Worcester cathedral-priory under St Wulfstan; Donngus (Donatus) at Canterbury where he was consecrated by Lanfranc in 1089; and Samuel, educated at St Alban's and consecrated by St Anselm at Winchester in 1096.[15] The close relationship between Dublin and Canterbury was evident in 1100 when Samuel was rebuked by Anselm for having expelled the monks of Canterbury from Christ Church and for giving away 'the books, vestments and ornaments of the church . . . [given by] the brothers, sons of the church of Canterbury'.[16] Under Benedictine rule at least for some of this period, Christ Church in the eleventh and early twelfth centuries was thus within the province of Canterbury rather than being part of the Irish church.

The twelfth century brought profound changes to Ireland in both the religious and the political fields, changes which would have a direct impact on Christ Church cathedral. For the first time the Irish church was organised along diocesan lines, bringing it into the continental European system,[17] but the position of Dublin initially remained unresolved: should it continue as a separate diocese under the rule of Canterbury or should it become part of the reformed Irish church? Eventually it was integrated into a national diocesan system at the synod of Kells-Mellifont in 1152 when the country was divided into the four metropolitan sees or provinces of Armagh, Cashel, Dublin and Tuam, with Gréne becoming the first archbishop of Dublin. The ecclesiastical landscape of Ireland was further transformed at this period by the founding of monasteries along European lines throughout the country, initially by the Augustinians and then by the Cistercians.[18] It is within this context that Lorcán Ua Tuathail (St Laurence O'Toole), who succeeded Gréne as archbishop of Dublin in 1161, introduced the

---

14   Gwynn, 'First Bishops'. The evidence for the consecration of Dúnán by the archbishop of Canterbury is circumstantial.

15   Gwynn & Hadcock, *Religious Houses*, p. 70.

16   Cited after Kinsella, 'Hiberno-Norse', pp. 38–9.

17   A process initiated at the synods of Cashel in 1101 and Ráith Bressail in 1111.

18   The impetus for the foundation of Augustinian and Cistercian houses in Ireland arose largely as a result of Archbishop Malachy (Máel Máedóc) of Armagh's journey to Rome in 1140, during the course of which he stayed at Clairvaux (leading directly to the founding of the first Cistercian house in Ireland at Mellifont in 1142) and made contact with a number of Augustinian houses including that of St Nicholas of Arrouaise in northern France. By the time of Malachy's death in 1148 it is estimated that there were about eight Cistercian and twenty-five Augustinian houses in Ireland, but these numbers would increase significantly into the early thirteenth century. Thereafter most new houses would be Franciscan, Dominican or Carmelite foundations. On the Augustinians in twelfth-century Ireland (including Christ Church) see Preston, 'Canons Regular'.

Augustinian canons regular of the Arrouasian order to Christ Church in 1162. Although a somewhat unusual choice, Augustinian cathedral chapters being rare even in England and France, Christ Church would remain an Augustinian cathedral-priory for nearly four hundred years until the Reformation.[19]

The religious reforms of the twelfth century were complemented by political developments which would shape the future not only of Dublin and its cathedral but of the entire country. When King Diarmait Mac Murchada of Leinster called on Henry II of England for help in a dispute with the high king Ruaidrí Ua Conchobair, Henry was given an excuse to carry out his plans for invading Ireland for which he had already gained authority from Adrian IV, the only Englishman ever to become pope. The first Anglo-Norman force landed in Ireland in 1169 and by the following year they controlled the south-east of the country. In 1170 Dublin was captured by Mac Murchada and his Norman allies under Richard de Clare (known as Strongbow). Henry II himself arrived in late 1171, attending Christ Church over Christmas and granting the charter of the city of Dublin to the 'gentlemen of Bristol', thereby formalising English control of Dublin. Large parts of Ireland were by now under Anglo-Norman control and Dublin became the centre of English rule in Ireland, a role which would be physically emphasised when King John built Dublin Castle in 1204. Following the death of Lorcán Ua Tuathail in 1180 subsequent archbishops of Dublin during the medieval period would all be Anglo-Norman. While the archbishop of Dublin was *ex officio* abbot of Christ Church, its priors (with the sole exception of Columbanus, c.1190–6) from c.1171 up to the Reformation would also be of Anglo- or Hiberno-Norman background, as also were the canons. English control of the Irish church was enforced by a statute of the Kilkenny parliament in 1366 which decreed that no native Irish could be admitted to ecclesiastical office.

The essentially English identity of medieval Christ Church is also seen in the oldest surviving parts of the cathedral which date from a building programme initiated by John Cumin. As Roger Stalley has shown, the closest architectural parallels are to be found in Wales and the south of England, most notably at St David's cathedral and at Wells and Glastonbury, while the thirteenth-century nave, described by Stalley as 'the most distinguished piece of Gothic architecture in Ireland', bears closest comparison with Worcester.[20] This is in marked contrast to the simpler architecture of other Irish medieval cathedrals, with the exception of St Patrick's, Dublin. The construction of a new cathedral which at the time was one of the largest and most imposing buildings in medieval Ireland (and it remains one of the larger Irish cathedrals) emphasised the power and wealth of Anglo-Norman rule in a newly conquered land. Nearly a century earlier the Normans had effected a comparable (if significantly grander) gesture in England with the construction of Durham cathedral in the northern borderlands of their

19 On Lorcán Ua Tuathail's choice of the Augustinian canons, see Empey in Kinsella, *Augustinians*, pp. 3–8.
20 Stalley, 'Construction', *passim*. Only the north side, itself much restored, survives of the medieval nave, the south side having been destroyed by the collapse of the nave in 1562 and rebuilt in the late nineteenth century. Otherwise the only substantial portions of the medieval cathedral to survive are the crypt and the south transept.

territories. Christ Church was thus the cathedral of a developing city which since its beginnings nearly two centuries earlier and continuing into early modern times was both culturally and ethnically distinct from (if not actually at odds with) the people of its hinterland: Dublin has never been an Irish-speaking city and in medieval times, as in most other medieval Irish towns which were likewise founded by the Vikings or the Anglo-Normans, the native Irish were kept at a distance and obliged to live outside the city walls in a suburb commonly known as Irishtown. The eastern part of Ireland under English rule, with Dublin as its capital, was protected by a defensive ring known as the Pale. Following the Reformation this ethnic and linguistic distinction between Dublin and so much of the rest of the country came to be further emphasised along religious lines: by the later seventeenth century Dublin was a predominantly Protestant city, its minority Catholic population living mainly outside the city walls.[21] It was only in the nineteenth century that Dublin became a predominantly Catholic city. As the cathedral of the capital city and for a long period also of the British administration in Ireland and recognised as the chapel royal in Ireland, Christ Church attracted support and prestige which ensured that its music could rival that of some of the greater English cathedrals. This unique relationship with both city and state has been a defining factor throughout most of the cathedral's history. Furthermore, during the centuries of British rule Irish cathedrals were closely linked to those of England through the appointment of cathedral personnel, the deans, dignitaries and choirmen at Christ Church, as also at St Patrick's, being overwhelmingly of English rather than Irish origin up to the later nineteenth century.[22]

Sources

The major primary sources for this history are the archival sources from Christ Church cathedral. Comprising documentary material transferred from the cathedral to the library of the Representative Church Body in the 1980s, those items now housed elsewhere but which can be identified as having strayed over the centuries from the cathedral, and a small number of items still held in the cathedral, they not only constitute one of the most significant Irish institutional archives, being unparalleled by any other Irish cathedral, but are also of importance in terms both of quantity and quality in the context of the British Isles as a whole.[23] The earliest documentary records of significant musical interest date from the late fifteenth century, though the originals have been lost.[24] Fortunately,

---

[21] Milne, 'Restoration', p. 279.

[22] With some notable exceptions, the practice initiated by the statute of the Kilkenny parliament in 1366 that only Englishmen would be appointed to positions within the choir continued as an unwritten principle at least into the eighteenth century (Bumpus, *Sir John Stevenson*, p. 5, but see also p. 80 n.69 below). The organists at Christ Church however provide an exception to this rule: following the appointment of Daniel Roseingrave from Salisbury as organist in 1698 (although he appears to have been of Irish descent, see p. 117 below) all organists were Irish (or at least living in Ireland at the time of their appointment) until Charles Kitson was appointed from England in 1913.

[23] See further Gillespie, 'Archives' and Refaussé in Milne, *Christ Church*, pp. 11–22.

[24] See Barra Boydell, ed., *Music: Documents*, pp. 34–7.

however, those deeds which were lost in the Irish Public Record Office fire in 1922 had been copied into the three volumes of the *Registrum Novum* compiled in 1741,[25] or were calendared in the late nineteenth century, or exist in isolated later copies or translations.[26] While some date back as early as the twelfth century, the earliest which refers to music dates from 1480. This is a charter making provision for four boys to serve in the choir and Lady chapel of the cathedral. The primary administrative records of the cathedral are the chapter acts. Commencing in 1574 (but including some earlier notes), these are the earliest surviving cathedral chapter acts in Ireland, the only others to predate the Restoration being those of St Patrick's cathedral, Dublin, which survive from 1643. Following the Restoration the cathedral reopened for services in November 1660 and, with the exception of one missing volume covering the period between September 1670 and January 1686, a complete series of chapter acts survives thereafter. In 1679 a fair copy was made of the first volume and copies of all subsequent chapter act books also exist.[27] The second largest category of administrative records which are a significant source for the history of music in the cathedral are the proctors' accounts, the earliest dating from 1541 and 1542. Thereafter, apart from the accounts for 1564–5 which are exceptionally detailed,[28] there is a break until 1589. The accounts are then sporadic up to 1626 but survive annually thereafter up to 1641 (a rent roll survives from 1645), in most cases both in their originals and in later fair copies.[29] After 1660 the proctor's accounts are complete except for the period between 1738 and 1766.[30] Following the disestablishment of the Church of Ireland in 1871 the chapter act books are supplemented by the board minute books, and the proctors' accounts superceded by various ledgers, payment journals, and cash and other account books.[31] Aside from the chapter acts and account books the other categories of written archives relevant to the cathedral's musical history range over a broad spectrum. A number of post-Reformation deeds relate to leases involving the payment of rent or of kind to the vicars choral, or to the granting of leases to individual choir members.[32] These are complemented by miscellaneous notes and volumes including matters relating to appointments, attendance, organs, the choir school and other matters. Choir attendance books survive, with breaks, from 1762.[33]

Surviving sources of music from Christ Church are rare before the eighteenth century. The only medieval source containing music which can be said with certainty to have come from the cathedral is the Christ Church Psalter, but musical notation is limited to brief antiphons and reciting tones to many of the psalms.[34] A small number of other medieval notated manuscripts which may

[25] C6/1/6/1–3.

[26] McEnery & Refaussé, *Deeds*.

[27] The original chapter act books form the series C6/1/7/1–, the copies form the series C6/1/8/1–; see also Gillespie, *First Chapter Act Book*.

[28] Gillespie, *Proctor's Accounts*.

[29] C6/1/26/3/1–29.

[30] C6/1/26/3/30–6; C6/1/26/16/13–22; C6/1/15/1–2.

[31] C6/1/16/3–6.

[32] In McEnery & Refaussé, *Deeds*.

[33] C6/1/23/1–13.

[34] *GB-Ob*, MS Rawl. G. 185.

possibly have originated in the cathedral are discussed in chapter one. No musical manuscripts that can be stated with any certainty to have originated in Ireland, let alone at Christ Church, are known to have survived from between the later fifteenth and early seventeenth centuries. The two known sources (one incomplete) of the anthem *Holy, Lord God Almighty* by Thomas Bateson, organist from 1609 to 1630, were copied in England in the 1620s and cannot be linked directly with the cathedral.[35] The Hosier manuscript, an early Restoration music manuscript which originated at Christ Church and St Patrick's cathedrals, is therefore of particular significance not only for the Dublin cathedrals but also as the earliest post-medieval music manuscript known to survive from Ireland.[36] In contrast to the small number of earlier sources of music, the collection of manuscript choir books dating from the eighteenth and nineteenth centuries comprises what Harry Grindle has described as 'undoubtedly the finest collection of part-, score- and organ-books in the country'.[37] This collection comprises thirty-three score books, twenty-four organ books, sixty-two part-books, and twelve 'loft-books' used by the soloists singing from the organ loft. The score books contain full voice and organ parts for 370 anthems and service settings by leading English church composers, mainly of the late seventeenth to early nineteenth centuries, as well as music by organists and choirmen of Christ Church. The part-books and organ books duplicate much of this repertoire but also include additional music.[38] A comparable but considerably less extensive collection of music, much of it copied by the same scribes, exists at St Patrick's cathedral.[39] The repertoire contained in the above music books, the survival of a small number of printed books of anthem texts sung at the cathedral and the evidence of service lists which only begin to survive intermittently from the mid-nineteenth century demonstrate that the choral repertoire at Christ Church consisted for the greater part of the regular canon of English cathedral composers current at any given period, but supplemented in some cases by quite a strong emphasis on local composers.[40] This repertoire emphasises the intimate links between Christ Church, indeed the Church of Ireland, and England through most of its history.

The present history falls into six chronological chapters whose divisions are suggested by developments both in the music and in the role of the cathedral itself as these changed in relation to the religious, social and political contexts. With the notable exception of the extensive documentation relating to the addition of boys to the choir in the late fifteenth century, information for music is sparse from the five centuries spanning the period from the cathedral's foundation in the eleventh century to the eve of the Reformation which are covered in the first chapter. The religious and cultural contexts of Christ Church and medieval Dublin provide a framework for a comparative study of practices elsewhere, largely on which basis the outlines of musical practices in the medieval cathedral can be drawn. Subsequent chapters, for which more extensive sources are available, provide accounts

35 *US-NYp*, MSS Drexel 4180–5; *GB-Lbl*, Add. MSS 17,792–6; see p. 59 below.
36 *GB-DRc*, MS B. 1; see pp. 88–96 below.
37 Grindle, *Cathedral Music*, p. xii.
38 O'Keeffe, 'Score-Books'; see ch. 4.
39 Houston, 'Music Manuscripts'.
40 See especially chs 4 and 5.

Plate 1. The modern cathedral from the south-west as restored by George Edmund Street in 1871–8. The covered bridge over the road leads to the former Synod Hall on the site of the church of St Michael. Compare the same view in the early nineteenth century, shown in Plate 7. From G.E. Street and E. Seymour, *Christ Church Cathedral Dublin* (London, 1882).

of the choir and its members, of organs, organists, music and repertoire, as well as examining the changing relationships between the cathedral and the city and political administration of the time as these influenced and affected music in the cathedral. Chapter two covers the period from the New Foundation in 1539 up to the cessation of cathedral services in 1647. Although documentary evidence for music now becomes more extensive and detailed, there is still relatively little direct information on the musical repertoire. It was during this period that close links were developed between Christ Church and Anglo-Protestant rule in Ireland which would have a direct bearing on the cathedral's musical life. The resumption of full cathedral services in 1660 following the Restoration marks the beginning of chapter three. Charles II substantially increased the incomes of the choirs of both Dublin cathedrals and acknowledged Christ Church as the chapel royal in Ireland, his reign marking the beginning of the greatest flourishing of the cathedral's music. There is a considerable degree of continuity and stability within the cathedral's music from the Restoration until the earlier nineteenth century when the wealth and influence of the Church of Ireland and its cathedrals began to be challenged by changing social and political circumstances. Nevertheless, the extent of material relevant to the cathedral's musical history including significant musical sources, and the acknowledged prominence of Dublin's musical life during the eighteenth century in which cathedral musicians played their part, have suggested a subdivision into two chapters for practical rather than for strictly historical reasons. Chapter four thus covers the period from 1698 until 1833 during which cathedral musicians including Roseingrave, Shenton, Woodward and Stevenson composed anthems and services preserved in the extensive collection of cathedral choir and organ books. The year 1833 marks both the death of Stevenson and the passing of the Irish Church Temporalities Act which significantly reduced the autonomy and status of the cathedral. Chapter five examines the period between 1833 and the disestablishment of the Church of Ireland in 1871 during which Christ Church's role and function within Dublin were increasingly being questioned, especially after 1846 when its deanery was combined for a period of about twenty-five years with that of St Patrick's. Although the choir could still attract good musicians, choral standards and morale began to decline and economies had to be effected. Disestablishment substantially stripped the cathedral of its remaining income, and in 1872 Christ Church cathedral closed for a period of six years during which the crumbling edifice was rebuilt by George Edmund Street, when it took on its present appearance (*Plate 1*). The final chapter covers the century following Distestablishment during which the cathedral would at times find itself starved of funds and largely irrelevant to the city whose spiritual centre it had so long been. No longer the cathedral of the established religion but serving a declining minority congregation, especially after Irish independence in 1922, the cathedral and its music went into sharp decline. When the choir school was closed in 1972 having been in existence for nearly five centuries, music reached its lowest ebb in the cathedral's history. The introduction of women to the choir in 1975 was one of the first steps towards the remarkable renaissance, both in the cathedral's music and in the life of the cathedral itself, which would mark the final decades of the twentieth century.

ONE

'Dulces Fecit Modos':
the Medieval Cathedral-Priory

Liturgy and chant

As the Introduction emphasised, it is to the south of England that one must look in order to understand the musical and liturgical practices at Christ Church during the first century or so of its existence. The Benedictine cathedral-priory of Worcester, where Bishop Pátraic of Dublin was trained between 1074 and 1084, was already noted by the ninth century for its classical tradition of Roman chant,[1] and surviving sources of the early eleventh century from Winchester and Canterbury demonstrate that English chant was closely linked to French and Rhenish forms of the Roman liturgy.[2] The early eleventh-century Winchester troper, the earliest surviving practical source of liturgical polyphony in western Europe,[3] provides clear evidence not only of the importance of music in the Anglo-Saxon liturgy but also of how advanced polyphony was in pre-Conquest England. One can reasonably assume that a comparable liturgy and chant repertoire, and possibly even polyphony similar to that of the Winchester troper, was sung at Christ Church during this period. Around 1075–80 Archbishop Lanfranc replaced earlier English practices at Canterbury by reforms based on those of Cluny and, particularly in the light of Bishop Donngus (Donatus) of Dublin's having been consecrated by Lanfranc in 1089, one must again suppose that these reforms were reflected at Christ Church.[4]

During the eleventh and twelfth centuries the liturgy as used at Salisbury cathedral became the most widely practised in England. Known as the Sarum use, it was officially established in Ireland at a synod at Cashel called by Henry II in 1172. The fact that a synod held fourteen years later in 1186 at Christ Church itself found it necessary to declare its adoption within the diocese of Dublin is a reminder that actual implementation could lag significantly behind the issuing of synodal decrees. While the liturgy celebrated in most monasteries followed monastic use rather than secular (such as that of Sarum), Augustinian houses

---

[1] *NG2* xxvii, p. 558.

[2] For summaries of liturgical music in the pre-Norman English church see Caldwell, *English Music* i, pp. 5–15 and Lefferts, 'Medieval England'.

[3] *GB-Ccc*, MS 473.

[4] On the liturgy and its musical implications at Canterbury during the eleventh century see Bowers, 'Canterbury', pp. 408–13.

being under the authority of their local bishop most often followed the secular use of their diocese.[5] That this was indeed the case at Christ Church under the Augustinian canons of the Arrouasian order introduced by Lorcán Ua Tuathail in 1162 is confirmed by the late fourteenth-century Christ Church psalter discussed below. The Salisbury connection is underlined by the fact that four archbishops of Dublin between 1280 and 1299 are recorded in Salisbury as having granted indulgences in connection with the cathedral there.[6] There can be little doubt therefore that by the later twelfth century plainchant corresponding to Sarum use was sung at Christ Church.

As a cathedral-priory Christ Church was essentially the private chapel of the canons whose primary function was the daily celebration of the divine office, the *cursus* or seven canonical hours of matins and lauds (these two constituting a single hour), prime, terce, sext, none, vespers and compline. Although details of internal structure varied between different regional uses, and between secular and monastic practice, the broad outlines of the divine office were common throughout Western Europe. The daily office was sung and consisted for the greater part of the psalms, the full cycle of which was chanted each week, together with scriptural readings and prayers. In addition a number of hymns and canticles were associated with particular hours, including the *Te Deum* which concluded matins, the *Benedictus* at lauds, the *Magnificat* at vespers and *Nunc Dimittis* at compline.[7] The times of the hours were not absolute but were linked to the natural cycle of day and night, there being considerable variation both geographically and seasonally. Matins was celebrated shortly after midnight, followed directly by lauds except in monastic use in which there was a short break between the two. Prime was sung after daybreak and the daytime was punctuated by terce, sext (around midday) and none. Vespers was celebrated at dusk and compline before retiring. Around this unchanging pattern were fitted the various daily masses according to each day of the church year, including morrow mass after prime and high mass. Later in the medieval period the Lady mass and other votive masses endowed by benefactors would be added. The regular divine office and daily masses would have been sung to plainchant, but it is possible that polyphony may also have been sung on more important days, as will be discussed below.[8] In contrast to more recent times the laity had little involvement in the medieval liturgy which was largely celebrated behind the choir (or rood) screen, often completely hidden from the people. The wider population of the surrounding city of Dublin would have looked to the various parish churches throughout the city for its regular spiritual needs, only entering the cathedral on important feast days or other special occasions, or as pilgrims to the various relics which made the cathedral into one of the major pilgrimage centres in medieval Ireland.[9] The

5   Harper, *Forms of Western Liturgy*, pp. 29–30.
6   Hawkes, 'Liturgy', esp. p. 34.
7   For a detailed outline of the divine office, see Harper, *Forms of Western Liturgy*, ch. 6.
8   See pp. 20–1 below.
9   The relics included the miraculous speaking cross (supposed to be a fragment of the True Cross), the *baculus Ihesu* ('the staff of Jesus which an angel had conferred on blessed Patrick'), a thorn from the crown of thorns, a piece of the cloth in which Jesus was wrapped as a baby, some of the milk of the Blessed Virgin Mary, and many relics of Irish saints including bones of St Patrick, St

priests and members of monastic communities prayed and celebrated mass on behalf of the people or, in the case of individually endowed masses which became increasingly common in the later Middle Ages, on behalf of specific benefactors whose presence at the mass was not essential. Many of these individually endowed (or votive) masses were celebrated at one of the side altars situated in the various chapels adjoining the nave or elsewhere in the cathedral outside the choir area and thus accessible to the laity. The extent to which the citizens endowed masses and made other donations to the cathedral-priory reflects the affection in which it was held and the extent to which it acted as a spiritual focus for the citizenry without their necessarily being present.[10]

Alan Fletcher has described the later medieval liturgy at Christ Church under three headings: 'regular', 'bespoke' and 'prestige'.[11] The regular liturgy included the daily celebration of the divine office and regular masses proper for each day of the year as outlined above. By 'bespoke' he distinguishes the various additional masses and other offices which were endowed and sometimes inaugurated by benefactors and other sponsors. This 'bespoke' liturgy is documented in some detail, endowments by both clerical and lay benefactors increasing steadily throughout the later Middle Ages so that

> By the eve of the Reformation, the cathedral priory had accumulated an impressive tally of the great and the good who courted liturgical recognition. The bespoke liturgy of Christ Church thus came to provide powerful local aristocrats with a showcase for their patronage. It was also used to blazon the civic piety and military interests of Dublin's magnates.[12]

Although none of the surviving deeds relating to this bespoke liturgy before the late fifteenth century mention music, plainchant must often have been sung, while the occasional use of polyphony cannot be ruled out. The 'prestige' liturgy falls into a number of categories. First of all there were those exceptional occasions when a significantly more elaborate liturgy would have been called for, such as the visit of Henry II in 1171–2 and the crowning of the young pretender Lambert Simnel as Edward VI in 1487, an event described by F.X. Martin as 'one of the most bizarre incidents in Irish history';[13] then there were certain recurring but infrequent occasions of celebration including those which must have accompanied the meetings of parliaments and great councils which habitually took place in Christ Church; finally there were annual occasions such as the celebration of Corpus Christi which was marked by a procession through the streets of Dublin, starting at the cathedral, and which developed in the fifteenth century into a major event of civic street drama.[14]

Brigid and St Columba. On the relics see further Lydon, 'Christ Church', pp. 93–4 and Stalley, 'Architecture', pp. 107–8.
10 See Refaussé & Lennon, *Registers*, pp. 18–23; McEnery & Refaussé, *Deeds*, pp. 24–5; Fletcher, 'Liturgy', pp. 133–8.
11 Fletcher, 'Liturgy'.
12 *Ibid.*, p. 133.
13 Martin, 'Crowning of a King'.
14 Fletcher, *Drama*, pp. 90–113.

Musical sources associated with Christ Church

A twelfth-century carved capital in the cathedral depicts (secular) musicians and dancers (*Plate 2*) and a mid-fourteenth-century account roll makes passing reference to visiting musicians, again secular and outside a religious context,[15] but otherwise there is little direct evidence relating to music at Christ Church before the late fifteenth century. Relatively few sources of medieval sacred music survive from Ireland as a whole, those associated with Christ Church being effectively restricted to a small handful of manuscripts which may possibly have originated in the priory although this cannot be proven. Evidence for musical practices at comparable institutions both in Ireland and in England must therefore be drawn on in order to propose some idea of musical practices in the medieval cathedral-priory.[16] Only one medieval liturgical manuscript can be linked with absolute confidence to Christ Church: the Christ Church psalter which was prepared on the orders of Stephen de Derby, prior of Christ Church from 1347 to c.1382, who is depicted in one of the miniatures as a kneeling supplicant.[17] It is thought to have been written and decorated in East Anglia and thus forms part of what by the late fourteenth century was a well-established trade in which English scriptoria were producing manuscripts for export.[18] In addition to the psalter this manuscript includes a calendar, creeds, litany and prayers, as well as later insertions including prayers and notes relating to the business of the priory in the later fourteenth and fifteenth centuries. The musical notation is limited to short antiphons to seventy-seven of the psalms (usually with the reciting tones and the endings also being given). Geoffrey Hand has suggested that these antiphons were inserted after the major part of the psalter was executed, and therefore probably in Dublin.[19]

The feature of this psalter which has attracted the most attention is the illumination which includes eight elaborate initials, two of which are of musical interest.[20] The illuminated initials serve a practical function in marking the beginnings of each day in the weekly cycle of the divine office. The eight psalms distinguished by illuminated initials, Psalms 1, 26, 38, 52, 68, 80, 97 and 109 (in the vulgate or Latin numbering) are the first psalms according to secular use for matins on each of the successive days of the week (starting on Saturday) and the first psalm for Sunday vespers, thus confirming that the Augustinian canons of Christ Church followed secular rather than monastic use. Psalm 80, *Exultate Deo* ('Sing aloud to God our strength; shout for joy to the God of Jacob! Raise a song, sound the timbrel, the sweet lyre with the harp'), is illustrated by a miniature showing five Augustinian canons, distinguished by their black hooded cope worn over a white rochet or surplice, making music on a triangular harp, psaltery, what

---

[15] See p. 24 below.

[16] Summary listing of medieval Irish manuscripts with musical notation in Buckley, 'Music and Musicians', pp. 187–8.

[17] *GB-Ob*, MS Rawl. G. 185. Hand, 'Psalter'; see also Hawkes, 'Liturgy', pp. 54–7.

[18] Pächt, 'A Giottoesque Episode'.

[19] Hand, 'Psalter', p. 312.

[20] Pächt, 'A Giottoesque Episode'; Hawkes, 'Liturgy'.

Plate 2. Romanesque capital depicting musicians and dancers, c.1200.
(Photograph: Roger Stalley)

might loosely be described as a rectangular 'harp', and two straight trumpets, together with two singers (*Plate 3*). The imagery is symbolic, reflecting the words of the psalm, and is certainly not an attempt to portray actual musical performance by the monks. While it does include instruments in contemporary use, others, notably the rectangular 'harp', are symbolic and do not bear organological scrutiny. A second miniature accompanying Psalm 97, *Cantate Domino* ('O Sing unto the Lord a new song'), belongs to a widely represented iconographical tradition in which this psalm is illustrated with a group of monks or clerics singing from music (*Plate 4*). Here six monks or canons sing from a music book placed on a lectern, in the manner in which notated sacred music was sung at the time. Four figures are visible full-length, three of whom are dressed in coloured copes and one at the back in what appears to be the black habit of an Augustinian. The monk nearest the lectern beats time with his right hand, while one of the monks behind holds the page open. In view of the widespread iconographical tradition associated with this particular psalm and of the English provenance of this manuscript, this illustration cannot be considered specific to Christ Church although there is no reason not to suppose that it broadly reflects practice there as elsewhere. Whether or not the music being performed is plainchant or polyphony cannot be determined, although some *Cantate Domino* miniatures do clearly show the singers performing polyphonic music.[21] Within the borders of the illuminated initial two grotesque rustics sing from music books in a parody of the more ordered singing of the monks.

[21] Cf. Page, 'English Motet'.

Plate 3. The Christ Church psalter (Oxford, Bodleian Library, MS Rawl. G. 185). Illuminated initial to Psalm 80, *Exultate Deo.*

Three Sarum manuscripts survive from the church of St John the Evangelist (demolished in the nineteenth century) which was situated immediately to the north-east of Christ Church and had been served by the canons of Christ Church from the time of Archbishop Luke of Dublin (1230–55). These manuscripts may very likely have originated in the cathedral-priory, but even if this is not the case they can at least be expected to reflect its liturgical practice. They comprise an antiphonal copied c.1435 and containing evidence of use at St John's in the early

Plate 4. The Christ Church psalter (Oxford, Bodleian Library, MS Rawl. G. 185). Illuminated initial to Psalm 97, *Cantate domino*.

sixteenth century, and two processionals dating from c.1400.[22] The antiphonal is a large volume clearly intended for choir use. As in the Christ Church psalter, the psalter section here includes brief musical antiphons as well as music for the opening words of each psalm. The sanctorale however includes a complete office for St Patrick with music, but it does not include chants or hymns associated with any other prominent Irish saints (although St Brigid, St Canice and others are cited in the calendars of many Dublin liturgical sources).[23] Patrick Brannon has examined the antiphonal together with three other broadly contemporary Irish Sarum manuscripts (an antiphonal used at Armagh cathedral, another possibly copied for use at St Canice's cathedral, Kilkenny, but showing evidence of use at Clondalkin, and a noted breviary used at Kilmoone) with a view to identifying possible remnants of distinctive early Irish (or 'Celtic') chant.[24] Two of the other

22 *IRL-Dtc*, MS 79, described in Hawkes, 'Liturgy', pp. 44–6; *IRL-Dm*, MS Z. 4. 2. 20; *GB-Ob*, MS Rawl. Liturg. d. 4, see below.
23 Hawkes, 'Liturgy', *passim*.
24 *IRL-Dtc*, MSS 77, 78, 80. See Brannon 'Search'.

manuscripts studied by Brannon include hymns or chants for other Irish saints (the Armagh antiphonal includes just three chants for the feasts of St Patrick), but the St John's antiphonal is the only one of these manuscripts to be associated exclusively with Dublin. The choice of St Patrick as the only Irish saint for whom chant is provided is repeated in the mid-fourteenth-century Dublin troper (see below). While the evidence of a mere handful of musical sources is admittedly slim, it may be that within the Anglophile environment of Dublin St Patrick was the only Irish saint to be accorded a full sung office, notwithstanding the presence of numerous Irish saints in the calendars of Dublin liturgical manuscripts, whereas in centres more distant from the capital closer links may have been retained with indigenous traditions, including hymns and sung offices for other Irish saints.

The two processionals from St John's are of particular importance as the sources for an Easter liturgical play referred to as the Dublin *Visitatio Sepulcri*.[25] This play stands very much within the western European tradition of liturgical drama, specifically that of resurrection plays, which goes back to the tenth century and was widespread by the fourteenth century. The Dublin play shares many individual portions of the dialogue with other resurrection plays from late medieval Europe but its particular form is unique. It is also unusual for the extent and details of its rubrics relating to staging and performance which enable many aspects of its performance to be reconstructed.[26] Placed securely in the liturgical context within matins on Easter morning, being framed by the Easter respond *Dum transisset sabbatum* and the hymn *Te Deum laudamus*, it presents the visit of the three Marys to the sepulchre to anoint Christ's body, their meeting with the angel, the announcement by the angel of the resurrection and the arrival of the apostles John and Peter. As Egan-Buffet and Fletcher have pointed out, the play would have been performed by male voices (probably the canons of Christ Church), with a boy or male alto possibly singing the part of the angel which 'would serve to maximise the dramatic impact, clearly intended by the author, of the angel's appearance to the women at the tomb'.[27] In addition to *Dum transisset sabbatum* and *Te Deum laudamus* the Dublin *Visitatio Sepulcri* features the sequence *Victime paschali laudes* as well as eleven further phrases which relate both textually and musically to Easter plays found in earlier Continental manuscripts; but it also includes music and text which is unique and which enhances the musical structure of the drama.[28]

The Dublin *Visitatio Sepulcri* evinces a high degree of artistry and sophistication amongst the Augustinian canons of Christ Church in the later fourteenth century. As Fletcher points out, the manuscripts from which it comes are reasonably close in date to the Christ Church psalter associated with the period when Stephen de Derby was prior 'when there seems to have been something of a small renaissance in the cathedral'. He suggests that 'it is tempting to regard the

---

[25] Transcribed in Egan-Buffet & Fletcher, *Visitatio Sepulcri*. See also Fletcher, *Drama*, pp. 61–77; Hawkes, 'Liturgy', pp. 38–44.

[26] For reconstructions of the play in performance see Egan-Buffet & Fletcher, *Visitatio Sepulcri*, pp. 166–79 and Fletcher, *Drama*, pp. 63–77.

[27] Egan-Buffet & Fletcher, *Visitatio Sepulcri*, pp. 201–2.

[28] *Ibid.*, pp. 182f.

appearance of a liturgy enhanced by drama as one of the signs of this artistic ferment', a point which makes the absence of more extensive musical records the more regrettable.[29] What is certainly clear is that the involvement of the canons in drama suggested by the *Visitatio Sepulcri* was not exceptional. Inserted into a mid-fourteenth-century account roll dating from 1337 to 1346 is the text of a morality play now referred to as *The Pride of Life*.[30] The only indication of musical participation in this play is a stage direction for the character of Nuncius to sing ('et cantat', in the context presumably a secular and not a religious song) when he says 'I must sing wherever I go', but as late as the sixteenth century on the eve of the Reformation the community of Christ Church was still actively involved in the performance of liturgical dramas specifically including music.[31]

Despite the presence of an *Ordo ad faciendum fratres et sorores secundum ordinem Sti Augustini* as well as a formula elsewhere for the reception of brothers and sisters into the Augustine order which might suggest links to Christ Church, the so-called Dublin troper dating from c.1360 (but with later additions) is generally accepted on more compelling internal evidence as having originated at St Patrick's cathedral.[32] The troper is however of the greatest interest in the context of both Dublin cathedrals during the later fourteenth century. The major part of this manuscript, the troper itself (fols 32r–131v), contains plainchant for the sung parts of the ordinary of the mass, the Kyrie, Gloria, Sanctus and Agnus Dei, frequently embellished with interpolated passages or 'tropes', along with sequences for various feasts including two in honour of St Patrick, and Marian sequences which are likely to have been sung at the votive mass of the Virgin. Dom Hesbert has noted that one of the two sequences in honour of St Patrick, *Laeta lux est* (fol. 50v), is only known from two sources of which this is the earlier, suggesting that it may have been composed in Dublin.[33] The second Patrician sequence *Laetabundus decantet* (fols 101v–102r) uses the same melody as the Christmas sequence *Laetabundus exsultet* (fol. 41v), a widely disseminated melody probably of French origin, but the text is only known from Dublin.[34] The Dublin troper is the only source for both text and music of thirteen of the Marian sequences, which suggests that these may have been composed in Dublin.[35] It is the earliest source for both text and music of eight further Marian sequences

---

29 Fletcher, *Drama*, p. 77. It is difficult to agree with Lydon's suggestion (Mills, *Account Roll*, p. xx) that 'the standards of literacy in the priory, certainly in the early fifteenth century, were low', although he does acknowledge the contrary evidence of the 'Pride of Life' play, some French verses scribbled into the back of another set of accounts, and the Christ Church psalter in which one miniature shows canons reading.

30 Mills, *Account Roll*, pp. xxii–xlii, 126–42; see also Fletcher, *Drama*, pp. 82–90.

31 See p. 31 below.

32 *GB-Cu*, Add. MS 710. Facsimile edition: Hesbert, *Tropaire-Prosaire*; see also Hawkes, 'Liturgy', pp. 33–67; Hand, 'Cambridge'. Despite the evidence presented by Hawkes and Hand, Hesbert, *Tropaire-Prosaire*, pp. 13–14 assigned the troper to Christ Church in the mid-fourteenth century.

33 Hesbert, *Tropaire-Prosaire*, pp. 21, 60, 79f (transcription), pls 39–40 (facsimile).

34 *Ibid.*, pp. 26, 60, pls 135–6 (facsimile).

35 *Ibid.*, pp. 65, 86–8, 92 (selected transcriptions and analysis); pp. 143–4, 159–60, 163–5, 169–72, 174–5, 178–81 (facsimiles). The sequences are *Ave spes angelico*, *Ave Verbum incarnatum*, *Ave Virgo virginum paradisi*, *Gaude Virgo concipiens de*, *Gaude Virgo quae de coelis per os*, *Jesu Fili Virginis*, *Laetare virginum flos*, *Miserere miseris*, *Nova venit genitura*, *Prophetarum*

which also occur in other later manuscripts, and the earliest source for the music but not the text of a further four Marian sequences.[36] It is also the earliest or sole source for four sequences in honour of St Clement (*Gloriosae mentis*), St Catherine (*Dilecto Regi*), St Edmund (king and martyr) (*Psallant coetus*), St Edmund (archbishop of Canterbury) (*In hac valle*) and one Sunday sequence (*Voce jubilantes*).[37] However, none of the tropes can be shown to be Irish.[38] The above sources from Dublin suggest that, with the exception of certain chants specific to the feast days of Irish saints (notably St Patrick, 17 March) and a handful of sequences which may have originated locally, the plainchant sung at Christ Church during the medieval period is unlikely to have differed significantly from what would have been heard in comparable English cathedrals.[39]

Polyphony

The Dublin troper is probably best known as the source of a three-voice setting of the Annunciation song *Angelus ad virginem* which has been inserted in a later hand. Of English or French thirteenth-century origin, this song enjoyed wide popularity in the late Middle Ages, being referred to by Chaucer in 'The Miller's Tale', but all other surviving notated versions are either monophonic or for two voices, the setting for three voices being unique to the Dublin manuscript and possibly a locally notated version of what was essentially an improvised polyphonic tradition, that of fauxbourdon.[40] One can readily appreciate *Angelus ad virginem*, whether in the three-voice version preserved in the Dublin troper or as a monophonic solo, being sung either by the canons of Christ Church or actor-singers under their direction as part of an Annunciation play within the tradition of sacred drama outlined earlier, but it is unclear to what extent polyphonic liturgical music may have been sung at Christ Church during the medieval period. The evidence from English cathedrals and monasteries does suggest that by the thirteenth and fourteenth centuries polyphony had become a normal part of the musical celebration of the office and mass especially on major feast days, with the practice of improvised descant being particularly widespread.[41] But even

---

praesignata, *Quicumque vult salvus esse poscat, Regina coeli flos Carmeli, Salve Mater misericordiae mundi.*

[36] *Ibid.*, pp. 63–4, 88–91, 92–5 (selected transcriptions and analysis); 145–6, 150–2, 156–9, 166–7, 172–4, 179–80 (facsimiles). Earliest sources for text and music: *Gaude Gabrielis ore, Mater avec plena, Coelum Deus inclinavit, Gaude gloriosa mundi* (later sources all insular), and *Maria Virgo concipiens, Gaude Virgo quae de coelis, Gaude Virgo salutata, Stabat juxta Christi crucem* (later sources also continental; melody of *Stabat juxta Christi crucem* earlier but to different text); earliest sources for music but not text: *Gaude Virgo gratiosa, Laetare puerpera, Dulcis ave poenitentis, Gloria sanctorum.*

[37] *Ibid.*, pp. 60, 82–5 (transcriptions of *Psallant coetus* and *In hac valle* for which this is the sole source).

[38] *Ibid.*, pp. 47, 57.

[39] Hesbert, *Ibid.*, p. 47, identified one *Kyrie* trope in the Dublin troper which is otherwise only known from one French source and which he suggested may not have been known in England.

[40] Dobson & Harrison, *English Songs*, pp. 176–83, 303–5; music: *ibid.*, pp. 266–8. See also Fenlon, *Music Manuscripts*, pp. 79–81; Hesbert, *Tropaire-Prosaire*, pp. 105–10, 186–7, 192–3.

[41] Harrison, *Music in Medieval Britain*, ch. 3.

where sacred polyphony was most widely practised it was essentially an elaboration of plainchant, sung usually on major festivals and other occasions of particular significance. As Roger Bowers has commented in the context of
fourteenth-century England:

> Nobody *needed* church polyphony; the plainsong liturgy was entirely
> self-sufficient, and composed polyphony was grafted onto it as a voluntary
> offering to God made by a few suitably informed enthusiasts, who pursued it
> largely as an unsolicited hobby.[42]

There is no clear evidence relating to polyphonic practices at Christ Church
before the late fifteenth century (apart from the association with *Angelus ad
virginem*) but the limited evidence for polyphony from elsewhere in Ireland
provides a context within which one can place Christ Church cathedral. Documentary references to sacred polyphony in medieval Ireland are enigmatic at best.
A mid-thirteenth-century life of Lorcán Ua Tuathail mentions the emphasis he
placed on music, alongside 'proper priests' and church decoration, as part of the
overall presentation of religion to the people. Apparently referring to the introduction of distinct new musical practices at the time when he introduced the
Augustinians to Christ Church in the 1160s, it also speaks of his making 'regular
singers [to stand] around the altar that they might praise the name of the Lord; and
he introduced order to the celebrations, *et in sono eorum dulces fecit modos* (and
added sweet measures [or modes] into their sounds)'.[43] This reference to 'sweet
measures/modes' could be interpreted as referring to polyphonic practices.
However, it might equally refer to new plainchant melodies including sequences,
the spread of the Augustinian order in the twelfth century being closely linked to
contemporary Gregorian reform including the spread of sequences.[44] A strong
tradition of polyphonic music is nevertheless associated with at least some
Augustinian houses in Britain.[45]

Despite the austerity and simplicity of the Cistercian rule which forbade the
singing of polyphony, three- and four-part singing had to be suppressed at two
British abbeys in 1217.[46] Following a visitation to Irish Cistercian houses eleven
years later Stephen of Lexington similarly found it necessary to send an injunc-
tion to each community that

> The rule of the Order in chanting and psalmody shall be followed according to
> the writing of the Blessed Bernard. No one shall attempt to sing with duplicated

---

42 Bowers, 'Performing Ensemble', p. 185.
43 'Fecitque regulares cantores circa altare, vt laudarent nomen Domini, et dedit in celebrationibus
    decus, et in sono eorum dulces fecit modos.' Copy c.1400 of lost mid-thirteenth-century(?) orig-
    inal cited after Plummer, 'Vie et Miracles', pp. 137–8.
44 Berry, 'Augustinian Canons'. Adam of St Victor, the most influential writer of sequences during
    the twelfth-century expansion of the form, was an Augustinian canon. See Fassler, 'Adam of St
    Victor'; Croker *et al.*, 'Sequence', pp. 101–2.
45 Most notable due to its parallels with Christ Church as an Augustinian cathedral-priory is St
    Andrews in Scotland from which there survives an extensive thirteenth-century collection of
    liturgical polyphony of the type associated with Notre Dame in Paris (*D-W*, MS Guelf
    Helmstadensis 628), see *NG2* xxiii, p. 872; Caldwell, *English Music*, pp. 23, 26.
46 Berry & Gellnick, 'Cistercian Monks'.

tones [*vocibus duplicatis*] against the simplicity of the Order . . . Anyone who transgresses this . . . shall be on bread and water on the day following and shall be flogged by chapter.[47]

If, as in England, at least some of the Cistercians in Ireland were singing polyphony, it is more than likely that the Augustinians at Christ Church, who were under no such restriction, would also have been singing polyphony.

The close links between Christ Church and centres in England such as Winchester where polyphony was sung as early as the late tenth and early eleventh centuries have already been noted. The earliest two examples of polyphonic music surviving from Ireland date from the later twelfth and thirteenth centuries and confirm that practices were in no way behind those elsewhere in western Europe. Although neither is associated with Dublin, both demonstrate close links with English and continental European practices. The so-called Cormac psalter written in the middle or second half of the twelfth century includes a colophon (*Cormacus scripsit hoc psalterium ora pro eo/ Qui legis hec ora pro sese qualibet hora*) set for three voices with no known concordance but using a *Benedicamus Domino* melody of the Sarum rite as the lowest voice.[48] This is very early in the European context for three-part music. A late twelfth/early thirteenth-century gradual whose provenance has been traced to the Benedictine monastery at Downpatrick includes a short piece of two-part polyphony which is unique in providing the only known musical concordance for a polyphonic work from before the later twelfth century, the same music occurring in a manuscript from Chartres dating from c.1100.[49] This gradual demonstrates links with Winchester which, as was noted earlier, was not only an important English centre of polyphony in the twelfth century but also had direct links with Christ Church cathedral during the eleventh century. A fourteenth-century missal of the Augustinian canons proper of the church of St Thomas the Martyr, Dublin, includes incomplete parts of a four-voice *rondellus* motet on three fly sheets used in the binding.[50] The specific link with Dublin Augustinian canons, while not of the same observance as those of Christ Church, makes this source of particular interest. The only other polyphonic music known from medieval Ireland is in the form of some fragments of textless mensural notation inscribed, probably in the later fifteenth century, on pieces of slate found at Smarmore in county Louth.[51]

[47] Stephen of Lexington, *Letters from Ireland, 1228–29*, trans. B.W. O'Dwyer (Kalamazoo, MI, 1982), p. 167, cited after Brannon, 'Medieval Ireland', p. 195.

[48] 'Cormac wrote this psalter, pray for him/ You who read this pray for himself [yourself] at every hour': *GB-Lbl*, MS Add. 36,929, illustrated and transcribed in Buckley, 'Music and Musicians', pp. 178–9; see also Harrison, 'Polyphony', p. 78.

[49] The verse *Dicant nunc* from the processional Easter antiphon *Christus resurgens*: *GB-Ob*, MS Rawlinson C. 892, fols 67v–68r concordant with Chartres MS 109, fol. 75r. Illustrated and transcribed in Buckley, 'Music and Musicians', pp. 180–1; cf. Gushee, 'Polyphonic Music', p. 151; Harrison, 'Polyphony'; see also Nicholson, *Introduction*, pp. lxxxiv f and pls lxi–lxiv.

[50] *Rota versatilis*, in honour of St Catherine, the complete music and text for which has been reconstructed from four fragments including this one. The motet is English in origin and dates from before 1325. *GB-Lbl*, MS Add. 24198; facsimile: Harrison & Wibberly, *Manuscripts*, pp. 3–8; Bent, 'Rota Versitilis', including transcription.

[51] NMI, accession nos 1961: 12, 24, 34, 41. Transcribed and illustrated in Harrison, 'Polyphony'; see also Bliss, 'Inscribed Slates'.

The fact that these came from a church not in a major religious centre or town suggests that more sophisticated polyphony was sung not only in the major centres, presumably including Christ Church cathedral, but also in smaller and more isolated communities.

The above examples of polyphony from Irish sources and the close links in the medieval period, as later, between Christ Church and English cathedrals provide little more than circumstantial evidence that polyphonic music was sung in the cathedral; how often, how elaborate, or how well we may never know. Augustinian houses of the Arrouasian observance were always small, many in England having a community of less than ten canons, and Christ Church was no exception: there were eleven canons in 1300, only eight in 1468, and ten when it was secularised in 1538. Hardly any Augustinian houses in the late medieval period reached double figures, and lay brothers never formed a major part of the order.[52] However a small community is not in itself an argument against the singing of polyphony: English polyphony of the fourteenth century required no more than three or four singers corresponding to the modern alto (countertenor), tenor and baritone ranges, singing one voice per part; while during the early fifteenth century 'a solo ensemble of four voices was considered to be the fundamental and irreducible medium for any major church to provide for the performance of polyphonic music'.[53] Unless sources of polyphonic music from the later medieval period which can firmly be linked to Christ Church do come to light (or evidence for the hiring of lay clerks who were sometimes employed in monastic cathedrals to sing polyphony), the question of the extent to which composed polyphony was sung within the cathedral before the late fifteenth century must remain unanswered. But by no means all medieval polyphony was composed and written down. Improvised polyphony, a practice which was referred to when four boys were endowed to sing in the cathedral in 1480, is likely to have been sung with greater frequency. Improvisatory musical practices, however, seldom leave their mark in the records.

Organs and other instruments

From the tenth century, primitive organs were used in some monasteries and cathedrals, most famously at Winchester as also probably at Canterbury by the later twelfth century.[54] The very nature and use of medieval organs remains problematic so that 'the organ remains the element of greatest obscurity among such musical resources as were available at the greater English fourteenth century churches'[55] and the question as to whether or not an organ was used in medieval Christ Church cannot be answered with confidence. In the early fifteenth century, however, organs were becoming more widespread, especially with the use of

---

52 Lydon, 'Christ Church', p. 77; Preston, 'Canons Regular', p. 35.
53 Bowers, 'Performing Ensemble', p. 184; cf. Bowers, 'To Chorus from Quartet', pp. 19–20.
54 Bowers, 'Canterbury', p. 417. There were also organs at York minster in 1147 and Westminster abbey in 1304 (Clutton & Niland, *British Organ*, p. 30).
55 Bowers, 'Performing Ensemble', p. 182.

small organs in Lady chapels. By the late fifteenth and early sixteenth centuries organs were widespread not only in cathedrals in Britain (there were no less than five organs in Durham cathedral) but also in parish churches,[56] and a cathedral of the relative importance of Christ Church is likely to have had at least one instrument.[57] Grattan Flood stated that there were indeed organs at Christ Church in 1358, in both Dublin cathedrals in 1450, and that a new organ was built in Christ Church in 1470 by John Lawless.[58] He gave no sources for this information which remains unsubstantiated but, while much of what Flood has written about Irish music history has proved to be unreliable, there is no good reason to doubt him in this instance. The use of a small organ at St Patrick's cathedral can be confirmed in 1471 when Archbishop Michael Tregury of Dublin left in his will his own 'pair of organs' for the celebration of the divine office in the Lady chapel.[59] The earliest evidence for organs at Christ Church which can presently be confirmed remains 1539 when the duties of the master of the choristers were to include those of organist.[60]

While musical activity in the cathedral-priory during the medieval period would have been overwhelmingly within the broad context of the liturgy, the cathedral's role within the city and its links with the secular administration called for occasions when music of other kinds might be heard within the precincts. Christ Church was the meeting place of the Irish parliament in which the prior held a seat in the upper house. In this role, and also as head of the leading religious house in Dublin, he frequently had occasion to entertain important visitors and benefactors on which occasions music might be called for, as in January 1338 when he entertained the visiting justices to dinner and payment was made to the justices' trumpeters in the refectory and also to 'a certain little harper'.[61]

Singing boys, the late medieval liturgy and the links between cathedral and city

During the fifteenth century it was increasingly becoming the practice for cathedrals and larger monastic institutions and collegiate churches to elaborate the liturgy, in particular the Lady mass which was celebrated in the Lady chapel, by the singing of polyphony and the addition of boys' voices. However, while the singing of polyphonic votive masses and antiphons became increasingly widespread, the presence of boy choristers does not in itself indicate that polyphony was sung. The statutes of many collegiate churches in England founded during the fifteenth century provided for a daily Lady mass to be observed with the attendance just of the boys and their instructor. Initially the intention was for the boys

---

[56] Harper, 'British Church Organ', p. 93.
[57] Cardinal Wolsey allowed the use of the organ specifically in Augustinian houses where, as was the case at Christ Church, the number of canons was low (Harrison, *Music in Medieval Britain*, p. 215).
[58] Flood, 'Irish Organ-builders', 'Organs of Christ Church'.
[59] Berry, *Register*, p. 26.
[60] See below, p. 33.
[61] Mills, *Account Roll*, p. 19.

to sing the plainchant on their own, their unbroken voices in themselves marking an elaboration of the music, but as their competence developed a polyphonic repertoire arose written specifically for just the boys and their master.[62] In Dublin this development is first noted at St Patrick's cathedral in 1431 when Richard Talbot, archbishop of Dublin, instituted a college of six minor canons and six choristers.[63] The six boys at St Patrick's would have sung the plainsong of the daily Lady mass and votive antiphon in the Lady chapel, and possibly also at masses celebrated within the cathedral itself, very probably also improvising a descant to the plainsong according to widely practised traditions of polyphonic improvisation. But composed polyphony involving boys does not arise within the English context (under which Dublin must be considered) much before the middle of the fifteenth century.[64] Participation by the boys in masses celebrated in the cathedral choir was possible in a secular cathedral such as St Patrick's. However, in monasteries and priories such as Christ Church, in which the conventual choir was isolated by the choir screen from those parts of the building to which the public had access, the participation of boy singers would typically be restricted to the Lady chapel and to votive masses and antiphons celebrated in the side chapels or nave of the cathedral itself, outside the choir.[65]

Provision for boy singers was first made at Christ Church in 1480 and the relevant documentation is amongst the most extensive surviving from anywhere in England or Ireland. It marks the most significant development in the musical life of the cathedral up until this time and the origins of the choral tradition which has formed the basis for the cathedral's music since the Reformation. This provision will be seen to have been instituted for reasons which underline the close links which had developed over the centuries between Christ Church and the people of Dublin. In 1480 Thomas Bennet, son of a former lord mayor, granted certain properties as an endowment for the sustenance in food, drink and clothing of four singing boys to serve in the choir and Lady chapel.[66] In honour of the Holy Trinity and of the Virgin Mary and for the souls of himself, his wife, parents and 'all my ancestors, sons and daughters and of all the faithful dead' Bennet endowed the rents of his properties at Ballymore in county Kildare and elsewhere to 'find, display and maintain honourably in clothes, food and drink' four boys, referred to unusually as *paraphonistis*, to sing in the high choir and the Lady chapel 'and for other divine services'. Four was usually the smallest number of boys specified in

---

[62] Bowers, 'To Chorus from Quartet', p. 38; cf. Bowers, 'Musicians', p. 223 in the context of the Lady chapel choir of the priory of Winchester in the mid-fifteenth century.
[63] Grindle, *Cathedral Music*, pp. 7–8.
[64] Bowers, 'To Chorus from Quartet', p. 27.
[65] It was at times questioned whether monks should be occupied in the study and singing of elaborate polyphonic music: significantly for the Augustinian context of Christ Church, Cardinal Wolsey's statutes written for Augustinian canons in 1519 forbade the use of polyphony in the choir, into which outsiders were not allowed during services. The canons were to sing plainsong 'chanted with modest gravity and in a sweet and tranquil style'. Laymen, seculars and boys were, however, permitted to sing with polyphony and organ at the Lady mass, the mass of the Name of Jesus, and on other such occasions when music might be sung outside the conventual choir (Harrison, *Music in Medieval Britain*, pp. 191–2).
[66] Barra Boydell, ed., *Music: Documents*, pp. 29–31 (translation *ibid.*, pp. 238–40); cf. Refaussé & Lennon, *Registers*, p. 68.

these contexts and may have been determined by the need for two each of trebles and meanes (i.e. alto or lower boy's voice) in order to ensure the possibility, with their master and two other adult singers, of attempting the five-part polyphony which was becoming common in English music.[67] The boys were to be 'competently' trained in the science of music 'for the honour of God and the aforementioned church'.[68] Although no specific mention is made here of a master or instructor to train the boys, this is implicit and would be more clearly defined in 1493 (see below). The four boys were to sing daily in the high choir in all sung divine services, at the daily Lady mass and to 'have sung some parts of the mass in the choir in praise of the maker of the world and the virginity of his most glorious mother, and for various other divine services and the observation of prayers inside the aforesaid cathedral church'.[69] Every Sunday after Vespers the four boys were to say prayers for the souls of Bennet and the others named in the deed. Because of the more usual exclusion of outsiders from the high choir in monasteries and priories, the specific mention that the boys would sing there on a regular basis 'in all sung divine services' is of particular interest. Bennet specifies the singing of composed polyphony on certain occasions: the daily Lady mass was to be sung with 'plainsong and musical songs known as set song or prick song at the least, and other more learned musical chants, so that those to be found thus step by step [i.e. the singing boys as each was appointed and trained] may be able to be more completely trained in them'.[70]

Five years later in October 1485 John Estrete, gentleman and sergeant-at-law, made an endowment for a daily mass to be celebrated after the choir mass and before the high mass in the chapel of St Laurence O'Toole.[71] On most days this mass was spoken by one of the canons, but on Thursdays 'with the helpe and assistance of the resydue of the said Convent and suche as kepyn the Queyr' it was to be sung 'be note . . . with playn song and sett song, yf it may be, and yf no, att the lest gode and tretable playn song'. The precise meaning is not clear, but the

---

67 In 1533 the Lady chapel choir of the Augustinian priory of Llanthony Secunda near Gloucester explicitly included 'foure childerne well and suffycyently enstructed that is to say too meanys and too trebles'; this was usual in a monastic context in which the number of monks or canons available to sing polyphony was small, as at Christ Church (Bowers, 'Vocal Scoring', pp. 56–7; 'To Chorus from Quartet', p. 35).

68 'Successive scientia musicali eruditos, et competenter pro honore Dei et Ecclesiae praed: scientia illa erudiendos.'

69 'Tam in alto Choro ejusdem Ecclesiae Cathedralis in omnibus Divinis serviciis cantandum et deserviendum prout talibus Paraphonistis hujusmodi Ecclesiis Cathed: incumbit deservire, et usualiter pro honore Dei habetur cantare, quam ad custodiendam et adjuvandam missam Beatae Mariae Virginis, quae cotidie celebrata est, et celebrari consuevit propter honorem Dei et ejusdem gloriosissimae Virginis infra magnam Capellam, vocatam Capellam Beatae Mariae Virginis, scituatam in parte boriali magnae altaris dictae Ecclesiae Cath: . . . et consonum nonullas partes Missae in Choro in laudem saeculi conditoris et virginitatis suae gloriosissimae Matris cantare et cantari facere, quam ad diversa alia divina servicia, et orationes infra dictam Cath: Ecclesiam observandas.'

70 'Cantari canticis planis, ac hujusmodi canticis musicalibus, vocatis Set Song, sive Priksong ad minus ac aliis majus scientificis musicalibus canticis, ut ipsi sic successive inveniendi in eisdem perfectius erudiri possint.' The terms 'set song' and 'prick song' both refer specifically to polyphonic mensural notation.

71 Barra Boydell, ed., Music: Documents, pp. 32–3.

reference to both 'the residue of the said convent', namely any of the canons of the priory not otherwise occupied, and 'such as keep the choir' is perhaps the strongest clue there is for the existence of lay clerks who are not unambiguously mentioned in the records.[72] The suggestion that the boys might be unable to sing a polyphonic mass infers that they were not receiving adequate training, a matter which was addressed in 1493 when the prior David Wynchester and the chapter presented a deed providing for a stipend for a music master to teach the four boys, as well as contributing to their food, clothing and accommodation.[73] This move put on a firmer footing whatever informal arrangement must already have been in existence since 1480 for the master of the boys. It was to be financed from the offerings made to the *baculus Ihesu* or staff of Jesus, the most important of the relics which made Christ Church such an important pilgrimage centre, as well as by rents from certain specified church properties and other donations. The deed (in Latin) specifies that the master should instruct the boys

> in plainchant, polyphony, descant and counter with the intention that the afore-said master and boys shall have the care each day of a mass for the Blessed Mary solemnly according to the learning and doctrine of the aforesaid master and boys, and of a mass and antiphon for Jesus every Friday only during Quadragesima and at other established times.[74]

Here their musical training specifically mentions not only plainchant and (composed) polyphony, but also the skills of polyphonic improvisation referred to as *discantum et counter* (descant and counter).[75] In addition, food and drink were to be provided each day for the master ('to suit his standing and as befits such a master') and the boys, as well as clothing and a room for sleeping and for teaching.[76] This deed of 1493 can therefore be regarded as marking the formal establishment of the cathedral choir school which had effectively existed since 1480 and would continue until 1972.

The daily liturgy involving the singing boys during the late Middle Ages can be summarised from the above documents. Into the daily *cursus* of the divine office (a pattern which was flexible due to the varying lengths of the daylight hours into which it was accommodated) were slotted the regular daily masses,

[72] References to 'clerks' in leases such as those in 1470 to James Power and in 1529 to William Power 'clerke' and his wife could possibly refer to lay clerks, as could undated references to *clerici* in the book of obits, but the term can cover a range of literate skills by no means necessarily related to music (McEnery & Refaussé, *Deeds*, nos 987, 1133; Refaussé & Lennon, *Registers, passim*).

[73] Barra Boydell, ed., *Music: Documents*, pp. 34–7; transl. *ibid.*, pp. 240–3.

[74] 'Planum cantum, fractum cantum discantum et counter ad intentionem quod dictus Magister et pueri custodient cotidie missam Beatae Mariae solenniter juxta scientiam et doctrinam dicti Magistri et Puerorum; ac Missam et antiphonam de Iesu in qualibet die Veneris tempore tantum quadragesimali aliisque temporibus legitimis.'

[75] For more on the practice of improvising over a plainchant see Meech, 'Musical Treatises'. The 1539 statutes for the New Foundation would again refer to the teaching of 'discant to four minims' (see p. 35 below).

[76] 'Et quod dictus Magister sive doctor dictorum quatuor puerorum habebit esculenta & poculenta honeste cotidie . . . unacum camera dicto Magistro sive doctori & pueris ad dormiendum & docendum eosdem pueros.'

namely the morrow mass, the high mass and the Lady mass. The morrow mass, which must be what John Estrete referred to in 1485 as the 'Quere Mass', was usually celebrated either immediately after prime, that is soon after dawn, or after terce in mid-morning. High mass might be celebrated at any time between prime and vespers and could vary according to the time of year.[77] Bennet's provision in 1480 for the four singing boys refers to their singing in all relevant services in the choir, which implies that they would have taken part in both the morrow and the high masses. As noted above, this does not necessarily mean that they sang polyphony which, if used, would probably have been reserved for Sundays and festal days. John Estrete's provision in 1485 for a new mass of the Holy Ghost to be celebrated daily states that it is to take place 'immediately after the Quere Masse . . . and are [before] the high Masses att the Auter [altar] . . . be begonnen' which implies that high mass followed fairly soon after the morrow (or 'choir') mass.[78] This mass of the Holy Ghost was spoken except on Thursdays when it was to be sung with plainchant and polyphony if possible (see above). Musically the most significant of the daily masses was the Lady mass which was the main focus of Bennet's endowment, but the placing of the Lady mass within the daily *cursus* at Christ Church is not known. The final mass referred to in the 1480 to 1493 documents is the Jesus mass on Thursdays which was to be celebrated each year in Lent from Quadragesima with an antiphon sung by the four boys with their master 'according to [their] learning and doctrine', in other words with improvised if not composed polyphony. In addition to the above masses there were other votive masses and occasions when the canons prayed for the intentions of the founders, but there is no indication that these involved anything more elaborate than the singing of plainchant.

The institution of Lady chapel choirs or singers was most often carried out not by the church but by wealthy individuals, whether lay as in the case of Thomas Bennet at Christ Church in 1480, or ecclesiastical as in the case of St Patrick's (archbishops were then as mitred earls). Bowers has commented that 'although the identity of the lay patron can often be readily discovered, one important factor often difficult to establish is the source of the initiative lying behind his donation'.[79] In Bennet's case the reasons for his initiative can be suggested. Thomas Bennet's endowment is but one, if a relatively elaborate, example of the many grants of properties and privileges made to the cathedral-priory by benefactors over the medieval centuries. The book of obits of Christ Church, compiled in the late fifteenth and early sixteenth centuries, records the names of over one thousand benefactors (including Thomas Bennet) and others for whose souls the community prayed.[80] This reflected a system that was of mutual benefit to both cathedral and the civic community: while those remembered in the book of obits received spiritual benefits through the prayers said on their behalf, the cathedral benefited through grants and bequests of land, money and valuables, or other benefactions. By the fourteenth century Christ Church had become the most

---

Harper, *Forms of Western Liturgy*, pp. 45–6.

Fletcher, 'Liturgy', p. 131 notes, however, that in Augustinian houses (as Christ Church) the daily chapter meeting was held after the morrow mass.

Bowers, 'Obligation', pp. 5, 6.

Refaussé & Lennon, *Registers*, pp. 37–86.

richly endowed of all the religious houses in Ireland, although by the early
sixteenth century its actual income placed it in the middle bracket of Irish
monastic houses.[81] The system of benefactors helped to create close bonds
between Christ Church and the citizens of Dublin: many of those commemorated
in the book of obits were members of the cathedral confraternity, three-quarters of
the names being those of lay people who comprise 'a roll-call of civic and gentry
families who were prominent in the Dublin area particularly in the later fifteenth
and earlier sixteenth centuries'.[82] The mayors of Dublin were regularly enrolled
in the book of obits where a number of highly placed officials in the central
government administration were also remembered. The annual swearing-in ceremony of the new mayor took place in Christ Church as did other important civic
ceremonies. The guild chapel of the Trinity (or Merchants') guild, the senior and
most powerful guild in the city, was in the south aisle of the nave,[83] and during the
troubled period in the mid-fourteenth century when the native Irish living in the
nearby Dublin and Wicklow mountains posed a constant threat, the priory
contributed to the defence of the city and its environs within which so much of its
property lay. The links between Christ Church and the city of Dublin thus went
far beyond its physical location at the centre of the medieval city: the
cathedral-priory was intimately linked into the lives of the citizens, physical and
spiritual.

While Bennet's concern was primarily spiritual – honouring the Holy Trinity
and the Blessed Virgin and providing for the salvation of his and his family's
souls – his grant also refers to the boys' serving 'as it behoves such *paraphonistae*
to serve cathedral churches of this type and to sing as custom demands for the
honour of God'.[84] Bennet was clearly looking at Christ Church within the wider
context of urban cathedrals and certainly aware of the presence of boy choristers
at St Patrick's already for nearly fifty years. In comparison music at Christ
Church must have seemed lean, even old-fashioned in the absence of the now
fashionable sound of boys' voices. Bennet clearly wished to bring the musical
elaboration of the liturgy at Christ Church into the forefront of contemporary
practice as it would have been understood in Dublin at the time, thereby adding
prestige to the city of which he was such a prominent citizen. His concern is
underlined by the relative detail of his grant, including the specific references to
'set song' and 'prick song' and the use of the boys not just for the daily Lady mass
as was becoming the norm, but also more unusually for all appropriate services in
the choir of the cathedral itself. The institution of a Lady chapel choir with boys
whose voices were also used within the wider context of the cathedral's liturgy
was thus initiated by a wealthy secular patron and reflected the important place
Christ Church held in the hearts and minds of the citizenry.

Bennet's deed combines with that of 1493 to suggest that there may not have
been an almonry school attached to Christ Church from which, as was so often the

---

[81] Mills, *Account Roll*, pp. ix–x; Gillespie, 'The Coming of Reform', pp. 160–1.
[82] Refaussé & Lennon, *Registers*, p. 21.
[83] For more on the Trinity guild see Clark & Refaussé, *Dublin Guilds*, pp. 23–5.
[84] 'Et deserviendum prout talibus Paraphonistis hujusmodi Ecclesiis Cathedralibus incumbit
      deservire, et usualiter pro honore Dei habetur cantare.'

case, choirboys might have been recruited.[85] The 1480 deed refers to boys being 'found', which does not suggest that they might be available from a corps of boys already associated with the cathedral, while in 1493 special provision was made for a room in which the boys could sleep and be taught, hardly a consideration had an almonry school already been in existence. The fact that it was felt necessary in 1493 to re-establish provision for the master and for the keep of the four boys (this had already been provided for in 1480) must indicate that the master had been paid on an informal basis and that the 1480 provision may not have proved sufficient for the boys' maintenance. It is also possible that the 1493 deed reflects the successful completion as it were of a period of probation: the duties and musical requirements laid down in 1480 may at the time have seemed ambitious but could have proved themselves in practice by 1493. If so, the prior and chapter may have felt it desirable to secure the longer-term existence and training of a choir of singing boys in order to assure the benefits which the music they represented must by then have been contributing in terms of both liturgical and civic prestige. David Wynchester, who had become prior relatively recently in 1489, may also have wanted to put his mark on the provision of music in the cathedral.

In view of this extensive documentation relating to the establishment of boy singers and a master to train them, it is all the more to be regretted that neither music nor any specific references to repertoire have survived from Christ Church from the entire period between the early fifteenth and the early seventeenth centuries. The growing elaboration of English sacred music over the course of the fifteenth century is reflected in the development of the 'florid' style of church music represented in the Eton choir-book compiled between 1490 and 1502, and of the festal masses and other sacred music of Fayrfax, Taverner and others in the early sixteenth century. The vocal abilities of the canons or other adult singers and of the boys at Christ Church are not known, but it seems unlikely that they would have approached the standards of the longer-established and more richly endowed choral establishments in England for which music such as that contained in the Eton choir-book was composed. Music of a more modest style would most probably have been sung at Christ Church, possibly including works composed by the master of the choristers of the time. Major church festivals including Christmas and Easter and those exceptional occasions which called for 'prestige' liturgy would by the late fifteenth and early sixteenth centuries have called for music of a more elaborate style. Undoubtedly the most elaborate of such 'prestige' occasions at which the newly established boys' choir participated would have been the crowning of Lambert Simnel as king of England on 24 May 1487.

Direct evidence for musical practices at Christ Church is again absent between the establishment of the boy singers in the late fifteenth century and the promulgation in 1539 of the statutes for the New Foundation of the cathedral which will be examined in the next chapter. During the early sixteenth century there is however continuing evidence for the involvement of the canons in religious drama which again emphasises that the Augustinian community at Christ Church existed very much as part of the civic community of Dublin. At Christmastide in

---

[85] See Bowers, 'Almonry Schools'.

1528 a series of entertainments was held in honour of the earl of Kildare on the Hoggen Green to the east of the medieval city. A special stage was erected on which a total of eight plays were presented:

> The Taylors acted the part of Adam, and Eue; the Shoomakers represented the Story of Crispin, and Crispiana. The Vintners acted Bacchus, and his story; The Carpenters presented the story of Joseph, and Mary. Vulcan, and what related to him, was acted by the Smiths; The Comody of Caeres, the Goddess of Corne, was acted by the Bakers . . . the Priors of Saint Johns of Hierusalem, of the blessed Trinity [i.e. Christ Church], and of Allhallowes, caused two playes to be acted; the one representing the Passion of our Sauiour, the other the seueral deaths which the Apostles suffered.[86]

Here we find the prior of Christ Church co-operating with the priors of two other Dublin monasteries, St John of Jerusalem and All Hallows, to produce plays on the passion and on the deaths of the apostles.[87] Just as the guilds represented the merchants and traders of the city through plays associated with their trades, the priories acted as representatives of the city's religious life in the presentation of religious drama. A passion play had earlier been performed, also on the Hoggen Green, in 1506.[88] In view of this tradition of the canons of Christ Church being involved in sacred drama at least since the *Visitatio Sepulcri* of the late fourteenth century, it is very possible that they were also involved in it and doubt-less too on many other similar occasions of which no records have survived. The strength of this tradition of religious drama associated with Christ Church is underlined by the fact that as late as 1541 and 1542, by which time letters patent had already been granted by Henry VIII confirming the New Foundation of the cathedral and the former prior and convent were styling themselves dean and chapter, payments were made 'For wyne to them that sanke the passon', to 'the syngers of the passyon at brekfast' and for 'the plaing of the resurrecton'.[89] As will become clear in the next chapter, the profound changes caused by the reli-gious reforms of the sixteenth century would take effect as part of a gradual rather than a sudden process and practices such as these associated with the old order would continue to make their presence felt into the new era.

---

86 Seventeenth-century copy of the lost sixteenth-century 'Dublin Chronicle' cited after Fletcher, *Drama*, p. 136.

87 The priory of the Knights Hospitallers of St John of Jerusalem lay some distance to the west of the city where the Royal Hospital, Kilmainham, now stands. All Hallows, a priory of Augustinian canons of the Arrouasian order like Christ Church, lay to the east of the medieval city adjacent to Hoggen Green. Having lain idle for over fifty years following its dissolution in 1538, it became the site of the University of Dublin, Trinity College, founded in 1592 by Queen Elizabeth.

88 Fletcher, *Drama*, p. 134.

89 Barra Boydell, ed., *Music: Documents*, p. 41.

TWO

'For the More Honour of God's Divine Service': the Reformation and Early Seventeenth Century

The New Foundation

In the autumn of 1537 royal commissioners arrived in Ireland charged by Henry VIII with authority to suppress monastic houses.[1] Archbishop George Browne of Dublin supported reform and may have had a hand in the resignation early in 1537 of William Hassard, prior of Christ Church since 1520. He ordered reference to 'the bishop of Rome' to be removed from all liturgical books, this being carried out in the case of the church of St John the Evangelist which was under the cure of Christ Church. The priory of All Hallows, the second Arrouasian house of the Augustinian canons regular in Dublin, was dissolved in autumn 1538 and in the following February the destruction of all shrines and relics was ordered, the jewels and precious metals being sent to the Irish exchequer. The value yielded by Christ Church, £35 15s 6d, was second only to Our Lady's shrine in Trim and reflected the cathedral's importance as a centre of pilgrimage. Amongst items lost to Christ Church was the *baculus Ihesu*, the offerings to which had supported the boys of the choir since 1493. The future for the priory of Holy Trinity at Christ Church must have seemed bleak. In May 1539 the remaining religious houses in Ireland were ordered to be dissolved and by December the commissioners, who had been travelling southwards from Dundalk, reached Dublin. For the first time they encountered popular resistance when they turned their attentions to Christ Church, the mayor and aldermen, supported by the lord deputy and council, protesting to the king's principal secretary of state that the cathedral, like St Paul's in London

> standith in the middes of the said citie . . . hit is the verie station place, wher as the Kynges Graces honorable Parliamentes and Counsailles ar kepyn, all sermons ar made, and wher as the congregacions of the said citie, in processions and station daies, and at all other tymes necessarie, assemblith, and at all tymes of the birth of our mooste noble Princes and Princesses, and othir tymes of victorie and tryumphe, processions ar made, and 'Te Deum laudamus' customabilie is songe, to the laude and praise of God, and the honor of our said Princes and Princesses.[2]

[1] Historical background based on Gillespie, 'Coming of Reform', esp. pp. 162–73.
[2] *State Papers. King Henry the Eighth*, p. 545.

As a result of this intervention dissolution was averted. Instead, statutes to convert the priory into a secular cathedral were drawn up and Christ Church was formally re-established as a cathedral of the New Foundation in 1541.

The statutes of the New Foundation, promulgated in December 1539, provide a detailed picture of the size and duties of the choir at this time.[3] In changing the choir from the existing canons (possibly supplemented by lay clerks or other secular members), four boys and master of the choristers (and organist) its structure and duties were consciously modelled on those of the secular cathedral of St Patrick's. The eight canons of the former priory who were not dignitaries became vicars choral rather than minor canons as was usual in cathedrals of the New Foundation. Like minor canons, however, they were all in holy orders. The first four were referred to as the principal vicars choral: the dean's vicar, the succentor or precentor's vicar (later more often called chanter's vicar), the chancellor's vicar and the treasurer's vicar, the first three of whom became prebendaries of St Michael's, St Michan's and St John's churches respectively. The remaining four regular canons were referred to as 'vicars minor'. In addition to the four boys there were three 'choral clerks': the organist and master of the boys, the sacrist who also assisted the singers at mass, and a third clerk who assisted the celebrant at mass. These additional positions suggest the presence in the former priory choir of at least two lay clerks in addition to the master of the boys, who also served as organist. The clerks or additional singing men, normally two in number up to the Restoration, came to be known as stipendiaries in the late sixteenth century, a term which would continue in use until Disestablishment.[4] The various lands and livings belonging to the former priory were allocated separately to the dignitaries and to the vicars choral for their maintenance, the vicars choral forming a distinct corporation. Exceptionally, all the vicars choral were made members of the chapter whether or not they were prebendaries. From 1543 leases were made by the dean and chapter 'with the consent of the vicars choral' who in other cathedrals had no such rights. This unusual arrangement may have arisen through the influence of prominent citizens, reflecting the cathedral's position within the city: the surnames of the canons at the New Foundation suggest that, with the exception of two Englishmen, they were all members of well-established and influential Dublin families with backgrounds in the law, land, trade or the church.[5] It was nominally the succentor's duty both to order the table of weekly services and to 'instruct the boys of the choir in singing'. In practice however the latter task was delegated to the organist and master of the boys. The chancellor's vicar was responsible for the correction of any mistakes in the Latin texts of the choir books,[6] and the organist and master of the boys was required to be 'learned in the musical art as well as in playing the organ and in singing plainchant and polyphony, and equally in sufficient descant for instructing the boys'.[7]

---

3   Sections relating to music in Barra Boydell, ed., *Music: Documents*, pp. 37–41, transl. *Ibid.*, pp. 243–6.

4   First recorded as 'stipendiaries' in 1593, *Ibid.*, p. 56.

5   Gillespie, 'Coming of Reform', pp. 154–5.

6   'Libros chori falso latino et incongruo corruptos.'

7   'Erit doctus in arte Musica[e], tam in pulsatione Organorum, quam in cantu plano et fracto, pariter et in sufficienti discantu, pro instructione puerorum.'

The choral duties following the New Foundation represent substantially a continuation of those contained in the deeds of 1480 to 1493. The four minor vicars officiated 'in their turns per week' at the daily Lady mass 'except on the great and principal feasts' when one of the dignitaries officiated. It is clear that at least improvised polyphony was sung on a daily basis at the Lady mass, the four boys being required to be present then 'and in all other masses *cum fractum habeant cantum*', the term *cantus fractus* being cited by Tinctoris as referring to a vocal line in metrical rhythm resulting from a longer note being 'broken' into smaller parts.[8] This would seem to refer to what is described elsewhere here as 'descant' or 'counter'. The second choral clerk (the sacrist) attended the daily Lady mass 'for assisting the singers there, in like manner at the high mass',[9] the organist and master of the boys also 'ministering' at the Lady mass, the daily high mass and as often as any other mass was celebrated *cum cantu fracto*. Other less clearly defined occasions on which the boys may have sung in polyphonic music were in the *missis gradalibus* ('stepped', or perhaps 'successive' masses?) 'and other necessary [masses] for the honour of God in the increasing choirs in which choristers are accustomed to be added'.[10] One of these 'other' masses was the Holy Ghost mass on Thursdays which the four minor vicars celebrated as a solemn mass 'with singing and choristers and other ministers as is the practice'.[11] When instituted by John Estrete in 1485 this mass was specifically to be celebrated with polyphonic singing if possible.[12]

In addition to the above masses when polyphony might be sung, whether improvised or composed, a number of masses and other offices specify or imply plainchant. The mass of the Holy Cross, or rood mass, was celebrated daily except Friday by one of the minor vicars 'with lowered voice'. Early on Friday mornings in lieu of the first mass, apparently referring to the above Holy Cross mass, the Jesus mass was celebrated by one of the dignitaries with 'solemn singing'.[13] Masses for the state of the king were celebrated thrice weekly by one of the four principal vicars at the high altar, specifically with plainchant (*cum cantu planu*). The four minor vicars together with two of the principal vicars celebrated masses at the altar of the Holy Ghost on Mondays, Wednesdays and Saturdays for the souls of Walter Kelly, former mayor of Dublin, of Alison Warde 'when she shall depart of this life' and of all the cathedral's other benefactors. With no less than six of the priest vicars present at these masses, they must also have been celebrated with plainchant. In addition, the four minor vicars were required to be present 'by day and night, especially when mass is celebrated with singing',[14] the former referring to the *cursus* of the divine office. The four chorister boys were

---

8 *NG2* v, p. 66.
9 'Pro juvandis cantoribus ibidem, similiter erit in alta missa.'
10 'Et in missis gradalibus et aliis necessariis pro honore Dei in choro augendis, in quibus solent onerari choristae.'
11 'Unam missam solemnem cum cantu et choristis, et aliis ministris prout decet et consuetem est.'
12 See p. 26 above.
13 'Et hoc solemnitur cum solemni cantu.'
14 'In coro convenientes, nocte dieque choris congruis et competentibus Divinis officiis personaliter intersint; praesertim quando Missa cum cantu celebrantur omnino intersint.'

also to be present at vespers 'for the singing of the versicles' and in the simple feasts 'for the singing of responses'.[15]

Further amplification of some of the musical practices following the New Foundation is provided in the deed establishing the salary and duties of Robert Heyward as organist and master of the boys seven years later, in March 1546.[16] As organist he was expected to play at matins on the eight principal feasts and major doubles, when polyphony was apparently sung. He was also responsible for the music of the daily Lady mass and antiphon and was present at the Jesus mass on Fridays, apparently as organist although this is ambiguous. Heyward's duties as master of the boys included instructing them 'in pricksong and descant to four minims', but most intriguing is the reference to his teaching them 'to play our Lady's mass, all instruments being found for them during the time of their child's voice'.[17] The four choirboys had specifically been provided for in 1480 to sing at the Lady mass and the 1539 charter also refers, as noted above, to their being present at the Lady mass when *cantus fractus* was sung. There is no reason on the evidence from elsewhere within the English tradition to suppose that unbroken boys voices were not being used in the music for the Lady mass at this period.[18] Does this then mean that at least some of the four boys played instruments in *alternatim* settings with voices, or was it a question of the plainchant *cantus firmus* being played instrumentally, above which one or two other boys sang the improvised 'descant to four minims'?

At Christ Church in 1539 the high mass and Lady mass remained the most important parts of the singers' daily observance as had been the case in 1480–93. The most significant change since that time was the substitution on three days each week of a mass for the king in place of the mass of the Holy Ghost, which had previously been celebrated every day, but on Thursdays the mass of the Holy Ghost continued to be sung polyphonically (whether improvised or composed) as had been established in 1485. The 'choir' mass referred to in 1485 as preceding the Holy Ghost mass is not mentioned in 1539. Instead there is a mass of the Holy Cross ('vulgarly styled "the rood mass" ') which appears to have replaced (or been a re-naming of) the former 'choir' mass since it was celebrated every day except Friday, on which day the Jesus mass was celebrated 'at the earliest part of the morning in lieu of first mass' and thus must have preceded both the mass of the Holy Ghost/for the king and the high mass. The Jesus mass, only mentioned in 1480–93 as being celebrated by the choirboys and their master 'according to their learning and doctrine' in Lent, is referred to in 1539 as a regular, weekly mass celebrated on Fridays 'with solemn singing'.

When Henry VIII issued letters patent in May 1541 formally establishing Christ Church as a cathedral of the New Foundation there was one significant

---

[15] 'In vesperis pro cantandis versiculis, et in simplicibus Festis pro cantandis Responsoriis.'

[16] Barra Boydell, ed., *Music: Documents*, p. 42; McEnery & Refaussé, *Deeds*, no. 1201. Since the Latin original has not survived one must rely on McEnery's not entirely unambiguous summary.

[17] Instrumental teaching for choirboys is also documented in English cathedrals in the sixteenth century. It is uncertain what type of instruments are being referred to here: while viols would have been most likely later in the century, it is more probable at this period that keyboard instruments were taught. See Payne, *Provision and Practice*, pp. 134f and Flynn 'Education', p. 189.

[18] Contrast my earlier comments in Milne, *Christ Church*, p. 240.

change from the 1539 statutes which would henceforth bind Christ Church even more closely with England. Whereas in the original scheme only the position of dean was a royal appointment, all other dignitaries being elected by the chapter, now all dignitaries became royal appointments. But Dublin now had two secular cathedrals so the future of Christ Church was not yet secured: the lord deputy, Sir Anthony St Leger, withheld the letters patent and proposed that Christ Church be converted into a parish church. However, in a repeat of the opposition in 1539 to the dissolution of the cathedral-priory, this proposal was countered by the argument that if the cathedral status of Christ Church were removed, the city would be 'totally defaced and disparaged'.[19] Ironically it was St Patrick's greater wealth which now attracted Henry VIII's attention and in 1547 he issued instructions for it to be suppressed. Christ Church's role as the cathedral for the diocese of Dublin was now assured, at least for the time being. The cathedral benefited through the transfer of the plate, jewels, ornaments and organs from St Patrick's and the choir at Christ Church was enlarged by six priests and two boys (referred to as *pueri personistae*).[20] At least two of the new priests, Richard Betagh and John Claregenet, were former vicars choral at St Patrick's.[21] The additional choral positions were funded out of money received by the exchequer, in recognition of which the choir did homage and sang in the court of exchequer at the end of the law terms, a tradition which continued into the late nineteenth century.[22] Additional incomes for the maintenance of the vicars choral were granted later in the same year by the archbishop of Dublin.[23]

At least in the shorter term, the Reformation brought about no sudden or profound change in Ireland which was to some extent cushioned from the rapidly changing religious climate in England. A conservative climate prevailed at Christ Church under Thomas Lockwood, dean from 1543 to 1565 and an astute politician and traditionalist in matters religious, and where the chapter was largely comprised of former canons of the cathedral-priory.[24] Despite the promotion of the first Edwardian prayer book in 1550, mass was still being celebrated at Christ Church in 1551 under the authority of the lord deputy, but the new English liturgy was also to be celebrated there for the first time in that same year. The new prayer book was at best vague as to the role of music and the evidence from English cathedrals shows an adapting of older musical practices to new circumstances rather than any profound change.[25] With the slower rate of change at Christ Church there is nothing to suggest that the survival of the choir was threatened during the Edwardian Reformation and the transition back to the Roman liturgy in 1553 following the death of Edward VI and the succession of his half-sister Mary was all the easier. By the time Thomas Radcliffe (who became earl of Sussex the following year) was sworn in as lord deputy in 1556 all the traditional aspects of Catholic worship were in place including processional crosses, censers, holy

---

[19] Gillespie, 'Coming of Reform', p. 166.

[20] Barra Boydell, ed., *Music: Documents*, p. 43; cf. McEnery & Refaussé, *Deeds*, no. 439.

[21] Gillespie, 'Coming of Reform', p. 168.

[22] Barra Boydell, ed., *Music: Documents*, pp. 43, 246.

[23] *Ibid.*, p. 43.

[24] On Lockwood see Gillespie, 'Coming of Reform', pp. 169–70.

[25] Payne, *Provision and Practice*, p. 23.

water sprinklers and copes for the clergy. One of the most significant events to affect Christ Church during Mary's reign was the restoration of St Patrick's as a cathedral in 1555. Although there were now two secular cathedrals in the one city, once again raising potential problems for the status of either cathedral, the enlarged choir at Christ Church which had ensued from the suppression of St Patrick's in 1547 was retained, at least for the immediate future.[26] Christ Church was also allowed to hold on to those items including organs or other instruments (the deed refers to *instrumenta musica sive organa*) which it had received from St Patrick's in 1547.[27] The unusual arrangement throughout following centuries whereby many choirmen sang in both Christ Church and St Patrick's cathedrals may first have arisen following the re-opening of St Patrick's as a cathedral in 1555. Certainly from the 1620s a majority of the vicars choral of Christ Church would be choir members of both cathedrals.[28]

The attendance and duties of the dignitaries, prebendaries and minor vicars at the various masses and the divine office were defined during Mary's reign.[29] In addition to ministering at the high altar according to their turns, the six minor vicars were to 'say or celebrate' the rood mass, and sing the daily Lady mass and Jesus mass during Lent. The three prebendaries or senior vicars choral and a senior dignitary (referred to as *calaber amises*, a term denoting a fur-lined hood which was traditional wear for Augustinian canons) were to sing high mass, all 'masses of the time' and 'second mass daily', and serve in the choir every day including Sundays, ferial days and all principal feasts. The three dignitaries sang mass on all principal double and major double feasts, but what is not defined is whether any of these references to singing are to plainchant or to polyphony. The chanter's vicar and chancellor were asked 'for the more honour of God's divine service' to appoint 'certain of basses and countertenors' for the daily Lady mass, indicating the need to have sufficient men's voices present for the singing of polyphony. Neither the choirboys nor the organist and master of the boys are mentioned.

The Elizabethan settlement

Following the accession of Queen Elizabeth in November 1558 religious change once again took some time to make itself felt at Christ Church, the mass still being celebrated at Easter 1559. When the lord deputy, the earl of Sussex, attended the cathedral on 26 August the litany was sung in English, but probably within the context of the mass as had been the practice in England in previous months.[30] The Irish parliament met at Christ Church in 1560 when the Acts of Supremacy and

---

26 McEnery & Refaussé, *Deeds*, no. 448. The number of boys on the foundation would return to four by 1604 (see p. 42 below).

27 Barra Boydell, ed., *Music: Documents*, pp. 45–6, 246–7.

28 See Cotton, *Fasti* ii, pp. 84–9, 202–12; although Cotton notes some common vicars choral in 1546, the paucity of records from St Patrick's before 1639 prevents a more accurate comparison of choir members at this time.

29 Barra Boydell, ed., *Music: Documents*, pp. 44–5; Gillespie, *Chapter Act Book*, pp. 23–4.

30 Gillespie, 'Shaping of Reform', p. 174.

Uniformity were passed, the latter differing from its English counterpart in that it allowed the use of Latin wherever priests 'had not the use or knowledge of the English tongue'; it also permitted much of the paraphernalia of medieval worship to be retained, including the wearing of traditional mass vestments.[31] The rood loft and screen would still be in place in 1565, a painting of the passion on the arch above the screen having only been removed in November 1564, and the structure of the liturgical year was still observed by a cycle of saints days of varying importance.[32] The gift of half a beef in 1565 by the (at least nominally) Protestant lord mayor Richard Fyan to ring a knell for the soul of the Catholic precentor of the cathedral under Queen Mary reflects this continuation of pre-Reformation practices into the Elizabethan period. The close links with the city were initially retained, Christ Church remaining as much a civic institution as a Protestant cathedral. Catholic and Protestant found common ground there, many Catholic citizens contributing to the rebuilding of the cathedral following the collapse of the nave in 1562.[33] However, the cathedral now began increasingly to fulfil the role of state church, a role not normal for cathedral churches. It was the place of worship of the lord deputy and ceremonies associated with his administration, including his swearing-in and the creation of knights, took place there, with the privy council usually meeting within the precincts where the Four Courts (the courts of the king's bench, exchequer, chancery and common pleas) would be located from 1608.[34] With the resurgence of Catholicism from the 1590s political and religious issues would begin to be more clearly demarcated and Christ Church would evolve into an island of state-sponsored Protestantism within an increasingly recusant city.

The conditions and duties of the choirmen

There is little information on musical practices following the Elizabethan settlement, but the fact that payments for candles 'for the choir at service' which were regularly bought for evensong through the winter of 1564–5 cease after early February 1565 suggests that perhaps polyphony was not then sung since this would have been sung from music books for which lighting would be needed.[35] During the period of the Marian restoration of the Latin rite the dean's vicar had been given authority 'to see good order in the hall, and commande others to shonne contencons and folishe arguments and disquietnes'. It was also ordered that

> Noe prebende nor vicare shall use or haunte unhonest, suspected houses by daie or by nighte nor be late forthe of ther close without honeste bretherne in ther company to avoyde all evill suspicon. And specyallye shall not sleepe in no

---

[31] See Jefferies, 'Irish Parliament'.

[32] Gillespie, 'Coming of Reform', p. 171; Gillespie, *Proctor's Accounts*, p. 39.

[33] *Ibid.*, pp. 15–16, 39.

[34] The courts remained within the precincts of Christ Church until 1796 when they moved to the present Four Courts building north of the river Liffey.

[35] Gillespie, *Proctor's Accounts*, p. 54. However, in 1565 Easter fell on 22 April (Old Style) which means that Lent would not have begun until the middle of March.

house of the cytie or suburbes out of their precyncte without a reasonable cause upon paine of forfiture of vi d tociens quociens.[36]

Like the canons of the former monastery which cast a long shadow over succeeding decades, the vicars choral were still living in the 1560s and 1570s within the precincts under the watchful eye of the dean and chapter and dining together in their common hall.[37] The earliest surviving chapter acts following the Elizabethan settlement, dating from 1574, and a set of regulations in Latin for the vicars drawn up in 1579 display little change from the above situation.[38] In 1574 all members of the cathedral were required to avoid 'dispitfull or slaunderus words', violent behaviour including shedding the blood of any of their colleagues, the wearing of arms within the precincts or city, and staying out of the precinct after 9pm. They were also to maintain the confidentiality of chapter business and attend daily morning prayer and 'high service'. Appropriate fines were outlined in each of the above cases. The 1579 orders specific to the vicars reiterate a number of the same concerns including that 'no strange women or of ill fame shall attend to the vicars chambers at undue times'. These orders also define aspects of the vicars' duties, including the precentor's (or precentor's vicar's) duty to arrange the tables of the services each week, assigning duties to each person, that is, to plan and arrange the music to be sung. Penalties for non-attendance at services in the cathedral and questions of general discipline amongst choir members would remain matters of continual concern to the dean and chapter, later chapter acts abounding in cases of vicars and stipendiaries being admonished for absence, appearance and hygiene, and unruly, drunken or irreverent behaviour.[39] In 1639 the lord deputy and council of state would have cause to complain that divine service was not 'conceived to be performed in a due formall and becoming manner and Decencie by the Viccars', and later in the same year the vicars were told 'to carry themselves Civill and in a becoming manner in the Quire and not to Laugh or Jeere at any one [of] the others singer fellows in reading or in Singing in the Quire'.[40]

The requirements for appointment as a vicar choral were outlined in 1579: each must be 'suitable in morals, knowledge, age and of legitimate birth', and within one year of being appointed must be prepared for promotion to holy orders. When Nicholas Begge, formerly described as a 'singing man' in 1561, was raised to the position of vicar choral in 1566 he agreed to serve at matins, evensong 'and all other services, except the administration of sacraments and matters relating solely to the order of priesthood' for a pension for life of £9 in addition to meat and drink in the vicars' hall and a room in the precincts.[41] The continuation of monastic practices in the vicars' hall is recalled in the

---

36 Barra Boydell, ed., *Music: Documents*, p. 45. Gillespie, *First Chapter Act Book*, p. 24.

37 Barra Boydell, ed., *Music: Documents*, pp. 51, 52–4, 79–80.

38 For the full texts see *Ibid.*, pp. 51–4, 247–9.

39 *Ibid.*, pp. 54, 56–7 (note that the date of the entry 'Vicars for Attendans in the quire' should read 26 January 1594, not 25 February), 60, 65, 70, 76; Gillespie, *First Chapter Act Book*, pp. 128, 136–7, 162, 165, 169–70, 203, 223; C6/1/8/2, pp. 13, 30, 49, 92, 110, 162.

40 Barra Boydell, ed., *Music: Documents*, pp. 74–5. These later concerns should be seen in the light of the Laudian reforms of the 1630s. See p. 48 below.

41 *Ibid.*, p. 84.

requirement that one vicar be assigned each week 'for the reading of any sacred book in the beginning of dinner and after shall say grace'. In common with most English cathedrals, however, as the century progressed and the links with the monastic past faded this practice of the vicars choral dining together in their common hall would decline and fall into disuse. By 1604 vicars choral were petitioning the dean and chapter that the rents and tithes still being collected and enjoyed by the vicars' steward and garner should be paid directly to themselves since 'ther comon table and manner of diet comonly called the Vicars hall, hath bene of long time discontinued, and dissolved, for that every one of them had his owne family within himselfe'.[42] When they contributed to the costs of the rebuilding of the cathedral tower in 1589 at least some of this money came from their not having used their accommodation allowances.[43] The decline of the communal style of living and eating together in the vicars' hall reflects the gradual change at Christ Church from the monastic heritage to the more open life of a modern cathedral. That this change should have taken more than half a century reflects the fact that the changes which the Reformation brought about were anything but abrupt.

The vicars' income came from property which was defined in the 1539 statutes and subsequently added to, but they also took out leases on properties elsewhere in the city either for their own use or to subrent as an additional source of income.[44] Rents due to the vicars were often paid in kind: in 1547 a lease included a requirement to 'supply daily the herbs necessary in hall and kitchen for the vicars choral and sufficient leeks at Lent, and to provide two pecks of onions yearly, or 5s in lieu thereof'; others included capons at Trinity Sunday and geese at Christmas, 'beeves' (i.e. cattle), and 'a table cloth for their [the vicar choral's] common hall every third year'.[45] When Robert Heyward was appointed organist and master of the 'choristers and children' in 1546 his payment in addition to the yearly stipend of £6 13s 4d had comprised

> 8 pecks of malt, payable at the feasts of the Nativity, Easter, Nativity of St John Baptist, and Michaelmas, a livery coat, a cart load of wood at Christmas, and the chamber by east of the churchyard; and the vicars choral grant him 4 pecks of malt, in equal portions, at said feasts, his daily finding, table and board, sitting and taking the same with them.[46]

In 1604 a new constitution for the vicars choral was drawn up under James I which provided the opportunity for a restructuring of the choir which would prevail until the late nineteenth century.[47] The anomalous situation whereby the vicars choral were members of the chapter but without there being any canonical

---

[42] *Ibid.*, pp. 58–9; compare Lehmberg, *Reformation*, pp. 194–5. The six vicars would again be described as all having families in 1638 (Barra Boydell, ed., *Music: Documents*, p. 72).

[43] *Ibid.*, p. 80; Gillespie, *First Chapter Act Book*, pp. 56–7.

[44] *Ibid.*, pp. 37, 43. The deeds and chapter acts make frequent mention of property leases to individual vicars choral and choir members (*inter alia* McEnery & Refaussé, *Deeds*, nos 1202, 1277, 1385, 1409, 1414, 1420; Gillespie, *First Chapter Act Book*, pp. 59–62).

[45] Barra Boydell, ed., *Music: Documents*, pp. 42–3.

[46] *Ibid.*, p. 42.

[47] Sections relating to the choir in *Ibid.*, p. 85.

prebendaries was reformed. The former vicars choral were transformed into three prebendaries who were no longer to be vicars choral, while the six priests who had been added in 1547 were now established as vicars choral. Thus, while the overall size of the choral foundation remained at six vicars choral as it had been in 1539, the vicars choral no longer held places in the chapter and the basis was laid for the later employment of choirmen who would be primarily musicians rather than churchmen. It was some time however before the full complement of vicars would be filled, the position of 'sixth vicar' being treated as of lower rank than the other five and singers typically being appointed specifically 'until a full vicars place shalbe voyd'.[48]

It became the practice for the vicars choral to assist the three prebendaries in their conduct of services but the 1604 charter did not specify that they need necessarily be priests. In 1634, only two of the five vicars then being priests, John Jewett was instructed to take orders as a deacon at the next opportunity, and William Ballard and William Betney were given six months to prepare themselves to receive the same orders.[49] In addition to the six vicars choral a number of other adult singers in the choir were engaged as stipendiaries, often in the expectation of promotion to a vicar's place, sometimes (after 1604) by way of the position of sixth vicar.[50] Once appointed, a vicar usually retained his post until his death unless he voluntarily resigned or was dismissed for absence or other misdemeanour.[51]

The shortage of basses was a recurring problem. In 1613 the vicars had received a special payment 'to prepare Songs and Anthems fitt for theire voices lacking Mr Hoskins who was gone for England . . . the Quire lackd voices at this time'.[52] Two vicars choral of St Patrick's, James Moyler (or Maylor) and Anthony Wilkes, received payment covering the same Christmas period, 'Mr Hoskins our base being in England'; Moyler later received further payments 'for suplying the place of a base' and was eventually appointed a stipendiary in 1617.[53] It is significant that Thomas Bateson's anthem *Holy, Lord God Almighty*, thought to have been composed around this period, has only a single bass part although scored for seven-voice choir. In 1626/7 a Mr Green was described as 'the bass', and in the chapter acts his appointment as a 'stipendiary base' is noted.[54] In 1638 a plan to increase the size of the choir to include ten vicars choral was proposed.[55] In view of their 'being very Sensible of the present disorder by

---

48 The allocation of rents, tithes and other dues to be assigned to the position of sixth vicar remained unresolved in 1609 when John Hoskins was accepted into this position which was described as having remained unfilled since 1604 (C6/1/8/1, p. 141); cf. Barra Boydell, ed., *Music: Documents*, pp. 60, 176, 180–1, 187 etc.

49 Barra Boydell, ed., *Music: Documents*, p. 69.

50 See for example Gillespie, *First Chapter Act Book*, pp. 140, 149.

51 See for example Barra Boydell, ed., *Music: Documents*, p. 56 (Walter Kennedy), 63 ('George Hely considering his age, did voluntarily yield up his place of viccar chorall'); Gillespie, *First Chapter Act Book*, p. 110 (John Ryce 'for the most part absent dureing this last halfe yeare, and alsoe in other respects is thought unmeet for the service of the quire').

52 Barra Boydell, ed., *Music: Documents*, p. 82.

53 *Ibid.*, p. 82; C6/1/26/3/9, fol. 5v; C6/1/26/3/10, fol. 3v; Gillespie, *First Chapter Act Book*, p. 139. On Anthony Wilkes see further note 62 below.

54 C6/1/26/3/13, fol. 4r; Gillespie, *First Chapter Act Book*, p. 149.

55 See p. 51 below.

the having of Soe many tenors and such a Scarcity of Bases and Countertenors in the Quire of Christchurch' it was recommended that the choir should include 'fowre Bases to reade prayers Usually, two Tenors and 4 Countertenors'.[56] The appointment of choir members does not seem necessarily to have been determined by voice type, although this could be a consideration. John Jewett from Fethard, county Wexford, was appointed specifically to a countertenor's place made void by the death of the long-serving John Bullock in 1620,[57] in 1634 Daniel Wiborowe successfully petitioned for a stipendiary's place since 'there is want of a Tenor on Decanus side',[58] and in 1644 Peter Stringer was appointed 'in respect there is great want of a base in the Quire'.[59]

The choirboys

By the early seventeenth century the number of choirboys, increased under Edward VI to six, had returned to four but it is not clear when this reduction in numbers took place. A position as a choirboy brought with it education, clothing and upkeep and must have been much sought after. Parents or a close relative sometimes petitioned for a place for their boy in the choir, and on one occasion a boy was presented with a plea on compassionate grounds supported by the organist.[60] The boys were engaged until their voices broke after which they might seek a place as an adult singer or stipendiary.[61] Boys with good voices may not always have been easy to find and in 1596–7 the mother of one choirboy was paid £2 'when she would have taken away him to keepe him', indicating the cathedral's desire to retain the services of this particular boy named Wilkes.[62] A fee was payable to the organist and master of the boys on admission and the boy was usually provided initially with a gown by their parent or sponsor.[63] At a later period the choirboys would be formally indentured to the cathedral as apprentices.[64] They were provided with new gowns on an annual basis and often too

[56] Barra Boydell, ed., *Music: Documents*, p. 73.
[57] See p. 56 n.149 below.
[58] Gillespie, *First Chapter Act Book*, p. 224. Wiborowe describes himself as having been 'exercised and imployed in that faculty and quallity [i.e. as a tenor singer] and was a Chorister bred and brought up in the said Church'.
[59] C6/1/8/2, pp. 146–7. For more on Stringer see note 166 below.
[60] In 1607 one of the vicars choral, Thomas Smith, and the chancellor Nicholas Robinson both put their sons forward as choirboys, the sexton Edward King his nephew (referred to as his 'son-in-law') and Richard Walshe, a stipendiary singer and later a vicar choral, his first cousin. All four boys were accepted. Barra Boydell, ed., *Music: Documents*, pp. 59, 78.
[61] In 1612 William Johnson and Richard Smyth entered as choristers to join the existing two, Rowland Phillips and John Congan, 'soe long as theire voices shall serve, and that they are serviceable for the Church', another boy Stephen Stephens being added the following year with a similar condition (Gillespie, *First Chapter Act Book*, pp. 134–5, 162, 165; C6/1/8/2, p. 58).
[62] Barra Boydell, ed., *Music: Documents*, p. 81; this is probably the same Anthony Wilkes who became organist of St Patrick's c.1606 (see also note 53 above) and a stipendiary at Christ Church between 1625 and 1627 (Grindle, *Cathedral Music*, p. 224; C/6/26/1/3/11, fol. 3r; Gillespie, *First Chapter Act Book*, p. 149). On the difficulties in finding talented boys see Lehmberg, *Reformation*, p. 203.
[63] C6/1/8/2, p. 58.
[64] See pp. 71 n.28, 79 below.

with new shoes, the purchase, washing and repair of their surplices, gowns and shoes being regularly mentioned in the accounts. The services on Trinity Sunday, the cathedral's patronal day, or at Christmas could provide the occasion on which the choristers were to appear in their new gowns, which were made of broadcloth with canvas collars.[65] Barbers were employed to 'poll and round' the choristers as well as to shave the vicars choral and the dean and members of chapter.[66]

The training of the choirboys remained the responsibility of the organist as master of the choristers, and he was required to ensure that there would always be sufficient boys to sing in the choir.[67] However, the boys might also receive training from others, as in the case of William Clayton who stated in 1644 that he had been taught pricksong by John Heydocke, a stipendiary in the cathedral choir since 1631.[68] There is ample evidence from English cathedrals of the choirboys being taught instrumental music, and although direct evidence is lacking at Christ Church, a list of books lent out by the cathedral in 1607 includes a 'set of *In nominees*'.[69] This indicates part books for viol consort, suggesting that the choirboys were taught the viol as part of their musical education. Most if not all of them would certainly also have been taught to play the organ.

In addition to the foundation choristers the cathedral choir school must have been attended by other boys, some only beginning their musical training, others possibly supplementing the choir at certain services. In 1575 William Wayrame (apparently not the music master) was allowed to miss morning prayer 'for that he must applie the youths in the grammer scole' suggesting that there were other boys in the school in addition to the choirboys who would have attended morning prayer.[70] The names of six choristers are listed for the period 1612–14 as well as there being a reference to the four 'chief choristers' (the number of foundation choristers at that time).[71] While the listing of six names over a two-year period may be accounted for by two new boys replacing others who had left the choir, the term 'chief choristers' does again hint at a larger number of boys who may on occasion have sung in the choir. The terms of a lease taken out in 1548 referred to monies being put towards

> the maintenance of Alexander, Anthony and George Browne, sons of Katherine Myaghe, wife of the said Robert Bathe, in good houses, meat, drink, clothes, and lodgings, and having them taught reading, writing, singing, and grammar, until the said Anthony shall be eighteen years.[72]

This probably represents the education provided to the chorister boys in the

---

65 Barra Boydell, ed., *Music: Documents*, pp. 44, 79–83; Gillespie, *Proctor's Accounts*, p. 79. In 1613 a furrier was paid for 'facing' the choristers' gowns (Barra Boydell, ed., *Music: Documents*, p. 81).
66 Barra Boydell, ed., *Music: Documents*, pp. 41, 84; McEnery & Refaussé, *Deeds*, no. 1398; Gillespie *Proctor's Accounts*, p. 83.
67 Gillespie, *First Chapter Act Book*, pp. 107, 108, 130, 161.
68 C6/1/8/2, pp. 147–8. For Heydocke's appointment as stipendiary, see Gillespie, *First Chapter Act Book*, p. 163.
69 Payne, *Provision and Practice*, pp. 135–45; Gillespie, 'Borrowing Books', p. 17.
70 Barra Boydell, ed., *Music: Documents*, p. 52.
71 *Ibid.*, p. 82.
72 *Ibid.*, p. 44.

cathedral school.[73] A reminder of the strict 'beat and treat' regime under which they were educated is given by the proctor Peter Lewis's account of the building of the new foundation for the tower following its collapse in 1562, when on 17 May 1565 he wrote:

> I brought all the corrystores to see the making of the fondacion and ewry of them brought a stone to the fondacyon and I bett ['beat'] them all that they myght ber in remembrance of the makying of the work and I bestouyd apone the chyldryn, at dener tyme, i terstyn.[74]

Music and the state

The Protestant Reformation in Ireland became increasingly identified with state policy as English political control of the country was strengthened from the late sixteenth century. Under the leadership of Adam Loftus, archbishop of Dublin and lord chancellor, the Church of Ireland was actively anglicised from the 1590s through the appointment of English personnel.[75] In 1575 only three of fifteen royally appointed bishops were English, the remainder being Irish or Anglo-Irish. By 1603 there were six English-born and ten Irish or Anglo-Irish bishops, but by 1625 only three out of the now twenty-three bishops were Irish.[76] These developments were closely reflected at Christ Church as the state increasingly began to stamp its authority not only on the administration and role of the cathedral but also on its musical life. In contrast to St Patrick's cathedral where the dean was elected by the members of the chapter who were themselves appointed by the archbishop, the dean and other dignitaries at Christ Church were royal appointments, these positions increasingly becoming a gift of royalty or of the lord deputy. John Garvey, who died in 1595, was the last Irish-born dean before 1660 and also the last Irish-born member of the sixteenth-century chapter. His successor Jonas Wheeler was a chaplain to Queen Elizabeth, and Ralph Barlow who succeeded Wheeler as dean in 1618 had been chaplain to Lord Chichester, the lord deputy.[77]

Where the late medieval cathedral-priory had developed artistic links with the city through its involvement in sacred drama, the cathedral musicians now began, as a professional body, to fulfil functions outside the cathedral for the benefit of the state and of the city corporation which included a small group of committed Protestant aldermen.[78] In 1568–9 the treasurer of the lord deputy Sir Henry Sidney paid the choristers for 'presenting . . . songs and new verse' and the 'singing-men of Christchurch' received payment one year later. Walter Kennedy, the cathedral organist, was admitted a freeman of Dublin in 1594 'with condicion that he shall attend with his boyes upponn the Mayor, and sing, on stacion dayes

---

[73] Cf. Flynn, 'Education of Choristers', pp. 180–99.
[74] Gillespie, *Proctor's Accounts*, p. 75. 'Terstyn' (or 'tester'): an Irish shilling of the sixteenth-century base issues which Lewis felt was worth 5¼d or 5⅓d.
[75] Ford, *Reformation*, pp. 32–5.
[76] *OCIH*, p. 96. See also Ford, *Reformation*.
[77] Gillespie, 'Shaping of Reform', p. 183.
[78] Lennon, *Lords of Dublin*, pp. 135–8.

and other tymes, when he shalbe called uppon, during his lyfe'.[79] The lord deputy also maintained his own band of musicians who became actively involved along-side the choir in the cathedral's music on important feasts in the liturgical year and on state days. In 1594 they were paid 'for their paines in the quire and helping our viccars', apparently on the Queen's Day (17 November, marking the accession of Elizabeth I), and given breakfast with the vicars on Christmas Eve; the following year they were again present on the Queen's Day as well as performing with the vicars on Christmas Eve.[80] Unspecified musicians, presumably those of either the lord deputy or the city, were employed on the occasion of the archbishop's visitation in 1615/17.[81]

Like church appointments, musical appointments were coming under state control. The lord deputy or lord lieutenant sometimes directly supported singers petitioning for a position in the choir and the dean and chapter had little alternative but to agree. In 1593 they had to accept as a vicar choral a singer named Inch recommended by the lord deputy despite the fact that the maximum number of vicars choral permitted by the foundation statutes had already been reached.[82] Objections were sometimes voiced, as in May 1623 when William Ballard presented letters from the lord deputy in support of his request for the vicar's place of Henry Burnett who had recently died:

> Many objections being layd against him by divers of the Chapter for severall misbehaviours yet to shew themselves by all meanes respective to those honorable letters they did agree that he should hold the sayd place with all the profits thereof as a Probationer for one yeare, Dureing which time, if he should so behave himselfe as noe just exception should be taken agaynst for to much sociablenes and good fellowshipp (as it is called) or drunkennesse or turbulent behaviour or proud or disgracefull speeches towards any of the Chapter or other misbehaviour that then hee should bee elected and installed full vicar.[83]

In 1646 Randal Jewett, who had formerly been organist but had since spent some years at Chester cathedral, similarly presented a letter from the lord lieutenant recommending him for a place as vicar choral. The dean and chapter again considered it prudent to accept the lord lieutenant's recommendation.[84] Petitioners might also plead special circumstances: in 1644 Edward Bankes petitioned for a vacant vicar choral's place on the grounds that he was 'bredd a

---

[79] Barra Boydell, ed., *Music: Documents*, p. 85.

[80] *Ibid.*, pp. 80–1. On Sir Henry Sidney's patronage of music and performance see Fletcher, *Drama*, pp. 214–22. State days commemorated the 'Protestant exaltation of secular authority' and focused on famous deliverances and triumphs of the monarch, and other key events of the Elizabethan regime (Cressy, *Bonfires and Bells*, pp. xi–xv).

[81] Barra Boydell, ed., *Music: Documents*, p. 82. These payments suggest the more regular appearance of the city or state musicians at Christ Church, but records only survive intermittently from this period.

[82] *Ibid.*, pp. 55–6.

[83] Barra Boydell, ed., *Music: Documents*, p. 64. In 1632 Ballard accused the sub-dean of misappropriating monies collected as fines, called him an 'Idle base and Sawcy Fellow' and even threatened his life, for which he was imprisoned for forty-eight hours (Gillespie, *First Chapter Act Book*, pp. 169–70).

[84] Barra Boydell, ed., *Music: Documents*, p. 78.

chorister in [Christ Church], and . . . was in the late rebellion deprived of his meanes and three of his children'.[85]

The appointment as organist and master of the boys in 1596 of John Farmer, following the appointment in 1595 of the Englishman Jonas Wheeler as dean and the (related?) resignation of Walter Kennedy as organist in November of the same year, may be linked to this growing anglicisation of Christ Church as a centre of state policy towards Ireland. Farmer's *Divers and Sundry Waies of Two Parts in One* (London, 1591) demonstrates his technical expertise in forty two-part canons and he was the single largest contributor to East's *The Whole Booke of Psalms* (1592) which includes twenty settings of psalms, canticles, etc, including the Lord's Prayer, Farmer's setting of which is his only sacred work to have remained in the repertoire. But the appointment of a prominent English composer to Christ Church may have been as much a political appointment as one based purely on musical ability. There is no information available on the backgrounds of earlier organists and master of the boys at Christ Church, but Farmer is nonetheless the first demonstrable appointment of an Englishman to the post.[86] Further evidence of Christ Church becoming more closely involved in the musical world of English cathedrals is provided by the appointment of John Fido as a vicar choral, master of the boys and, apparently, organist in May 1600.[87] This may be the same John Fido, described by Ian Payne as a 'purveyor of ready-to-sing anthologies of sacred music', who is recorded variously as organist, master of the boys, singer and/or music copyist at Hereford, Lincoln, Worcester, Wells and King's College, Cambridge in the 1590s and early seventeenth century.[88]

If the appointment as organist of Farmer, and possibly also that of Fido, can be interpreted as reflecting this state-sponsored policy of the anglicisation of Christ Church, then that of Thomas Bateson in 1609 had demonstrably political connections. Organist at Chester cathedral before coming to Dublin, Bateson had already established his reputation as a composer through his first book of madrigals published in 1604. The importance placed by the dean and chapter on securing the services of Bateson, the most distinguished musician to hold the position of organist at Christ Church during the sixteenth and seventeenth centuries, is seen in the fact that in no other case was the contract appointing an organist deemed worthy of being copied into the chapter acts.[89] In the dedication of his second book of madrigals in 1618 to Lord Chichester, who had been lord deputy between 1605 and 1616, Bateson states that '. . . it is not the least of your Honours favours conferred upon me, to grace me with your Honourable service, and to call me to a more immediate dependency upon your Lordship', later referring to 'that relation I have to your Honour' and 'your Honours favours unto me'. What favours was Bateson referring to? As organist at Christ Church at a time when the cathedral was acknowledged as the state cathedral, Bateson's position was effectively

---

[85]   C6/1/8/2, p. 147.

[86]   On Farmer's tenure as organist see p. 54 below.

[87]   Barra Boydell, ed., *Music: Documents*, p. 58.

[88]   Shaw, *Organists*, pp. 134–5, 306; Payne, *Provision and Practice*, pp. 76–7; Morehen, 'Fido'. See also pp. 54–5 below.

[89]   Barra Boydell, ed., *Music: Documents*, pp. 60–3. On the terms of Bateson's contract see p. 55 below.

within the lord deputy's official household. His reference to his being called to 'a more immediate dependency' strongly suggests that his appointment was at Chichester's direct request. Furthermore, the initiative for Bateson's receiving, in 1612, the first music degree to be awarded by the recently founded University of Dublin, Trinity College may also have come from Chichester.[90] At this period music degrees (awarded by Oxford and Cambridge, and now by Dublin) were awarded to musicians of proven ability or upon recommendation, the recipient submitting an exercise as evidence of his skill in music. Bateson's only surviving sacred work, his anthem *Holy, Lord God Almighty* whose text is taken from the epistle for Trinity Sunday, was very likely written for the occasion of his conferring (which may have taken place in Christ Church and quite possibly on Trinity Sunday), being unusually scored for seven voices and honouring as it does the Holy Trinity to which both Trinity College and Christ Church were dedicated.[91]

Counter-Reformation Catholicism had been growing vigorously in Ireland during the early part of the seventeenth century. After the accession of Charles I in 1625 this was seen as presenting a serious political threat which needed to be countered by more positive action. Following their defeat at the Battle of Kinsale in 1601 many of the Gaelic nobility had fled to France and Spain, and England feared the potential explosiveness of Irish-Spanish and Irish-French Catholic links: recusants began to be regarded as the main threat to the government.[92] When Lancelot Bulkeley, archbishop of Dublin, carried out his visitation at Christ Church in April 1627 one of his major concerns was the propagation of Protestantism in the face of the potential Catholic threat. The regular celebration of holy communion was emphasised and lax practices were addressed. A set of orders was drawn up which required the vicars and stipendiaries to attend communion whenever it was held and morning and evening service daily (the choristers wearing their gowns), for which they were to assemble within a quarter of an hour at most after the bell was rung.[93] On Fridays all choir members were to attend in their gowns, and in surplices if it was a holy day; on Sunday mornings and afternoons they were to wear gowns and surplices ('clean and decently') and they were to remain until the end of service and sermon, neither taking off their surplices in the choir nor leaving their places before the 'state' (i.e. the lord deputy and other state representatives) and congregation had departed. The organist was to serve in the choir when not needed at the organ, and all vicars and stipendiaries were required to take communion whenever it was served in the cathedral.[94] All these requirements were to be enforced under threat of specific fines.

The appointment as sub-dean in 1630 of John Atherton, an English cleric who had formerly been private chaplain to Adam Loftus, lord chancellor and lord justice (nephew of the earlier archbishop and chancellor of the same name),

---

[90] Brian Boydell, 'Thomas Bateson', p. 59.

[91] Barra Boydell, ed., *Music: Documents*, pp. 187–93; on the dedication of the anthem see Grindle, *Cathedral Music*, p. 164.

[92] McCurtain, *Tudor and Stuart*, p. 132. See also pp. 49f below.

[93] Barra Boydell, ed., *Music: Documents*, p. 64.

[94] On the increasing emphasis on the celebration of the eucharist at Christ Church at this period see Gillespie, 'Crisis of Reform', pp. 197–8.

resulted in a further tightening of discipline amongst the choir. In July the whole choir was reminded of the 1627 orders and the following month the organist (Randall Jewett, Bateson having died the previous March) was 'admonished not to walk in the body of the church in time of divine service, as also to teach daily the choristers their art of singing'.[95] But Lord Deputy Wentworth, sworn in at Christ Church in July 1633, would set about the wider reform of the Church of Ireland with the assistance of his close adviser John Bramhall, treasurer of Christ Church and subsequently bishop of Derry, and the support of Archbishop Laud of Canterbury. Arminian clerics from England were appointed and Puritan and Presbyterian clergy removed.[96] The Laudian emphasis on elaborate worship, the 'beauty of holiness', made itself felt at Christ Church which was to be what Raymond Gillespie has described as 'the flagship for a religious experiment which could not be allowed to fail'.[97] The building was repainted, the altar refurbished, new communion silver acquired, taverns and tobacco shops removed from the crypt (which had long served as a location for shops and stalls), and the behaviour and decorum of members of the cathedral improved (including an order that 'noe person presume to make urine against the Walls of the said Church'!).[98] A new set of orders to be observed by the vicars choral in performing divine service, 'especially upon Sundays and Festival days', was drawn up in 1634.[99] Apart from the choir members being required to sit together and not to talk during services, each was told to 'respectively performe his due part' when singing 'hymns or anthems' and to sing the doxology at the end of every psalm. Those vicars who were not priests took turns by the week to read the first lesson and also the epistle at the communion table 'plainly and distinctly'. The orders to remain in the choir 'soberly and reverently' until the congregation had departed were reiterated, as well as their requirement to attend and receive communion on all occasions. Aside from those orders relating directly to the choir and its duties, the role of Christ Church as the state cathedral is reflected in aspects of the liturgy being specifically modelled on that of the Chapel Royal:

> And after the Anthem or Psalme at the end of Sermon, he [the vicar choral in holy orders] whose turne it is, standing up in his usuall place, [shall] audibly say, O Lord save our King. The rest of the Quire answering, And mercifully heare us when we call upon thee. And after saying the prayer for the King by it selfe, for the Queen, the Kings Children, the Lady Elizabeth etc. and for the Lord Deputy, and bishops Blesse the people with the peace of God, as is accustomed in the Kings Chappell.

There is also clear evidence for the elaboration of music: already since Archbishop Bulkeley's time instruments had regularly accompanied the choir. William Bedell (later bishop of Kilmore and Ardagh) preached every fortnight at

---

[95] Barra Boydell, ed., *Music: Documents*, p. 65.

[96] Ford, *Reformation*, pp. 214–15.

[97] Gillespie, 'Crisis of Reform', p. 199. On the Laudian experiment at Christ Church see *Ibid.*, pp. 195–202.

[98] See in particular Gillespie, *First Chapter Act Book*, pp. 202–4.

[99] *Ibid.*, pp. 66–9.

THE REFORMATION AND EARLY SEVENTEENTH CENTURY

Christ Church when he was provost of Trinity College Dublin between 1627 and 1629. A contemporary biographer wrote of him that he

> desired no instrumental musick in his cathedral (or organ or the like), but vocal and spiritual singing with grace in the heart to the Lord. He was much displeased with the pompous service at Christ's church in Dublin, which was attended and celebrated with all manner of instrumental musicke, as organs, sackbutts, cornets, viols, etc., as if it had been at the dedication of Nebuchadnezar's golden image in the plain of Dura; and discovered his dislike of those things (now in the time of the Gospel) to a leading prelate, who told him only this, that they served much to the raising of the affections etc. To whom he replied, that all things that are used to work upon the affections ought to tend to edification under the Gospel, as this did not.[100]

The object of Bedell's complaints is corroborated by a payment in 1629/30 of 2s 6d 'To them that plaid on the Cornetts'[101] but his more puritanical views were in marked contrast to developments which would subsequently take place under Wentworth and Bramhall. Specific provision of places for instrumentalists was made a few years later: in 1636/7 a 'place for the violin' was made and a 'Seate for the Sacke-but' in the following year, while in March 1638 the proctor was instructed to 'Pay to the two Sagbutts and two Cornetts for their Service and Attendance in this Church the Summe of 20 nobles eng[lish]', a payment corresponding to the £6 13s 4d (equalling twenty nobles) made in 1637/8 to 'the Lord Deputies Musicke' confirming that it was the state musicians who played in the cathedral.[102] This growing use of instruments reflects contemporary practice at many English cathedrals, although the specific use of a violin in 1636 is exceptional before the Restoration.[103] While they may also have played voluntaries and other purely instrumental music, the musicians playing 'in the choir and helping our vicars' in 1594–5 shows that they did accompany the voices as well.[104]

The role of music, including the use of instruments, as part of the cathedral-state links was further emphasised in 1638 within the context of government attempts to control the recusant guild of St Anne, an episode which demonstrates the use of the cathedral choir as a tool in the religious and political struggles of the time. Wentworth's reforms included an active policy of reclaiming the revenues of the church, most particularly where these had remained in Catholic hands, and attention turned to the chantries and religious guilds or confraternities which, despite the attempts of reformers, had remained undissolved in Ireland.[105] The guild of St Anne, whose guild chapel was located in St Audoen's parish church (usually referred to at the time as St Owen's) not far from Christ Church, was one of a number of such lay confraternities which persisted under Protestant rule. The guild had appointed chantry priests (also referred to as chaplains) down to 1564;

100 Stuckburgh, *Biographies*, pp. 153–4.
101 Barra Boydell, ed., *Music: Documents*, p. 83.
102 *Ibid.*, pp. 70, 83 (and cf. also p. 84).
103 Cf. Payne, *Provision and Practice*, pp. 148–9.
104 Barra Boydell, ed., *Music: Documents*, p. 80.
105 Some of these organisations even survived into the nineteenth century (Lennon, 'Survival of Confraternities').

in the 1540s they were required to sing at all divine services, and there were also two clerks who sang and read daily in the choir, one of whom played the organ at all services, principal feasts and holy days.[106] Links between the guild and the parish were close and continued into the seventeenth century, but the guild concerned itself increasingly with social and charitable rather than spiritual concerns, stressing its role as an adjunct to the city council, its membership including a high proportion of the aldermen of the city. By the late sixteenth century the guild, which was manifestly recusant in its membership and sympathies, was becoming the object of scrutiny by the established church. As late as c.1597 high mass was celebrated at St Audoen's with (unspecified) musical accompaniment,[107] but a series of direct challenges to the guild from officials of church and state seeking to acquire the guild's revenues and to enforce conformity had begun in 1593–4. In 1599–1600 Henry Fitzsimmons, described as 'born in this city of Dublin, the son of an alderman of good account, and by his profession a priest and a Jesuit', was attracting congregations in Dublin of four to five hundred every Sunday to mass which was sung 'in prycksong'.[108]

By 1606 the positions of the guild's six chantry priests and two clerks had been transformed into six singing men and two choirboys who thereafter received regular salaries from the guild for singing in St Audoen's. These positions were filled by members of the choirs of both Christ Church and St Patrick's (of which St Audoen's was a prebend) together with the organist of Christ Church.[109] In March 1609 the guild paid Thomas Bateson (who had just arrived from Chester to become organist at Christ Church) for 'making up' the organ and to play on Sundays and holy days.[110] Evidently, between the late 1590s and 1606 control of the guild had been largely assumed by the Protestant minority. By 1606 the guild was thus supporting a fully fledged musical establishment at St Audoen's which was drawn from the members of the two cathedral choirs.[111] Such was the identity of the guild with the parish church that when the organ in St Audoen was repaired in 1624 it was paid for by and described as belonging to St Anne's guild.[112]

Wentworth's interest in St Anne's guild resulted from the discovery by Revd Thomas Lowe, one of the vicars choral of both Christ Church and St Patrick's cathedrals,[113] of the rent book of St Anne's guild which showed that a majority of its properties were leased to Catholics, in accordance with a papal bull of 1569

---

106 Lennon, 'Chantries', p. 14.
107 E. Hogan, ed., *Ibernia Ignatiana* (Dublin 1880), p. 41. I owe this and several other references relating to St Audoen's and the guild of St Anne to Dr Colm Lennon.
108 *Calendar of the State Papers*, p. 76.
109 Account book of St Anne's guild, *IRL-Da*, MS 12. D. 1, fol. 29r.
110 *Ibid.*, fol. 23v. This reference to Bateson (9 March 1608/9) predates the earliest reference to him at Christ Church by a fortnight.
111 The annual salaries of organist, choirmen and choristers were respectively £10, £4 (£5 6s 8d for the choirman who had responsibility for the boys) and £5 6s 8d for the two choristers (*Ibid.*, fols 25v, 29r, 32r).
112 *Ibid.*, fol. 33v.
113 Thomas Lowe (formerly a stipendiary) was appointed vicar choral in 1631 following the death of Thomas Bateson; subsequently prebendary of St Michan, he died in 1644 (C6/1/8/2, p. 147). Not to be confused with the Thomas Lowe who was organist and master of the choristers at Gloucester cathedral, 1665–6 (Shaw, *Organists*, p. 121).

enjoining Catholic members of confraternities to lease properties to their co-religionists only.[114] Wentworth accordingly established a commission in 1635 which recommended in June 1638 that the guild's revenues be appropriated for the benefit of the cathedral choir and to enhance its music, the cathedral being described as lacking 'competent Means for the Maintenance of an Able and Sufficient Quire'.[115] The existing five vicars (Revd Thomas Lowe, Revd John Allen, John Jewett, William Ballard and William Betney) and one other singer (Richard Dagnall) were each to receive an increase in salary and the number of vicars was to be increased to ten through 'the other foure' (i.e. stipendiary singers) being 'incorporated with the said 5 viccars and Dagnall to Remaine for ever a Corporacion of ten persons'.[116] Of the ten, at least four were always to be priests, the first of these to be dean's vicar (Thomas Lowe) and all four priest vicars to have precedence over the others both in rank and salary.[117] Furthermore two additional boys were to be added 'because fowre boys be an insufficient Number to make an harmony in the Quire'. Increased accommodation was to be arranged: the college belonging to the guild of St Ann at St Audoen's was described as being 'not soe Capatious of 6 priests with families as formerly it was of soe many single men' and, while five of the vicars are noted as having rooms 'near Christchurch', it was determined that the college building should be made larger so that the other five could be provided with chambers therein.

The commission also proposed that the guild should meet in the cathedral, ostensibly because Christ Church was a more appropriate location than St Audoen's; in reality this request seems to have been a bid to keep the guild under closer supervision. Protestant control of the guild was effected by the admission to its membership of some heavyweight representatives of the Protestant establishment including the archbishop of Dublin, Bishop Bramhall of Derry, the bishop of Waterford and Lismore, the vice-treasurer, the lord chief justice, the deans of both Christ Church and St Patrick's cathedrals, and other prominent members of church and state.[118] St Audoen's was to be compensated by an increase in the salary of its organist Randall Jewett who, like his predecessor Bateson, was also the Christ Church organist.[119] The enlarged cathedral choir was to attend on the two anniversaries of the guild (the feasts of St Anne and of the Purification) which would continue to be celebrated in St Audoen's church when the dean and chapter of Christ Church would attend together with the lord deputy

---

[114] Ware, *Romish Fox*, pp. 120–8; Lennon, 'Chantries', p. 22.

[115] Barra Boydell, ed., *Music: Documents*, pp. 71–4. Although entered under the chapter meeting held on 2 October this certificate is dated 18 June. A chapter meeting held on 19 June (but entered in the chapter book after 2 October) gives this as the date on which the above certificate was adopted and admitted by the dean and chapter. Appointments to vicars' positions specifically referring to the certificate were made on 19 June and also on 16 October (C6/1/8/2, pp. 89, 98).

[116] The only other named choirman at this time is John Heydocke who appears alongside Richard Dagnall in the accounts as a stipendiary (C6/1/26/3/26, fol. [1r]).

[117] Barra Boydell, ed., *Music: Documents*, p. 87.

[118] *IRL-Da*, MS 12. D. 1, fol. 41r; these new Protestant members were subsequently expelled in 1653 when the established church was in disarray after the Cromwellian settlement (Clark & Refaussé, *Dublin Guilds*, p. 34).

[119] *IRL-Da*, MS 12. D. 1, fol. 72v.

and council. Further evidence for the regular use of instruments in Christ Church at this period is contained in the provision which was made for two cornetts and two sackbuts to accompany the choir every Sunday.[120]

The deed providing for these changes was not enacted until September 1643, but the guild accounts show an increase to at least ten 'singing men' between 1639 and 1640, all of whom were members of the choir of Christ Church and some of whom were specifically appointed according to the terms of Wentworth's order of 19 June 1638.[121] The singers' salaries were increased and the direct involvement of Christ Church is apparent in the petitioning by the dean for the payment of salaries due to the choir and to the 'sackboots and stipendaries to the guilde serving in Christchurch'.[122] An enhanced choir with regular instrumental support thus provided compensation for the guild's having to move to the cathedral, but even on those occasions when the guild still met in St Audoen's its ceremonies were brought under the direct control of the established church and state. However, by February 1645 services in the cathedral choir would be described as 'slenderly performed for want of Number, and fitt and able men'.[123] It appears that the expansion planned under the St Anne's guild certificate of 1638 was overtaken by events and was at best short-lived.[124]

Organs and organists

Information is scant about the organ or organs in the cathedral during this period. In 1594 and 1595 payments had occurred for 'removing the organs' to the choir and Henry Alyngton was paid for mending the organs in 1612.[125] A year later some structural work to the building was carried out in the vicinity of the organ and the 'door to the organs' was rehung.[126] In October 1616 Bateson (who had previously been paid both in Chester and in Dublin at St Audoen's church for mending the organs) was contracted for the sum of £35 (sterling) to 'make, or cause to be made, a sufficient Instrument or organ' for the cathedral, with an additional £5 being allowed if needed. Subsequent payments for hooks and nails for the 'doore of the Organ place' and to a carpenter for making the organ case are also recorded.[127] At the same time an organ-blower is first mentioned, payments to the organ-blower becoming normal in subsequent accounts.[128] The organ is

120 Barra Boydell, ed., *Music: Documents*, p. 80.
121 *Ibid.*, pp. 86–8. *IRL-Da*, MS 12. D. 1, fols 43v–51r, 72r–73r.
122 *Ibid.*, fols 51r, 72r.
123 Barra Boydell, ed., *Music: Documents*, p. 78.
124 In the proctor's accounts for the years after 1638 the names of only five vicars and continuing references to only four boys still occur. The accounts between 1641 and the cessation of cathedral services in 1647 do not survive.
125 Barra Boydell, ed., *Music: Documents*, pp. 80, 81. The payments in 1594 and 1595 apparently relate to the celebration of the Queen's Day in November, on which occasion the lord deputy's musicians were also paid (see p. 45 above) and special payment made for bell-ringing.
126 'For a piece of long timber to stay the Crosse beame and bordes over the organs and a sawen sparre 16d. A paire of hinges for the doore to the organs on the north side 8d . . .' (*Ibid.*, p. 82).
127 *Ibid.*, pp. 63, 82. The accounts only record a total of £20 paid to Bateson for the organ.
128 'To Patrick for blowing the bellows' (C6/1/26/3/10, fol. 7r). John Hignot is first named as

next mentioned in 1633/4 when a 'staffe to blow the organs' was paid for and in 1635 it was noted that

> the organs were hurte by the admitance of to many to Sit behinde them, The Deane and Chapter did admonish John Hignet Organ-blower to bee hereafter more carefull and not to admitt of any to Sitt or Stand neere to the Organs where they or the Pipes may receive any hurte upon payne of loosing his place.[129]

This poses the question of where the organ was situated. The normal location at this period would have been on the choir screen which separated the choir area from the nave. If this was the case there must have been considerable space around the organ to enable members of the congregation to make use of this area.[130] While in England a parliamentary ordinance in May 1644 had commanded that 'all Organs, and Frames or Cases wherein they stand in all Churches . . . shall be taken away, and utterly defaced, and none hereafter set up in their places',[131] this order had little or no effect in Ireland and there is no reason not to believe that the organ was in use up until cathedral services ceased at Christ Church in 1647.

The names of the organists and masters of the choristers are not known between Robert Heyward in 1546 and the end of the sixteenth century. Walter Kennedy is first specifically identified as organist in 1594 although he had been a vicar choral (as were subsequent organists including Farmer and Bateson) possibly since 1586, probably in 1589 and certainly in 1592.[132] On 19 November 1595 Walter Kennedy resigned his position but was paid a pension which he was warned a few months later would be withdrawn if he did not 'come to sermons' every Sunday and receive communion on the first Sunday of the following month.[133] A reference noted above to Kennedy attending with 'his boys' in 1594 to sing before the lord mayor indicates that he was master of the boys as well as organist.

organ-blower in June 1629 and is often named in the proctor's accounts up to 1641 (Gillespie, *First Chapter Act Book*, p. 157; C6/1/26/3/17–28).

[129] C6/1/26/3/22, fol. 3r; Barra Boydell, ed., *Music: Documents*, p. 70.

[130] Routine repairs to the organ included 'organ ropes' (for the bellows) twice in 1636/7, leather (for the bellows) and the 'organ mender' in 1637/8, ropes twice (including once 'for the Organ bellies [sic]') and the 'organ mender' in 1638/9, with further unspecified work carried out in 1641 (Barra Boydell, ed., *Music: Documents*, pp. 83–4).

[131] Cited after Spink, *Restoration*, p. 3.

[132] Referred to as organist in a lease dated 2 Aug. 1594 (McEnery & Refaussé, *Deeds*, no. 1419). Cotton, *Fasti* ii, p. 82 records Kennedy as a vicar choral since 1586 but his source is lost or unknown. Shaw, *Organists*, p. 408 cites Kennedy as 'named as organist in 1586 by Finlayson (1852)' although Finlayson, *Anthems*, [pp. xxx–xxi] does not mention Kennedy in his succession list of organists. The earliest record of Kennedy which can presently be confirmed is when he was listed alongside known vicars choral in 1589 (C6/1/26/3/4, fol. [7r]). He is specifically named as one of the vicars choral in 1592 (Gillespie, *First Chapter Act Book*, p. 84; McEnery & Refaussé, *Deeds*, no. 1404). His signature is appended to a payment of his wages on 12 December 1594 (C6/1/26/3/6, fol. [8r]). Kennedy took out a number of leases in 1591 and following years, including several of property owned by the vicars choral (Gillespie, *First Chapter Act Book*, pp. 71, 80–1, 88; McEnery & Refaussé, *Deeds*, no. 1414; C6/1/26/3/6, fol. [9r]).

[133] Gillespie, *First Chapter Act Book*, p. 93. Kennedy countersigned here with a crude 'W'.

The possible reasons behind the appointment of John Farmer as Kennedy's successor were discussed above, but Farmer did not become organist immediately after Kennedy's resignation. Farmer was paid 'as master of the Children and Organist . . . from Candelmas daie last [2 February 1596]', but later in the same year there is a payment 'for Goshans Chardges for coming to Dublin to be our organist and for hiring horse'.[134] George Goshan had been a stipendiary singer at Christ Church between 1589 (or earlier) and 1594.[135] Having perhaps demonstrated his abilities as an organist while serving under Walter Kennedy and left Dublin to take up an appointment elsewhere, he appears to have returned to act as organist between November 1595 and Farmer's arrival, apparently in February 1596. Thereafter he remained at Christ Church as a singer, apart from a temporary absence later in 1596 when payment was 'sent' to him or given to his wife, possibly while he fulfilled the terms of his employment elsewhere or arranged his affairs there.[136]

There is very little information (and indeed some confusion) relating to Farmer's tenure as organist. He was installed as a vicar choral on 10 August 1596 but in July 1597 was threatened with dismissal and ordered to return by the first of August 'for departing the land without lysence'.[137] Exactly when he ceased to be organist is not clear: he is thought to have been living in London in 1599, the year in which his *First Set of English Madrigals to four Voices* was published, the work by which he is best known.[138] The next organist, or more precisely the next master of the choristers, for whom there is evidence is Richard Myles who, already described as 'one of the vicars choral', was formally installed in that position in November 1599 which suggests that Farmer remained in Dublin until sometime earlier in that year.[139] Two months later Myles was to be paid 'for the trayning and instructing in singing and Makeing fitt for the Quire such boyes as the said Deane and Chapter and Myles shall from tyme to tyme provide for queristers'.[140] In May 1600, only four months after Myles's appointment, John Fido (who was noted earlier as active for brief periods at a number of different English cathedrals) was elected vicar choral and charged 'to teache and bring up the Queristers instructing in songe so manie as shalbe requisite and necessarie for furnishinge of the Quire . . .'.[141] In the absence of any evidence to suggest the separation of the posts of organist and of master of the boys at this period it may

134   Barra Boydell, ed., *Music: Documents*, pp. 56, 81.
135   *Ibid.*, p. 80; C6/1/26/3/6[b], fol. [3r].
136   Barra Boydell, ed., *Music: Documents*, p. 81; C6/1/26/3/7[a], fol. [7r]. Goshan subsequently appears in the accounts for 1597/8, the last set to survive before 1612/14 (Barra Boydell, ed., *Music: Documents*, p. 81; see also Gillespie, *First Chapter Act Book*, pp. 95, 97).
137   *Ibid.*, p. 57.
138   Fellowes, *English Madrigal Composers*, p. 241 stated that Farmer returned to Dublin where he remained until the spring of 1599 but the available records do not support this claim. Cf. Shaw, *Organists*, pp. 408–9. The possibility that Farmer did not return to Christ Church after 1597 cannot be ruled out.
139   Barra Boydell, ed., *Music: Documents*, p. 57.
140   *Ibid.*, pp. 57–8.
141   *Ibid.*, p. 58. John Fido is not otherwise recorded in the chapter acts or the accounts. Shaw, *Organists*, p. 409 comments 'I include [Richard Myles] somewhat tentatively as Farmer's successor, bearing in mind that he is not mentioned by either Finlayson (1852) or Crawford (1881)'. Neither Shaw nor Grindle, *Cathedral Music*, mention John Fido.

be assumed that Myles and Fido each served as organist as well. Neither is mentioned again in the cathedral records. John Fido next appears (assuming this to be the same person) as a vicar choral in deacon's orders at Wells cathedral in 1605, so it is possible that he remained at Christ Church for up to five years.[142]

The next mention of the organist or choirmaster is the appointment in 1609 of Thomas Bateson who, prior to his appointment to Christ Church, had served as organist of Chester cathedral since 1599. Bateson was admitted and installed as a vicar choral on 24 March 1609 and his contract as organist and master of the choristers was entered into the chapter acts on 5 April, on which date he was also granted leave to spend a month in England 'about his necessarie business', presumably to arrange for the removal of his family and belongings to Dublin.[143] The terms of Bateson's contract provide as detailed an account as is available of the organist's duties and conditions of employment at this period. His appointment was for life (he was to remain at Christ Church until his death in 1630), being required to 'teach and instruct foure Choristers to sing sufficiently from time to time',[144] to 'serve the Quire' and to fulfil his duties 'either by himselfe or his Sufficient deputie (for skill and conversacon)'. He was also entrusted with the 'placeing and displaceing and ordering of all the Choristers in the said Church which now are placed and hearafter shalbe placed, as to him shalbe thought fitt and convenient'. Since it was not considered that the living of a vicar choral's place was 'sufficient to countervayle his labour and paines in the premises', he was to receive an additional £8 13s 4d (English) annually as well as being granted 'a convenient house within the preceincts of our said Church, to dispose of the same att his will and pleasure, as to him shalbe thought fitt and convenient'. A new lease on Bateson's house was granted to his widow in April 1630, but he appears also to have held the lease on another house in the precincts mentioned in 1631 when it was agreed that the rent on it due to Bateson shortly before he died should be paid to his widow.[145] At the end of Bateson's contract there is added the condition that he must not absent himself from his job for more than one month without permission. Bateson appears to have fulfilled his duties conscientiously and repaid Lord Chichester's trust in him, there being only one recorded minor reprimand for misbehaviour during the twenty-one years he served the cathedral.[146] Bateson's will, the original of which was lost in the Public Record Office fire in Dublin in 1922, makes no reference to music or other matters directly related to his profession.[147]

Randall (or Randolph) Jewett took over as organist directly after Bateson's death in March 1630.[148] The son of a singer of the same name at Chester Cathedral

---

[142] Shaw, *Organists*, p. 135.

[143] Barra Boydell, ed., *Music: Documents*, pp. 60–3.

[144] Later in the same document this is given as 'shall teach and instruct the Choristers of the said Church, in singing fitt for the said Quire'.

[145] Barra Boydell, ed., *Music: Documents*, pp. 65, 66.

[146] In 1620 Bateson was admonished for 'divers abusive and Contemptuous tearmes and Speeches given by him to Mr Thomas Low, one of the Prebends of the said Church' (*Ibid.*, p. 63). Grindle, *Cathedral Music*, p. 16 cites a further reprimand as made against Bateson, but this is in fact dated after his death, being directed at 'the organist' who by that time was Randall Jewett.

[147] Bridge, 'Chester', p. 75; Barra Boydell, ed., *Music: Documents*, p. 86.

[148] *Ibid.*, p. 82.

from at least 1612–15, Jewett was simultaneously organist at St Patrick's Cathedral, the first of many to combine the two posts.[149] The succession of two organists at Christ Church who had come from Chester may reflect no more than the historic links between the two cities, Chester at that time being the usual port of embarkation for Dublin. Bateson and Jewett were not however the only musicians to serve both in Chester and Dublin: John Allen, appointed a stipendiary at Christ Church in 1620 and a vicar choral at least from 1626 up to 1646 or 1647, could possibly be the same John Allen who was organist of Chester from 1609 to 1613 and Peter Stringer, also from Chester, would become a vicar choral in 1644/5.[150] Within months of taking up the position of organist Randall Jewett had crossed with the dean and chapter, being admonished under threat of losing his quarterly salary

> not to walke in the body of the Church in tyme of divine service, as alsoe to teach dailie the queresters theire Art of Singeing, and being convicted of contumancy to Mr John Bradley Chancellor and Proctor of this Church in not delivering the keys of the Organs as he was enjoyned.[151]

The following year his salary was increased to £15 annually 'conditionallie he being verie diligent in his place of Organist which he nowe holdeth' and on the same day Richard Galvan was given an allowance of £5 per annum not only to sing in the choir on a daily basis but also 'uppon necessitie or otherwise as occasion shall serve to supplie the Organist place'.[152] This is the earliest evidence for the formal recognition of an assistant organist although Bateson's contract had allowed for the use of a deputy. This, and a further increase in Jewett's salary as organist in 1634 to £20 a year, may reflect additional duties associated with the musical elaboration of worship during this period of Laudian reforms discussed above. Jewett was admitted as a vicar choral in June 1638.[153] The request in July of the same year for him to inform the chancellor 'what bookes he hath had that belong to this Church' may relate to his ceasing to be organist, for in October 1638 Benjamin Rogers is noted as having already served as organist for three months although he was not formally established in the post until the following September. Jewett nevertheless remained on as master of the choristers, the first time that the two posts are known to have been held by different people at the same time.[154] Benjamin Rogers' tenure as organist at Christ Church was

149 Le Huray, 'Jewett'; Grindle, *Cathedral Music*, p. 224. The Jewetts were a long-established Chester family (Le Huray, 'Jewett'), but a countertenor named John Jewett from Fethard, county Wexford, had entered the choir of Christ Church in 1620, was raised to a full vicar's place in 1628 and died in 1640. The relationship if any to Randall Jewett is not known; the coincidence of this unusual surname in Ireland is striking (C6/1/26/13/20, 16 March 1619/20; Gillespie, *First Chapter Act Book*, p. 155; C6/1/8/2, p. 110). The death of a chorister named James Jewet, possibly a son of either Randal or John Jewett, is noted in 1636 (C6/1/8/2, p. 43).

150 Gillespie, *First Chapter Act Book*, p. 143; C6/1/26/1/3/11, fol. 2v; Barra Boydell, ed., *Music: Documents*, p. 78; Shaw, *Organists*, p. 63. On Stringer see note 166 below.

151 Barra Boydell, ed., *Music: Documents*, p. 65.

152 *Ibid.*, p. 66.

153 *Ibid.*, p. 69; C6/1/8/2, p. 89. Shaw, *Organists*, p. 409 stated that Randall Jewett was in deacon's orders by 1638 but this reference is in fact to John Jewett, not Randall.

154 C6/1/8/2, p. 79; Barra Boydell, ed., *Music: Documents*, pp. 70, 74–5.

short-lived, for in 1641 he was a lay clerk at Windsor, his departure possibly prompted by the rebellion of that year or by the worsening conditions at Christ Church which were themselves a reflection of the troubled political climate: the following year the organist's salary was to be cut by half to £10 'in respect of the poverty of the meanes of the Church and the Slowe payments thereof'.[155] Why Jewett ceased to act as organist remains unclear but by 1643, possibly already by September 1642, he was organist at Chester Cathedral and it must be assumed that he stayed at Christ Church until then.[156] By January 1645 he was back in Dublin as a vicar (and apparently organist) at St Patrick's and in July 1646 he presented a letter from the lord lieutenant supporting his successful petition for a vacant vicar choral's place at Christ Church.[157] Whether or not he acted as organist during this final year before cathedral services were suppressed in 1647 is not clear: the position of organist at St Audoen's church (usually held by the organist of Christ Church) was granted in July 1645 to John Hawkshaw (who would be organist in both Dublin cathedrals after the Restoration in 1660) 'in the absence of Randall Jewett', but reverted again to Jewett in July 1648.[158]

Music and repertoire

The period between c.1590 and the 1640s is regarded as the golden age of Anglican church music, but no music sources of this period survive from Christ Church. There was however considerable activity in the copying and purchase of music which parallels the evidence from English cathedrals at the same period, although information is sparse before the later sixteenth century.[159] Payments for 'a quyer [of] paper for songs' and to the precentor's vicar for the 'repairing of songs' (probably the rebinding of choir books) in 1541 and 1542, and the specification of the duties of the organist in 1546 as including the procuring of 'suitable songs' at the expense of the cathedral are the only references to the cathedral's music books before the end of the century.[160] The increased evidence for the provision of music from the 1590s reflects the survival of more extensive records from this period. 'Paper for prickyng songes' was bought twice between 1594 and 1596 and this may be what was bound into ten choir books in 1597/8.[161] The presence noted earlier in 1600 of John Fido who was associated with the copying and supply of choir music at a number of English cathedrals in the 1590s and early seventeenth century also suggests opportunities for further additions to the musical repertoire. What this repertoire contained cannot however be known beyond assuming it to be similar to that of English cathedrals with the possible

155 Holman, 'Rogers'; Barra Boydell, ed., *Music: Documents*, p. 77.
156 Shaw, *Organists*, p. 64. Jewett is also recorded at Chester under the name of Robert Jewett (Mills, 'Music in the City', p. 58).
157 *Ibid.*, p. 417; Barra Boydell, ed., *Music: Documents*, p. 78.
158 *IRL-Da*, MS 12. D. 1, fol. 74r; Jewett was organist and master of the choristers at Winchester cathedral from 1666 until his death in 1675.
159 See Payne, *Provision and Practice*, pp. 73–8.
160 Barra Boydell, ed., *Music: Documents*, pp. 41–2; cf. McEnery & Refaussé, *Deeds*, no. 434.
161 *Ibid.*, pp. 80–1.

addition of locally composed works. The vicars and choristers were given a special payment for 'severall meetings to exercise and try theire Songs before the Nativity' in 1612, suggesting new repertoire.[162] In 1613 Andrew Auden, a stationer not otherwise recorded in Dublin, was paid for delivering '11 rul'd paper bookes for Church Songs' to Thomas Bateson. In the following year two service books were bought for 15 shillings, and three services were copied by a Richard Wyborne whose identity is not known (he may have been a stipendiary).[163]

In line with other musical developments the 1620s and 1630s saw increased activity in providing new music, but again neither composers nor works are named: a service book was repaired in 1625/6, three service books bought in 1629/30, four service books, 'rul'd books' (probably referring to music manuscript) and a 'Sett of bookes for the Quire' in 1632/3, existing music repaired or bound in 1634/5, another four service books and 'a service book for the organist' bought in 1637/8, and 'certain anthems and services' in 1638/9.[164] A set of choir books bought in 1632/3 had to be collected from Drogheda, a day's ride north of Dublin. These may have come from St Peter's church in Drogheda which was used at that time as a pro-cathedral by Archbishop Ussher of Armagh (Drogheda lies at the south-eastern corner of the ecclesiastical province of Armagh) with a choral foundation since 1619 of six 'singing men' and three boys.[165] In 1639 Peter Stringer was paid for 'certaine Anthems and Services procured by him'.[166] What appears to be an adjustable music desk was provided in 1594 when 'a deske for the quire to remove up and downe' was paid for, with another 'desk in the quire and making sellers to Sett it in each place' in 1595.[167] In 1632/3 the carpenter was paid 'for making boxes in the quire for each viccar to putt his bookes in'.[168]

Despite this ample evidence for the purchase and provision of music, actual music which can be linked to Christ Church, directly or indirectly, is limited to a handful of works by composers associated with the cathedral and surviving in sources not directly linked to Dublin. John Farmer's four-voice syllabic setting of the Lord's Prayer predates his period in Dublin and can therefore be assumed, like his other settings from East's *The Whole Booke of Psalms* of 1592, to have been in the repertoire during his tenure as organist. Despite its apparent

[162] *Ibid.*, p. 81.
[163] *Ibid.*, pp. 81–2.
[164] Barra Boydell, ed., *Music: Documents*, pp. 75, 82–3; C6/1/26/3/23, fol. [1v] ('New binding Service booke').
[165] Little, 'Discord', p. 356.
[166] Barra Boydell, ed., *Music: Documents*, pp. 75, 84. The close connections between Dublin and Chester make it likely that this was the same Peter Stringer who was a lay clerk at Chester from 1637, having formerly been a choirboy there, and would return to Chester after the interregnum as a minor canon and subsequently organist and master of the boys (Shaw, *Organists*, p. 217; Bridge, 'Chester', pp. 91f). He was not a member of the Christ Church choir in 1639 but was appointed in 1644 to a vacant vicar's position at Christ Church (C6/1/8/2, pp. 146–7). This raises the question of why he should have been involved in the supply of choir music to Christ Church when he was still at Chester cathedral: was he another 'purveyor of sacred music' like John Fido at the beginning of the century?
[167] Barra Boydell, ed., *Music: Documents*, p. 80; C6/1/26/3/7[b], fol. [2v].
[168] Barra Boydell, ed., *Music: Documents*, p. 83.

simplicity, it has an attractive, almost wayward quality with some striking modulations.[169] A service by Bateson, sung at Chester until the early years of the nineteenth century and doubtless used by him in Dublin too, has since disappeared.[170] His only surviving sacred music is the full anthem *Holy, Lord God Almighty*, which he is thought to have composed for the occasion of his being conferred with a Bachelor of Music degree from Trinity College Dublin in 1612. The music survives in two sets of part-books, both copied by John Merro in Gloucester probably in the 1620s.[171] It is scored for two trebles, two altos, two tenors and bass, a combination noted earlier as reflecting the paucity of basses in Christ Church in the early seventeenth century. Although otherwise imitative in style, the words 'Worthy art thou O Lord [to receive glory, honour and power] . . . For thou has created all things' which form the central message of the text are given emphasis by being set in a declamatory, chordal style in which the rhythm is determined by that of the words (*Ex. 2.1*). This anthem answers to David Brown's description in the context of his madrigals of Bateson as 'an accomplished, if not faultless, craftsman'.[172]

The greater majority of the fifty-one verse anthems in a printed volume representing the repertoire at Christ Church immediately after the Restoration in 1660 are by composers active during the first half of the century.[173] It can reasonably be assumed that most of these works would have been in the cathedral's repertoire prior to 1647. The composers of twenty-eight anthems are named, but indications of verse or chorus sections in the texts allow a further eighteen to be identified with reasonable certainty.[174] The twenty-two composers thus identified include Orlando Gibbons (six anthems), Byrd (four), Bull and John Hutchinson (three), Nathaniel Giles (two or possibly three),[175] and Tomkins (possibly two),[176] Batten, Morley, Peerson, and Ward amongst those represented singly. Two, possibly three, composers associated with Christ Church during the first half of the seventeenth century are also present: Randolph Jewett, Benjamin Rogers and possibly John Fido. Gillen and Johnstone have suggested that Jewett's *O God, the King of Glory* may very well date from his years in Dublin between 1628 and 1639(?) and again between 1643 and c.1650, but that *I heard a voice* (which is unattributed in this collection) most probably predates his Dublin period since it survives in a manuscript which appears to have originated c.1625.[177] The dating of Jewett's

---

[169] Modern editions: *The Treasury of English Church Music* ii, ed. le Huray (London, 1965), p. 132; ed. Morehen (Oxford University Press, 1965); ed. Duley (Dublin: Cathedral Imprint, 1995).

[170] Brown, 'Bateson'.

[171] *GB-Lbl*, Add. MSS 17,792–6; *US-NYp*, Drexel MSS 4180–5. See *NG2* xxiv, p. 17. Modern editions: ed. Hill (Chichester: Cathedral Music, 1988); Barra Boydell, ed., *Music: Documents*, pp. 187–93. See also Grindle, *Cathedral Music*, pp. 163–5.

[172] Brown, 'Bateson'.

[173] *Anthems To be Sung . . . in the Cathedrall Church of the Holy and Undivided Trinity in Dublin* ([Dublin?], 1662). Copy in *IRL-Dtc*. For more on this collection see ch. 3 below.

[174] Cf. Clifford, *Divine Services*, Daniel & Le Huray, *Sources*. I am indebted to Richard Andrewes, Fitzwilliam Museum, Cambridge, for many of these identifications; see also Gillen & Johnstone, *Anthology*, pp. 15–17.

[175] *O Lord turn not away thy face* (no. 18 and unattributed) could be by either Giles or Hooper.

[176] *O Lord, let me know mine end* (no. 23 and unattributed) could be by either Tomkins or Ramsey.

[177] Gillen & Johnstone, *Anthology*, pp. 71–2; both anthems ed. in *Ibid.*, pp. 41–70.

Ex. 2.1 Thomas Bateson, *Holy, Lord God almighty*: (a) bars 21–5,
(b) bars 37–40

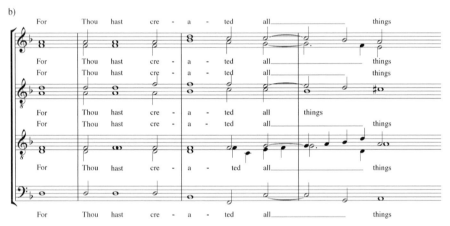

two other anthems in the collection, *Bow down thine ear O Lord* and *The King shall rejoice*, is not known beyond the fact that they are likely to predate the Commonwealth. The two anthems by Rogers, *Everlasting God, which hast ordained* and *Hear me when I call, O God*, could date from his Dublin years between 1638 and 1641 although this is not certain.[178] An unattributed anthem, *Hear me, O Lord, and that soon*, corresponds with a setting by John Fido, who has already been noted as master of the boys and probably organist at Christ Church in 1600.[179]

---

[178] The text of both anthems in Clifford, *Divine Services* but music of *Hear me when I call* in *GB-WRch*, MSS 1–3, copied c.1660 (Daniel & Le Huray, *Sources* ii, p. 110). Another anthem by Rogers which may date from his Dublin period is *I beheld and lo* which is unattributed in the Hosier MS (see p. 89 below).

[179] Gillen & Johnstone, *Anthology*, p. 16.

The cessation of cathedral services

In January 1643 the English parliament passed a bill 'for the utter abolishing and taking away all archbishops, bishops . . . deans and chapters . . . and all vicars choral and choristers . . . out of the Church of England'.[180] Cathedral services ceased over the following years as the Puritan parliamentary forces gained control, some cathedrals being suppressed already from late 1642 (for example Canterbury, Lincoln and Hereford).[181] The political and religious situation at the time was more complex in Ireland and under the lord lieutenant, the marquis of Ormond, the Puritan momentum was largely kept in check. However as early as 1639 the 'musicians of this church' had petitioned for payment 'in respect of the uncertainty of the State of the Church' and in 1641 a series of arrears in payments to members of the choir were made.[182] A number of choirmen, amongst them Benjamin Rogers, appear to have left Dublin rather than risk being caught up in the troubles (the leaders of the 1641 rebellion had planned to take Dublin Castle but were betrayed in October 1641). The reduction in the organist's salary in 1642 has already been noted and in November 1643 the vicars choral and prebendaries complained that their tenants, on whose rents they were largely dependent for their income, had 'not for a long time paid them any rent'. By February 1645 the chapter could complain that 'Gods Service in the quire [was] slenderly performed for want of number, and fitt and able men', but cathedral services were to continue until 1647.[183] In July 1646 Randall Jewett was able to return from Chester cathedral, which had been suppressed, to become again a vicar choral at Christ Church and on the same day John Heydocke (who had been a stipendiary since 1631 and is described here as 'the oldest stipendiary') was promised 'the next viccars Choralls place that shall fall voyde either by Death resignacion or any other way'.[184]

Difficult though life had been for the cathedral during the previous few years, it was the capture of Charles I by parliament which ultimately precipitated the end of cathedral services. Left without clear instructions the marquis of Ormond travelled to England in July 1647 to consult with the king. He had little alternative but to surrender Dublin to the parliamentary forces which had been imposing an economic blockade and, while trade was restored and the economic fortunes of the inhabitants began to recover, the days of Christ Church as a cathedral were numbered. Stipendiaries were appointed in May 1647 and again on 14 June at what was to be the final chapter meeting, the minutes of which give no immediate sign that they would not meet again in formal session for over thirteen years.[185] The abolition of the Book of Common Prayer was proposed the following week and, as Gillespie has commented, 'without the rationale of liturgical worship the

180 Spink, *Restoration*, p. 3.
181 Collinson *et al.*, *Canterbury*, p. 450; Owen, *Lincoln*, p. 75; Payne, *Provision and Practice*, pp. 170–1.
182 Barra Boydell, ed., *Music: Documents*, p. 78; C6/1/26/3/28, fol. 4v.
183 Barra Boydell, ed., *Music: Documents*, pp. 77, 78.
184 C6/1/8/2, p. 163.
185 *Ibid.*, p. 172; Barra Boydell, ed., *Music: Documents*, p. 79.

cathedral began to disintegrate'.[186] But unlike the physical destruction wrought on numbers of English cathedrals by the parliamentary forces, at Christ Church the administration rather ground slowly to a halt, as it did at St Patrick's although over a longer period. The chapter at Christ Church was still issuing leases in 1648 although cathedral services has long since ceased, but the personnel were gradually leaving.[187] During the Interregnum Christ Church would continue in use as a place of worship, but music would not be heard again until after the Restoration in 1660.

[186] Gillespie, 'Crisis of Reform', pp. 207–8, on which the above summary is based.
[187] A number of leases of former cathedral property are recorded between 1647 and 1660, most of which are transfers of leaseholders, although some still acknowledge rents due to the dean and chapter (McEnery & Refaussé, *Deeds*, nos 1559–79).

THREE

'So Great and Solemn Service': the Restoration and Later Seventeenth Century

The Restoration in 1660 initiated a period of exceptional activity and creativity in the musical life of Christ Church cathedral. This activity is closely related to the cathedral's role as the state cathedral and chapel royal for the English administration in an Ireland whose political and religious landscape had been transformed since the 1640s. More than a decade of warfare had followed the rebellion in October 1641 in which the lines of conflict were not simply defined. Initially the Irish Catholics had risen in rebellion in Ulster where the largest numbers of Protestant plantations and land seizures had taken place. They were soon joined by many of the 'Old English' throughout Ireland, the Catholic gentry and landowners who traced their ancestry back to English settlers of the medieval period and who most often supported the English Royalist cause. Matters were complicated by the outbreak of the Civil War in England, the insurrection against English rule and appropriation of land becoming clouded by many of the Irish Catholic gentry's support for the English Royalist cause, the rebellion increasingly taking the form as much of a religious war as of a war of independence.[1] Oliver Cromwell's arrival in Ireland in 1649 marked the beginning of nine months of ruthless repression and reconquest which have ever since made Cromwell into 'a by-word for brutality, and the worst personification of that English racial and religious animus against the Irish which stretched over several centuries'.[2] By the late 1650s the exclusion of Ireland's majority Catholic population from land ownership, public office and political rights had begun, a process which would culminate in the discriminatory penal laws enacted from the 1690s. The Restoration in 1660 thus marked not just the return to power of the monarchy and the re-establishment of cathedral services after the Commonwealth: it also saw the consolidation of English rule in Ireland after nearly two decades of unrest and political uncertainly and defined the demarcation of political difference along religious lines which has haunted Anglo-Irish relationships ever since.

The Restoration also ushered in a new era in cathedral music following the complete break in the practice of cathedral music since the 1640s. During his exile in France Charles II had maintained the liturgy in his private chapel with elaborate ceremony including music, and following the Restoration the Chapel

---

[1] For a succinct account of the war in Ireland see 'Confederate War', *OCIH*, pp. 115–16.
[2] T.C. Barnard, in *BCMIC*, p. 149.

Royal became the model which cathedrals sought to emulate. The new solo style of music 'after the Italian way',[3] which had originated around the beginning of the seventeenth century with composers such as Monteverdi, was being widely adopted throughout Europe but had only tentatively begun to make its presence felt in English sacred music before the Civil War. Now, following the Restoration, it began to take over from the earlier polyphonic style, a change which can be clearly traced in musical developments at Christ Church. The position of music in the Anglican liturgy was also formally recognised for the first time: allowance had been made in earlier editions of the Book of Common Prayer for the singing of the psalms, *Te Deum*, canticles, etc., but the 1662 Book of Common Prayer for the first time specifically contains the rubric 'In Quires and Places where they sing here followeth the Anthem' after the third collect at morning and evening prayer, thus giving formal expression to a practice which had in fact pertained since the Reformation.[4]

Cathedral services resumed

Although Christ Church had 'ceased to be in any sense a cathedral church' since 1647, it had remained open as a centre of worship throughout the 1650s.[5] Sermons were regularly preached on Sundays by Independent and Presbyterian ministers and it functioned as the church of the parliamentary commissioners in Dublin. In contrast to many cathedrals elsewhere, therefore, the building remained largely undamaged and continued to fulfil important civic functions such as the ringing of bells to regulate civic life. Following the death of Oliver Cromwell in 1658 and the decline of the Commonwealth, the process of reviving episcopacy and restoring Christ Church to cathedral use proved to be quite rapid. In December 1659 the congregation had rejected puritan austerity by ordering a red pulpit cushion with crimson silk lining and a gold fringe.[6] A sermon to mark the proclamation of King Charles II was preached on 24 May 1660, by which time the Book of Common Prayer was beginning to be used again. Robert Mossom was appointed the new dean on 25 September, the new cathedral chapter holding its first meeting on 2 November 1660.[7] In February 1661 the carpenter was paid for making the 'Singing mens Seates' and, although first referred to the following November, an organ of some description was clearly already in use by this time.[8]

The restoration of the monarchy and of the established church and its liturgy (not to mention ecclesiastical property and rents)[9] was marked by an elaborate ceremony in Dublin on 27 January 1661 which served as much as a demonstration

---

[3] William Child, *The First Set of Psalmes of III Voyces* (London, 1639), title page. Cited after Dennison, *Humfrey*, p. 11.

[4] The musical aspects of the restored liturgy are outlined in Spink, *Restoration*, pp. 6ff.

[5] Gillespie, 'Crisis of Reform', pp. 209–15.

[6] C6/1/26/6/15.

[7] Mason, *History and Antiquities*, p. 191. William Fuller had been appointed dean of St Patrick's on 3 July 1660.

[8] On the organs see pp. 85–6 below.

[9] Milne, 'Restoration', pp. 264–5.

of political strength by Ireland's Anglo-Protestant rulers as a religious celebration. The climax of the ceremony was the consecration of two new archbishops and ten bishops. This service of consecration, held in St Patrick's cathedral, was preceded by what can best be described as a triumphal procession by representatives of the religious, intellectual and municipal pillars of the Anglo-Protestant establishment across the city of Dublin which was still substantially contained within its medieval walls (*Plate 5*). The lord primate Archbishop Bramhall, the bishops elect and the bishop consecrators, the deans and other dignitaries of the two Dublin cathedrals, Christ Church and St Patrick's, the members of the University of Dublin (Trinity College) headed by the pro-vice-chancellor and doctors of divinity and law, and 'the ministers and civilians of the city' gathered at Christ Church 'in their several gowns and formalities'. Accompanied by the combined cathedral choirs, they processed 'with silent, solemn gravity' to St Patrick's cathedral, into which they were led by the choir singing a *Te Deum* accompanied by the organ (the identity of neither this *Te Deum* setting nor of the other hymns sung during the ceremony is recorded). The office of morning prayer was celebrated, after which the lord bishop elect of Down, Dr Jeremy Taylor, ascended the pulpit while the choir sang the hymn *Praeveni nobis*. An unnamed anthem followed.[10] After the office of consecration of the twelve archbishops and bishops the choir sang an anthem *Now that the Lord hath readvanc'd the crown* specially composed by Richard Hosier, the recently appointed dean's vicar and master of the choristers at both cathedrals, to a text by William Fuller, dean of St Patrick's and former treasurer of Christ Church.[11] As the lord primate went from

---

[10] Possibly *O God that art the well-spring of all peace* by John Holmes, see pp. 68–9 below.

[11] Further on Hosier's anthems see pp. 88–95 below. Possibly the stipendiary of the same name noted at Christ Church in August 1634 but dismissed the following December for 'wilfully [deserting] his service in this church' (Barra Boydell, ed., *Music: Documents*, p. 69), Richard Hosier was appointed a vicar choral at St Patrick's in October 1660 (St Patrick's chapter acts, C2/1/3/2, 24 Oct. 1660) and is first named at Christ Church in November 1660, subsequently being appointed dean's vicar and master of the choristers (see pp. 70, 82 below). He took holy orders prior to December 1665 when he was admitted as a weekly reader of common prayers (C6/1/7/2, fol. 141r). Hosier died sometime before 17 March 1677. The possible identification of Hosier with other eponymous cathedral musicians is unclear. If at Dublin in 1634, he cannot be the Richard Hosier baptised on 8 February 1624 in Gloucester, son of the master of choristers and organist Philip Hosier (*GB-GLr*, MF 554; I am grateful to Brian Crosby for bringing many of these references to my attention; on Philip Hosier see Shaw, *Organists*, p. 119). A Richard Hosier is recorded at King's College, Cambridge, in 1637 and as a gentleman of the Chapel Royal in 1641 (Crosby, 'Early Restoration', pp. 462–3; see also Spink, *Restoration*, p. 225) while a 'Mr Hosier' became organist at New College, Oxford, in January 1637 and is noted there the following year as *informator* in music (Shaw, *Organists*, p. 388). A Richard Hosier baptised on 4 March 1592/3 at Gainsborough, Lincolnshire (Gainsborough parish registers, Lincolnshire Archives) would seem to be too old to be the Dublin Hosier of the early Restoration since he would already have been approaching seventy in 1660. A 'Richard Hosier diaconus' was admitted as a probationary minor canon at Bristol cathedral in April 1622 and (the same person?) as a lay singing man following the Restoration, on 17 September 1660 (Bristol cathedral, DC/A/8/1, fols 5v, 6v). It is not inconceivable that this Bristol Hosier might have learned of the vacancies at the Dublin cathedrals and decided to move there in time to be appointed at St Patrick's in late October (records are sparse from Bristol in succeeding years, but there was no Hosier there in 1662–3; information from Brian Crosby). A Richard Hosier applied unsuccessfully for a minor canon's place at Peterborough in March 1662 (*GB-PB*, MS 52).

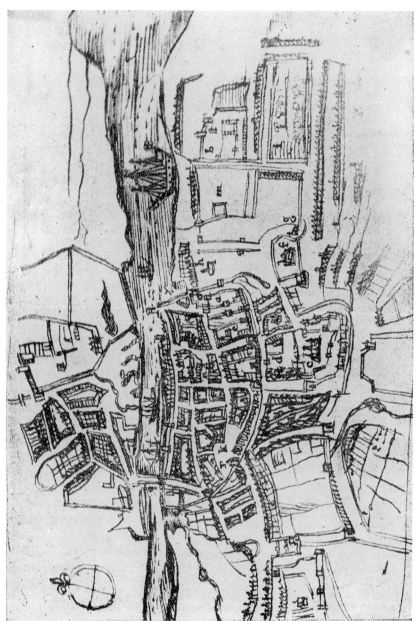

Plate 5. Sketch map of Dublin, c.1680, by Thomas Dineley. Christ Church cathedral is in the centre of the walled city, marked 'n', Dublin Castle in the south-east corner of the walled city, marked 'a', and St Patrick's cathedral to the south, marked 'c'. (National Library of Ireland, Dublin)

the choir to the west door at the end of the service the hymn *Laetificatur cor regis* was sung, the whole procession then accompanying him to his house. The description of the ceremony concluded by stating that it took place 'without any confusion, or the least clamour heard, save many prayers and blessings from the people, although the throng was great, and the windows, throughout the whole passage, filled with spectators'.[12] This description of unanimous public support may reflect little more than Protestant royalist propaganda, but it is true that seventeenth-century Dublin was an overwhelmingly Protestant, English-speaking city in contrast to most of the country.

Dean Fuller's text of the anthem *Now that the Lord hath readvanced the crown*, also referred to as the 'Consecration anthem', focuses on the restoration and synthesis of church and monarchy after the turbulent years of the Commonwealth, the final lines articulating contemporary belief in the doctrine of divine right:

> Now that the Lord hath readvanced the crown
> Which thirst of spoil and frantic zeal threw down,
> Now that the Lord the mitre hath restored,
> Which with the crown lay in the dust abhorred:
> Praise him ye kings, praise him ye priests, all sing
> Glory to Christ our high priest, highest king.
> May Judah's royal sceptre still shine clear,
> May Aaron's holy rod still blossoms bear.
> Sceptre and rod rule still and guide our land,
> And they whom God anoints feel no rude hand.
> May love, peace, plenty, wait on throne and chair
> And may both share in blessings as in care.
> Angels look down and joy to see,
> Like that above, a monarchy,
> Like that above, a hierarchy.
> Hallelujah.[13]

This anthem is the penultimate entry in a printed collection of anthem texts (without music) published in 1662 and entitled *Anthems to be Sung at the Celebration of Divine Service in the Cathedrall Church of the Holy and Undivided Trinity in Dublin*.[14] The final anthem in this collection is John Holmes's *O God that art the well spring* which makes specific references to King Charles, to the one ('true') religion, and to the hoped-for union of England, Scotland and Ireland:

12 Mason, *History and Antiquities*, pp. 192–4, citing contemporary accounts by Dudley Loftus and the *Kingdom's Intelligencer*, 11 Feb., 1660/1.
13 Edited in Barra Boydell, ed., *Music: Documents*, pp. 195–9; recorded on *Sing* (CD). See further pp. 91ff below. Spink, *Restoration*, pp. 329–30 records another setting of this text, by William King, organist at New College, Oxford, between 1664 and 1680.
14 The place of printing or publication is not given, but a payment on 2 May 1662 to Dr [Thomas] Bladen 'for printinge and bindinge the Anthems' almost certainly refers to this book (Barra Boydell, ed., *Music: Documents*, p. 132). William Bladen, since c.1626 Dublin's only printer and for much of the period only bookseller, was succeeded c.1663 by Nathaniel Thompson (see note 148 below) under the nominal direction of Bladen's son Dr Thomas Bladen (Pollard, *Book Trade*, pp. 37–9). For more on *Anthems to be Sung* see pp. 59–60 above and 87–8 below.

O God that art the well-spring of all peace,
Make all thy gifts in CHARLES his reign increase.
England preserve, Scotland protect,
Make Ireland in thy service perfect.
That all these kingdoms under Great Britain's king
May still be watered with the gospel spring.
Oh never let unhallowed breath have space
To blight/blast those blooming buds of union;
But let us all with mutual love embrace
One name, one king, and one religion.
Ah, let this peace be thought the only gem,
That can adorn King CHARLES his diadem.
Hallelujah. Amen.[15]

Like that of Hosier's 'Consecration anthem', the music of this anthem is contained in the Hosier MS (*GB-DRc* MS B. 1) and also in an earlier organ book not linked to Dublin, the so-called Batten Organ Book (*GB-Ob* MS Tenbury 791).[16] The music of *O God that art the wellspring* as it is preserved in the Hosier MS comprises vocal parts with an organ bass, but there has been much crossing-out and re-writing: the organ part contains many more notes in length than the voice parts it accompanies, which themselves do not always correspond with each other musically. As a result much of the anthem is more or less impossible to transcribe with any degree of confidence from this source alone. The music in the Batten organ book consists of a two-stave organ part without text or other identification of vocal entries except when 'Chorus' is marked, but it is for the most part clearly written. The anthem is identified by composer's name and by title, including the subtitle 'Anthem for the King' (which also occurs with others of Holmes's anthems in MS Tenbury 791). It is notated a fourth lower than in the Hosier MS[17] but the opening bars of the Hosier MS version are not present. Despite this, the Tenbury organ part can be married reasonably well with the version in the Hosier MS. The Tenbury organ book contains several of Holmes's anthems 'prickt from his own pricking in the year 1635' by Adrian Batten, a choirboy at Winchester and pupil of John Holmes who was organist there from 1599 to 1621 and thereafter master of the choristers at Salisbury until his death in 1629. The subtitle 'Anthem for the King' and the nature of the text indicate an anthem composed either for the coronation of Charles I in 1625 or, if 'Charles' in the text as preserved in the Hosier MS and the 1662 *Anthems to be Sung* is a substitution for 'James' as is quite possible, an occasion such as when Holmes travelled in 1613 with some of his choristers to Salisbury to augment the cathedral choir there during James I's stay in the city.[18] Whatever its origins, *O God that art the wellspring* must originally date from before 1629 although the text may

---

[15] *Anthems to be Sung*, p. 33 (textual repetitions not reproduced here). Attributed to John Holmes in *Anthems to be Sung* and to his son Thomas (d.1638) in the Hosier MS.

[16] For more on Tenbury MS 791 see le Huray 'Towards a Definitive Study' and Clark 'Adrian Batten'.

[17] The lower pitch and the notation, with C2 and F5 clefs both on six-line staves, implies the by then old-fashioned *in contrabasso* use of transposing clefs.

[18] Le Huray & Morehen, 'Holmes'.

Ex. 3.1 John Holmes, *O God that art the well spring*

subsequently have been adapted to suit the circumstances at Dublin in 1661.[19] While clearly appropriate for the consecration service in January 1661, it could alternatively have been performed on 23 April 1661, the day of Charles II's coronation in London, which was marked in Dublin by a state procession of the lords justice with 'all sorts of music played before them' from Dublin Castle to Christ Church, where 'after divine service and anthem the lord primate made a most excellent sermon'.[20] The text certainly encapsulated the hopes and aspirations of the Anglo-Protestant ascendancy gathered in Dublin in the early months of 1661: while the lines 'England preserve' and 'Scotland protect' are stated once each by the two treble soloists, both combine to sing 'Make Ireland in thy service perfect' as a duet, each voice repeating these words twice (*Ex. 3.1*).

The re-establishment and duties of the choir

The choir of Christ Church cathedral appears to have been active more or less as soon as services were resumed although it took some time to be re-established formally. St Patrick's cathedral appointed nine vicars choral in October 1660, all

[19] Where the vocal parts as they appear in the Hosier MS can be followed in the organ part of Tenbury MS 971 the precise syllable/note count does not always correspond, lending weight to the suggestion that the text may have been altered in order to adapt it to the particular needs of Dublin in c.1661. On the dating of this anthem contrast the opinion I expressed previously in Milne, *Christ Church*, p. 309 and Barra Boydell, 'Now that the Lord', p. 241, both before its presence in Tenbury MS 791 had come to my notice.

[20] *Mercurius Publicus*, xvii (2 May 1661); *The Kingdom's Intelligencer*, xviii (6 May 1661), cited after Gillespie, 'Crisis of Reform', pp. 216–17.

of whom would become members of the choir of Christ Church as well (in effect from this period up to the late nineteenth century the one choir would serve both cathedrals), but appointments at Christ Church did not follow as promptly.[21] Although Richard Hosier petitioned in November 1660 to be 'the first vicar choral that shall be elected into this church' and the following February both he and John Hawkshaw were appointed vicars choral,[22] the full complement of vicars choral and stipendiaries were not appointed before September 1661.[23] References to the choir singing at the consecration service in January 1661, the installations of the dean and other dignitaries in February and March 1661 and the service to mark the coronation of Charles II in April 1661 nevertheless indicate that a choir was already in place.[24] In 1641, the last year before the cessation of cathedral services for which a complete list survives, the choir of Christ Church had comprised five vicars choral (the place of sixth vicar not having been filled for many years), two stipendiaries and four choirboys, in addition to the organist.[25] After the Restoration, however, the size of the choir was increased: while the number of vicars choral remained at six (as defined by James I's grant of 1604) there were initially eight stipendiary choirmen.[26] Within a few years their

21   St Patrick's chapter acts, C2/1/3/2.

22   C6/1/7/2, fols 79v, 80v; Barra Boydell, ed., *Music: Documents*, p. 96. John Hawkshaw was organist at both Dublin cathedrals but there were two musicians of the same name, both organists and probably father and son, whose separate identities are not always clear: an undated list of choir men and organists serving both cathedrals (c.1664) distinguished between a 'Mr Hawkshaw senior Organ' and a 'Mr Hawkshaw Organ' who also sang tenor (see note 26 below). The 'John Hawkeshaw, organist from Chester' named in 1664 in a list of those who took the oath for Protestant strangers under the 1663 act (21 Apr. 1664, *GB-Lbl*, Egerton MS 77, fol. 117v) must be the latter since he cannot be the John Hawkshaw appointed organist at both cathedrals in 1660/1, who had lived in Dublin before the Commonwealth and was certainly living there in October 1660 wherever else he may have spent some or all of the intervening years. It seems that Crawford's conjecture that two John Hawkshaws served as organists of St Patrick's between 1660 and 1685 may be correct (*Cathedral Anthems* ('Succession of Organists') cited but questioned by Shaw, *Organists*, p. 419). The Christ Church deeds include leases granted to 'John Hawkshaw' in 1645, often in the 1660s, as well as in 1697 and 1709 (McEnery & Refaussé, *Deeds*, nos 1556, 1596, 1637, 1640, 1662, 1702, 1711, 1814, 1878, 1939, 1947, *inter alia*), these later dates well after the death of the cathedral organist John Hawkshaw (senior) in late 1688 or early 1689 (Barra Boydell, ed., *Music: Documents*, p. 102); see also p. 86 below.

23   C6/1/7/2, fols 78v, 88r; Barra Boydell, ed., *Music: Documents*, pp. 96–7.

24   C6/1/7/2, fols 85r, 87r, 89r. The formulaic description of these installation ceremonies ('the organs playing and the singers of the church going before . . . singing holy hymns [sometimes 'anthems']') is repeated with little variation into the nineteenth century.

25   C6/1/26/3/28, fol. 3r. Vicars and stipendiaries can be identified by name and amount of payment.

26   The chapter act of 24 September 1661, re-appointing the full complement of choir men, and an undated list (c.1664), indicating allocation of their duties between Christ Church and St Patrick's, together allow the full adult membership of the choir at this period, with most of their voices, to be established. The six vicars choral were Peregrine Darling (countertenor), John Tadpole senior (countertenor?), Richard Hosier (tenor), Robert Essex (bass), Faithful Tadpole (bass?), and John Hawkshaw (organist, see note 22 above); the stipendiaries were Nicholas Seaward (countertenor), Michael Leigh (or Lee, tenor), Michael Newton (tenor), Richard Bury (or Berry, bass), Walter Howard (bass), John Tadpole junior (bass?), John Blett and Anthony Tankersley (voices not known). In addition the younger John Hawkshaw (tenor and organist) is listed as singing at Christ Church in the c.1664 list (Barra Boydell, ed., *Music: Documents*, pp. 96–7, 157; see also names listed in payments made in November 1663, C6/1/26/4/12). Identification of the three Tadpoles is uncertain: here they are listed as 'Mr Tadpole Sen.', 'Mr Tadpole Jun.' and John

number settled at six which would remain normal throughout most of the period up to Disestablishment in 1871. Occasionally this number declined, most notably during the unsettled period during the Williamite War when there were only two or three stipendiaries in 1689 and 1692 and four in 1692/4.[27] Despite a proposed increase to six in 1664 which was not apparently realised, the choirboys normally numbered four into the early eighteenth century when they were increased to six.[28] However, as was observed in the previous chapter, other boys may have attended the cathedral school and sung in the choir in addition to the foundation choirboys. Shortly after the Restoration the full complement of the choir thus stood initially at eighteen members, all of whom (including the four boys) were also members of the choir of St Patrick's cathedral.[29] Two of these choir men, John Tadpole senior and John Hawkshaw senior, had been members of both cathedral choirs in the 1640s,[30] while Faithful Tadpole had become a choirboy at Christ Church in 1639 (and also, like his brother(?) John the younger, at St Audoen's church under the patronage of St Anne's Guild).[31] What these and other choir members who had sung in cathedral choirs before the Commonwealth, whether in Ireland or England, did during the intervening years is seldom recorded. Some former cathedral musicians in England found employment as private household musicians, music teachers in the larger cities, or as theatre musicians. The same certainly applied to at least some of the Dublin cathedral musicians, a matter of considerable concern to Edward Wetenhall who as precentor of Christ Church cathedral in the 1670s would later regret that during this period

> The rage of the War, having scattered our Quire-men, and ravisht from them their subsistence, had also put them to seek their bread in mean, miserable and illiberal waies: and those few Principles of Literature, which any of them had, were, by that means, extinguisht or lost, rather than improved, their natural parts lowerd and debased, or worse: so that the thin number of them, who survived these calamities to see the Restauration, retained nothing but their

Tadpole, while a contemporary list of choir absences and penalties (also undated) names 'Mr Tadpole the Father', 'Mr Tadpole Jun' and 'Mr Tadpole Sen' (C6/1/26/12/6[/3]); however another, dated 28 Mar. 1664, names 'Tadpole senior', 'Tadpole junior' and 'Faithful Tadpole' (Barra Boydell, ed., *Music: Documents*, p. 158); see also note 31 below.

27 C6/1/15/1/24–27.

28 See pp. 109–10 below. The four foundation choirboys indentured in December 1662 (the earliest date for which choirboys' names are known after the Restoration, this being a rare occurrence at Christ Church of the choirboys' names) were Joseph Shepard, John King, Bartholomew Chadderton and Samuel Chadderton. Grindle incorrectly stated that there appear to have been six choirboys in the choir from the Restoration (*Cathedral Music*, p. 29). The number of choirboys is seldom specified but the proctor's accounts 1664–5 and chapter acts 27 Mar. 1666 clearly specify four choirboys (Barra Boydell, ed., *Music: Documents*, pp. 101, 133).

29 Cf. Cotton, *Fasti* ii; Lawlor, *Fasti*; St Patrick's chapter acts C2/1/3/2, *passim* (annual dean's visitation lists).

30 Cotton, *Fasti* ii, pp. 84, 204,

31 In 1641 the cathedral accounts mention 'Mr Tadpoles 2 sons' but without naming them (C6/1/26/3/28, fol. 4v; C6/1/7/2, fol. 39r; *IRL-Da*, MS 12. D. 1, fol. 48r). As one of the two choirboys paid by St Anne's guild, John Tadpole junior was almost certainly also a choirboy at Christ Church. John Tadpole senior, together with 'his two boys', was paid by St Anne's guild for singing in St Audoen's up to May 1652 (*ibid.*, fol. 92r).

Musick, which possibly they would have lost too in a great part, but that their
necessities would not permit them to *hang their harps upon the willows*, their
Musical skill being the most considerable means of support then left them.
Neverthelesse, they were not then to *sing the Song of the Lord*, nor any of the
songs of Zion, but to contrive their melodies to the humour of such who would
feed them: The influence hereof, both upon our Musicians, and Musick, is
sadder than I will speak of.[32]

The only former choir man of Christ Church whose activity during the Commonwealth is recorded is John Tadpole who remained in Dublin throughout the 1650s
as a parish clerk of the neighbouring church of St John.[33]

A draft text of the oath sworn by vicars choral on their admission in the early
years of the Restoration cites their duties of obedience to the dean and to the rules
of the church and of the corporation of vicars choral, of daily attendance at
services, and of confidentiality (a clause swearing that the applicant has neither
committed simony in seeking this position nor would be so involved in the future
was subsequently added in by another hand).[34] A set of orders dating from
17 September 1662 itemises details of behaviour and fines or other punishments
including dismissal.[35] The first of the eighteen orders (and thus one assumes
considered most important) states that every vicar, stipendiary and choirboy must
attend morning and evening service daily, various fines being specified for late
arrival at different stages of the service. The second order requires all vicars and
stipendiaries to take communion on solemn feasts and at least once quarterly
(reference is made here to communion being celebrated monthly). The third order
concerns their musical skills:

> That every Vicar, and Stipendiary diligently apply himselfe, to the improving
> his Skill in Song, That hee may bee able to perform his parte at first Sight in
> Ordinary Anthems of the Church, Otherwise, That, after admonition hee bee
> put out of his place, or Office at the discretion, and Sentence of the deane and
> Chapter, for his insufficiency.

Thereafter attention moves to a range of aspects of behaviour and appearance.
The requirement for the organist to serve in the choir on 'ordinary days' except
when needed at the organ suggests that much of the singing was unaccompanied
(verse anthems clearly being an exception). Choir members were required to be
'modest and grave in their attire, hair and gesture' at all times and in all places,
this particularly applying to services when they were to wear their gowns during
weekdays with clean surplices on Sundays and festivals. Reverent behaviour was
expected during services 'without laughing, or talking, or any indecent behaviour' and they were all to stand when singing anthems, sitting down only being
allowed during lessons and sermons. While they were not to wear their hats in the
nave of the church, in the aisles they were to wear them when walking in the

---

32 Wetenhall, *Of Gifts and Offices*, pp. 538–9 (original italics).
33 Gillespie, 'Crisis of Reform', p. 209.
34 Barra Boydell, ed., *Music: Documents*, p. 158.
35 'Orders and statutes . . . for the government of the vicars choral, stipendiaries, and choristers',
    ibid., pp. 97–100.

presence of the dean or subdean. Attendance was strictly enforced, vicars taking turns by the week to note down the names of defaulters (a number of surviving contemporary attendance lists bear evidence to this practice).[36] They were to converse together 'peaceably . . . without any reproachful language or other injury offered', not to strike another 'with hand or foot or any instrument of hurt' and avoid 'lying, railing, or any other enormity of living'. Conviction of being 'a common swearer, drunkard, or incontinent liver' would result in expulsion and none was to keep any alehouse, wine tavern or 'house of resort to drinking'. Broadly speaking these orders of 1662 re-established norms of behaviour and duties which had been current prior to the Commonwealth, but the need for such rules of conduct and penalties was very real. Earlier in the same year there had been complaints of

> scandalous differences and much reproachful language amongst several persons of the choir . . . to the violation of that amity and unity which ought to be amongst them as brethren of the same society, thereby bringing great dishonour unto God, disturbance unto the church, and offence unto us, entrusted with the government of this cathedral.[37]

A month later Robert Essex, a vicar choral, and Anthony Tankersley, a stipendiary, were involved in a tavern brawl as a result of which Essex was rendered 'unfit for the service of the choir by reason of the blackness of his eye'.[38]

The practice of sacred music

From 1661 the choir met on Wednesday and Friday afternoons 'to practice in singing [and] to make them fit for the service of the choir' and in 1665 practices were specified on Thursday mornings and on Saturdays after evening prayers, for two hours in each case.[39] There are however few indications of musical standards beyond what can be read into the requirement cited above relating to the choirmen improving their skills in order to be able to read at sight 'Ordinary Anthems of the Church', a point specifically raised by Dean Moreton on the occasion of his visitation in January 1679.[40] The dean and chapter's response to Moreton's visitation leaves out any order relating to this particular point, perhaps indicating that no remedial action was deemed necessary.[41] Closely reflecting the concerns expressed by Edward Wetenhall, however, the dean wished to know if the anthems usually sung were 'such for matter and form as are fit to excite and employ Christian devotion' and whether anthems and services were performed 'with due art and decency'. Wetenhall had devoted considerable attention in his treatise to this question of the style and appropriateness of anthems. But

---

[36] E.g. *ibid.*, p. 158; C6/1/26/12/6/[1–7] (Feb.–May 1664).

[37] Barra Boydell, ed., *Music: Documents*, p. 97 in which the date incorrectly appears as 31 Mar. (rather than 21 Mar.) 1662.

[38] C6/1/7/2, fols 106v–107v.

[39] Barra Boydell, ed., *Music: Documents*, pp. 97, 101.

[40] *Ibid.*, pp. 164–6.

[41] *Ibid.*, p. 166.

Wetenhall was no Puritan, expressing rather a deep love and appreciation of music as part of worship and commenting that 'it is not impossible, that there may be some men of such an odd temper, as to be neither delighted with Poetry nor Musick, yet it is most certain the spirit of God is no such enemy to either'.[42] His central concern was that sacred music should emphasise the clarity and meaning of the text which should not be obscured by the musical invention or interest:

> Great care therefore ought to be taken in all our Church-Musick, that the Musick as little as may be, prejudice the distinct perceiving of the words, and so attending the sense. For whether the Hymn, or Psalm, become unintelligible to the Commonalty by the strangeness of the language, or curiosity of the Musical form, in which it is performed, devotion is equally destroyed, be it howsoever unintelligible.[43]

An overriding concern, therefore, is that sacred music should eschew all popular, secular influences and remain in the service of the text without drawing attention to itself:

> Much less is it tolerable, that things should be foisted in to the Public Lauds, because the words in which they are expressed, are of a rowling or jingling sound, and tickle the ear or fancy of an empty Musician . . . there is a *Decorum*, as to the very manner and kind of Musick, which is to be observed. Musick is therefore used in the Worship of God, because of the power it hath upon the mind of man, to raise good affections and calm disorderly ones. That Musick therefore, which in stead of exciting devotion, and composing the soul to a sedate and fixed temper, onely moves light and giddy thoughts, induces an aiery humour, and sporting, frisking dancing passions, is altogether to be banished [from] the Christian Worship. To set Anthems or Services in the way of Madrigals or Galliards (as some of late have in a manner done) is to debauch Devotion, to pervert the Worship of God, and as it were to take pains to make men wanton therein.[44]

Wetenhall later criticizes further the prevailing musical style of anthems and services and the choice and treatment of the text:

> First, it may be conceived, that some of our Anthems and Services, as our Church-composers have ordered the matter, savour more of *curiosity* of *musick*, than design of devotion. Whereas all Musick used in the worship of God, ought to be reverential, grave and easie, accommodated as well to the intelligibleness of the words, as to such tender affections and meltings of soul, as we profess it intended to beget, we may observe, on the contrary, our Gentlemen sometimes bring us aiery, and even mimical composures, difficult and distractive of the Performers thoughts, and not consistent enough with the hearers understanding. They contrive our Church-musick, in compliance with the vanity and vices of the age, and are more concerned to shew themselves *Artists a la mode*, than to fit their Melody for the engaging their own and others hearts in pious affections towards God. From hence it comes to pass, that, Secondly, we have, in several

---

[42] Wetenhall, *Of Gifts and Offices*, p. 223.
[43] *Ibid.*, p. 239.
[44] *Ibid.*, pp. 246–7.

of those new pieces strangely needless and nauseous, not to say senseless, repetitions; of such words or clauses I mean, on which no *Emphasis* lies fit to detain thought, or exercise devotion. If any word consist of consonant and voluble syllables, fitter than others to bear some little sequel of Notes, which the Musician fancies, it shall be dallied with, and tost as a feather in the air, for no other reason but because the Artist would shew his skill thereby, and tickle the ears and fancies of vainer minds . . . Thirdly, it may be adjudged another fault, neer a kin hereto, that these Gentlemen choose out *words* for Anthems as the *sound*, and not as they *signifie* . . . words may be unfit for Anthems, not onely because the soundness of their sense is suspicious, but, because they do not properly suit with the business of divine praise. Unsound, we will suppose, nothing of Scripture can be, but, it is not the hundreth part of Scripture that was designed for Lauds, nor ought therefore to be sung to God Anthem wise.[45]

And yet Wetenhall is not conservative in his musical taste, calling for sacred music to be composed in a contemporary style when he writes '. . . I would fain know, why I may not sing to God in the Musick of the age, as well as pray or preach in the language of the age.'[46] Closely linked with the question of what music was appropriate were the attitudes of the choir members (and, indeed, of composers of anthems) towards the music. Here Wetenhall raised the question of a perceived lack of adequate religious education of choirmen, a point to which he would return in his discussion of the training of choirboys (see below), commenting that 'our Church-composers generally want that deep judgment in things sacred, which they have in sounds'.[47] When it comes to the singers themselves, Wetenhall is despairing of their behaviour:

Alas! may it not daily be upbraided to many, according to the very literal truth, that they who officiate in the Divine Service, and the Service it self so officiated . . . hear not, or heed not the words, but listen onely to the Musick, and rest therein? . . . Besides, what a disturbance must holy indignation give to any good mans devotion, when he shall be diverted, and put besides his attention of Worship, by beholding men, that pretend to be worshipping of God, tyed fast by the ears, staring, gaping, anon smiling, whispering, busie with every one neer them, unable to conceal the secret titillation with which their curiosity, in attending Musick while they neglect the matter, strikes and affects them.[48]

Wetenhall does not expand on choral standards, least of all specifically at Christ Church. He does however reveal some interesting aspects of congregational involvement, not only in the singing of psalms as might be anticipated, but also in the anthems. In explaining that the congregation need not actually take part in the singing in order to be part of the act of worship, he writes that

There are few, if any of our people, who are the least used to Cathedral Service, but can, and do sing with the Quire the plain Tones of the Psalms, in which too very often, we sing our most usual Hymns, the *Te Deum, Magnificant*, and the

45 *Ibid.*, pp. 535–7; cf. Barra Boydell, ed., *Music: Documents*, pp. 162–3.
46 Wetenhall, *Of Gifts and Offices*, p. 310.
47 *Ibid.*, p. 386.
48 *Ibid.*, pp. 262–3; cf. Barra Boydell, ed., *Music: Documents*, p. 161.

rest. The same I must say of the Responds, when (as most commonly) plainly sung. Nay, even in the very *Chorus's* of our Anthems, as many as can sing musically may, and in the Versicles, or any other part of the Service, if any cannot or may not vocally join, it is sufficient, that the consent of their hearts distinctly go along with the voices of those who sing.[49]

Here, in addition to referring to the singing of the *Te Deum, Magnificat* etc. to simple psalm tones rather than necessarily in polyphonic settings, Wetenhall describes the practice of certain members of the congregation on occasion singing along with the choir in cathedral services, even in the choruses of those verse anthems with which they were familiar. Writing within the context of a some-times heated discussion amongst several Irish churchmen about the place of music in worship which had developed by the late seventeenth century, Joseph Boyse would later complain that 'the generality of the people complain that the Chanters and Choristers are just such Barbarians to 'em, because their voice is not so articulate as to enable 'em to understand what they play or sing'.[50] The words of anthems were however made available to the congregation, complete with indications of solo and chorus sections, a practice reflected in the 1662 book of *Anthems to be Sung* from Christ Church cathedral. Wetenhall explains that 'each Church has particular Books of its particular Anthems, which are disperst amongst the people with intimation, which is the Anthem to be sung at that time'.[51]

This conjunction of Edward Wetenhall as precentor of Christ Church publishing what was one of the most extensive and detailed of contemporary Anglican treatises on church music, and Dean Moreton's express concerns regarding the choir suggests that the practice of music at Christ Church achieved a new level of significance, perhaps even of excellence, during the late 1670s and early 1680s.

Choirmen's incomes and the augmentation estate

Following the Restoration there was a flurry of activity aimed at re-establishing the claims of the corporations of dean and chapter and of prebendaries and vicars choral to their properties, rights and revenues. As the two senior choir members (and variously serving as vicars' steward),[52] John Hawkshaw and Richard Hosier visited properties held from these two bodies in order to certify their value,

[49] Wetenhall, *Of Gifts and Offices*, p. 489.

[50] Boyse, *Remarks*, p. 19. On the debate concerning music in worship see further Neary, 'Music' (1995), pp. 22–9 and Nestor, 'Post-Restoration Attitudes'. Boyse's *Family Hymns for Morning and Evening Worship . . . All taken out of the Psalms of David* (Dublin 1701) includes the earliest known dated music printing from Ireland (Barra Boydell, 'Development of Music Print Trade').

[51] *Ibid.*, p. 487; cf. Barra Boydell, ed., *Music: Documents*, p. 161. On *Anthems to be Sung* see pp. 59–60 above, 87–8 below.

[52] Hosier is cited as vicars' steward in 1661 and 1662 and Hawkshaw in 1665 (C6/1/26/5, fol. 26v; C6/1/26/12/2, fol. 2v; C6/1/7/2, fol. 136r). Hawkshaw also served as vicars' steward at St Patrick's (chapter acts, C2/1/3/2, 8 Apr. 1661).

collected rents and tithes, and assigned or witnessed leases.[53] The return of forfeited rents and properties would continue to concern the vicars choral for some years, their tithe entitlements and those of the choirs of both cathedrals not being confirmed until 1671.[54] Some choir men appear individually to have supplemented their incomes through property and other leases. For example in October 1662 Faithful Tadpole took out a twenty-one year lease of several acres of land north of the city in Glasnevin and Grangegorman belonging to the prebendaries and vicars choral, a holding which he assigned a month later to John Hawkshaw.[55] Hawkshaw himself was one of the major landholding vicars choral: already in 1645 he had leased sixteen acres near Glasnevin from the dean and chapter, undertaking to build two houses on the premises, and he was still identified as landholder of this property in 1666.[56] In the early 1660s his holdings also included a tenement and over thirty-five acres of land in north county Dublin as well as being assigned several acres north of the city previously leased to Ralph Roseingrave (which a year later he re-assigned to Daniel Bellingham, alderman and subsequently lord mayor of Dublin). Both of these properties belonged to the dean and chapter.[57] However only a very small number of choir members were leaseholders and all of these were either already living in Dublin in the 1640s (members of the Tadpole family and John Hawkshaw) or acting as vicars' steward (Hosier and Hawkshaw) and thus involved by virtue of their office in the management of property and rents belonging to the vicars choral.[58] Except occasionally as witnesses, none of the other choir members listed in 1661 or in the immediately following years are named in any of nearly 250 deeds recorded from the 1660s and 1670s.[59] This suggests that rental from leases was an exceptional source of income only availed of at this period by choirmen belonging to settled Dublin families. It may be that, however long they eventually remained in Dublin, many choir members (most of whom appear to have been English) did not feel ready for the longer term commitment to living in Ireland which the taking out of leases on property would suggest (leases at this period were normally for a twenty-one year term). Memories of the divisions of the Civil War were certainly fresh at home in England, but living in Ireland, even in the overwhelmingly Anglo-Protestant environment of Dublin, many must have felt haunted by the threat of Irish Catholic reprisals, a fear nurtured by the savage language and iconography of contemporary sectarian propaganda.

53 Barra Boydell, ed., *Music: Documents*, pp. 95–6; C6/1/7/2, 8 Apr., 30 Apr., 9 July, 16 July 1661; C6/1/26/5, fol. 29v (1 Apr. 1661); C6/1/26/12/2, fol. 2r, etc.
54 Milne, 'Restoration', p. 264.
55 McEnery & Refaussé, *Deeds*, no. 1637 (cf. C6/1/26/5/94).
56 *Ibid.*, nos 1556, 1702.
57 *Ibid.*, nos 1640, 1596. This Ralph Rosingrave is also named elsewhere as a tenant of property owned by Christ Church (C6/1/26/3/30, fols 2r, 3r etc.; C6/1/26/5/81). He may be a direct forbear of his namesake, the early eighteenth-century organist of Christ Church.
58 Other miscellaneous leases included Richard Hosier's being assigned the tithes on all fish taken from the Liffey in Dublin and also 'a small waste spot of ground containing about eight foot in length and about six foot in breadth' in the cathedral close (C6/1/26/5, C6/1/26/10/36), and the older John Tadpole's being granted all profits from butchers' stalls in St John's Lane, adjoining the cathedral, in return for paving and keeping the same area clean (C6/1/7/2, fol. 153v, 154r; McEnery & Refaussé, *Deeds*, no. 1710).
59 McEnery & Refaussé, *Deeds*, nos 1581–1826.

As musicians the choir members were beginning to supplement their incomes outside the cathedral, although not necessarily with the approval of the dean and chapter. When the tenor Michael Lee was discovered to have 'sung amongst the stage players in the play-house' in February 1663 he was strongly admonished for having brought 'dishonour to God's service' and 'disgrace to the members and ministers of this church'.[60] This is the first recorded occasion on which a member of the choir performed in a theatre, a situation which would cause grave concern to the dean and chapter on a number of occasions in the following century.

Soon after the Restoration the income of the cathedral choir was significantly increased and put on an altogether more secure footing. In May 1664 the duke of Ormond and the privy council wrote to the archbishops and bishops stating that

> We are sufficiently informed that the yearly revenue belonging to the two choirs of the cathedral churches of the Holy Trinity [i.e. Christ Church] and of Saint Patrick's in Dublin though established by royal charter and seated in the metropolis of this kingdom . . . is notwithstanding very small and insufficient to maintain a fit number of persons qualified for the discharge of so great and solemn service as is there to be performed.

Acknowledging the two Dublin cathedrals' roles as pillars of Anglo-Protestant rule in Ireland, Charles II responded by more or less doubling the choirs' incomes through the allocation of rents and tithes forfeited during the rebellion. Known as the 'augmentation estate' this was to be 'disposed and settled upon the vicars and choirmen of each cathedral church as an additional provision for the increase of their maintenance', the relevant act being passed in December 1665.[61] The revenues of this estate, divided equally between the two cathedral choirs, would ensure that, up to the late nineteenth century, the two Dublin cathedral choirs would be among the wealthiest in the British Isles. The lord deputy or lord lieutenant had a stall in Christ Church and regularly attended services there, the cathedral effectively serving as the Chapel Royal in Ireland, a status formally acknowledged in 1672 when Charles II referred to Christ Church as 'our said cathedral and royal chapel'.[62] With the Anglican faith reaffirmed as the established church, English control of Ireland consolidated, Christ Church confirmed as the spiritual *locus* of English rule in Ireland and its properties and revenues regained and, in the case of the choir, substantially increased, the future for the cathedral and its music was perhaps more secure than it had ever been before. Furthermore, the practice now became firmly established of offering singers the combined incomes of positions in both Christ Church and St Patrick's, services

---

60 Barra Boydell, ed., *Music: Documents*, p. 100. The occasion in question was a performance of *Pompey* with songs between the acts set to music by John Jeffries, Dr Pett, Le Grand ('a Frenchman belonging to the Duchess of Ormond') and an unnamed 'Frenchman of my Lord Orrery's' at the Smock Alley Theatre which had opened the previous October (Morash, *Irish Theatre*, pp. 21–9, esp. pp. 28–9). Lee would most likely have appeared as a soloist in one or more of these songs.

61 Promulgated 26 May 1664, C6/1/27/3/1, pp. 169–71; list of rents and tithes, *ibid.*, pp. 181–5.

62 Letter dated 14 June 1672. Copy, Public Record Office, Dublin, State Papers 63/331/89. On his visit to Ireland c.1680 Thomas Dineley described Christ Church as 'the King's Chappel, or Christ Church Dublin' (Ball, 'Extracts', p. 289).

being so arranged that the choir could attend both cathedrals. The exceptional level of income enjoyed by choir men meant that Dublin could attract cathedral musicians of the highest quality from England, a factor which would contribute significantly to the flourishing of music at Christ Church from this period into the nineteenth century when the wealth and influence of the Church of Ireland, and in particular of the Dublin cathedrals, began to be challenged by a series of legislative acts reflecting changes in the social and political climate.

The choirboys and the 'master of song'

From the later seventeenth century choirboys were formally bound apprentice for seven years and were taught 'in the art of singing, reading and writing', each being given 'competent meat, drink, lodging and apparel, according [to] his quality, during that term'. Each boy swore to be obedient, to keep secrets, to suffer 'no injury to be done to said church', to avoid taverns, unlawful houses, gambling, and 'immoral practices', and even (remembering that the boys were probably aged about eight or nine when entering their apprenticeship) 'not to marry or absent himself without leave'.[63] At the beginning of their apprenticeship their parents provided them with 'two whole suits, one coat, one cloak and linen' and the master of the boys received an annual maintenance allowance of £8 per boy (which remained unchanged into the eighteenth century), in addition to which the dean and chapter paid for their bedding and other incidentals including washing of their clothes and coal for heating their school room.[64] The boys were also cared for when ill and in 1688–9 the dean and chapter contributed to funeral expenses when a choirboy died in service.[65] Discipline, while severe by modern standards, was probably no harsher than normal for the period. Following a mere 'complaint or rumour' that he had 'departed from his tutor's service', one of the choristers in 1664 was committed to Bocardo, described as 'the ancient prison and place of restraint belonging to this church', while the proctor considered his offence and determined his punishment.[66] Unless they went on directly into the choir as adult members,[67] when boys completed their apprenticeship term (or when their voices broke) they were paid a gratuity of £5 (occasionally less if they had only fulfilled a portion of their apprenticeship contract) for clothing or towards being apprenticed out to 'some suitable trade'.[68] The fact that each choirboy was treated 'according to his quality' suggests that

[63] Barra Boydell, ed., *Music: Documents*, pp. 100, 156–7; McEnery & Refaussé, *Deeds*, nos 1648–9.
[64] Barra Boydell, ed., *Music: Documents*, pp. 156–7; C6/1/26/3/30, C6/1/15/1.
[65] Barra Boydell, ed., *Music: Documents*, pp. 134, 135, 139, 140.
[66] Another boy would spend time there in 1676/7 (Barra Boydell, ed., *Music: Documents*, pp. 101, 136).
[67] E.g. C6/1/7/3, 30 Oct. 1700. In 1766 former choirboys Samson Carter and John Wann would respectively be ordered to serve as an adult choir member and encouraged to rejoin the choir, Wann also being provided with a spinet at the expense of the cathedral (Barra Boydell, ed., *Music: Documents*, p. 117).
[68] References to gratuities (or 'bounties') abound in the eighteenth century, but the earliest date from 1676/7 and 1678/9 (Barra Boydell, ed., *Music: Documents*, p. 136; C6/1/15/1/15).

they might come from a range of social and economic backgrounds. While the vast majority must have been local, in many cases the sons of adult choir members, others might be attracted from further afield. In 1697/8 the master of the boys, Nicholas Sanderson, travelled specially to Cork to bring a choirboy up to Christ Church.[69]

It was in the longer-term interests of the dean and chapter that the boys should be well looked after and receive a proper education and musical training since they formed the essential foundation for a cathedral choir comprising devout, literate and obedient, not to say musically able, adult choir men. In the early Restoration years such concerns must have been foremost in the minds of deans and chapters as they re-established choirs comprised largely of singers not brought up in the cathedral choir tradition, broken as this had been under the Commonwealth for the first time in its history. On the occasion of his visitation in January 1679 Dean Moreton asked whether the choristers were 'well instructed in the catechism of the church, in musical skill, in reading and writing, [and in] such other learning as they may attend'.[70] Here Morton was again echoing the words of his precentor Edward Wetenhall, who had urged in the previous year that

> A greater *care* [should be taken] in the *education* of our *choristers*, that they be not taught musick alone, but, together therewith, *Grammar*, and some *Humane Learning*; but especially, that they be well instructed in *Religion*, by being brought not onely to repeat their Catechism, as usual, but intimately to understand it, and carried a little further into the doctrine of the Church . . . 'tis certain, there is no surer way to make men serious and sincere in Religion, than by bringing them to a clear and good understanding of it . . . by this means, our Quire-men being in part bred scholars, would be more intelligent and serious, not onely in their Office in the Church, but abroad in their conversations; and in private too, they would be able to entertain themselves, and delight in reading, study and meditation, which might both improve them in knowledge, virtue, and even in Divine musick it self, . . . I dare put it under my hand, there will never be a devout religious succession of young people in our Quires, without a diligent School-master, and a consciencious Catechist, or some good persons, who will discharge to the Choristers those parts. And, except our Quire-men do approve themselves, in *divine offices* serious and devout, *worshipping God in spirit and in truth*, and paying to him a *rational*, as well as an harmonious service, and, in their *ordinary conversation*, discreet, sober, and, in some measure, exemplary persons, at least free from ignorance, impiety, luxury and idleness, we can expect no other fate to our Quires, than what befell the Nests of lewd and ignorant Monks. God forbid, I should say or think, all at the Dissolution deserved that character, but, if we may believe History, so great a number of them were such, as, in all probability, brought the judgment of God on the rest.[71]

---

69   Barra Boydell, ed., *Music: Documents*, p. 141; who this boy from Cork was and whether or not he became a regular choirboy is not recorded. Seymour, *Christ Church*, p. 28 stated in 1869 that 'no Irishman [was] admitted even as a vicar choral [at Christ Church] until Sir John Stevenson was enrolled among the pupils of its music school late in the eighteenth century'. This assertion has been widely repeated but, while true to a large extent, it does not stand up to close scrutiny, as in the case of the boy from Cork cited here (see also below, ch. 4, note 59).

70   C6/1/26/12/7, fol. 1v.

71   Wetenhall, *Of Gifts and Offices*, pp. 543, 545–7 (original italics).

Following the dean's visitation these concerns were acted upon when the chapter determined 'that the Choristers be farther instructed in the Church Cate-chism, and be taught to write and read as well as sing, and that the Master of them take care that they be so instructed'.[72] The boys boarded with the master who had overall responsibility for their general education, although a second teacher was employed for 'grammar' or 'writing'.[73] As Wetenhall commented, the church would

> breed [the boys] up in the art of Musick, and in some other parts of good litera-ture, as we find them capable . . . After a year or two sole attending song, if the boyes are capable, and the Masters diligent, some lesser practice daily will perfect them, and a good part of each day may be allocated to such purpose as I contend for [i.e. grammar, 'some humane learning' and religion].[74]

Relatively few names of choirboys at Christ Church are recorded for the period covered by this chapter, but of these a number reappear as choirmen at either or both of the Dublin cathedrals, confirming the continuity of experience and choir membership.[75]

---

[72] Barra Boydell, ed., *Music: Documents*, p. 167.

[73] Payments in 1669/70 'to Mr Jackson for 2 boys' schooling' and in 1682/3 to Nicholas Sanderson (master of the boys) 'for writing master' are amongst the earliest specific references to a separate school teacher; in 1676/7 'grammars for the boyes' were bought from 'Mr Wild', presumably the bookseller Joseph Wilde of Castle Street (Barra Boydell, ed., *Music: Documents*, pp. 135, 136, 138; Pollard, *Book Trade*, p. 614).

[74] Wetenhall, *Of Gifts and Offices*, pp. 532, 545.

[75] The names of more choirboys are recorded at St Patrick's thanks to full listings of choir members in the dean's annual visitations (St Patrick's chapter acts, C2/1/3/2, *passim*) and it is probable that most of these were also choirboys at Christ Church. Although neither appears as an adult at Christ Church, Samuel Chadderton and Joseph Shepard, both of whom were choirboys at Christ Church from December 1662 and at St Patrick's from before January 1664, became vicars choral at St Patrick's in 1671 (Barra Boydell, ed., *Music: Documents*, p. 100; St Patrick's chapter acts, C2/1/3/2, 11 Jan. 1664; Cotton, *Fasti* ii, p. 205). Thomas Burnet, a choirboy at Christ Church until 1678/9 and at St Patrick's from before January 1673, was appointed a stipendiary at Christ Church and a vicar choral at St Patrick's in 1687 (C6/1/7/3, 13 July 1687; Cotton, *Fasti* ii, p. 206). John Vinigam (or Vinicom) and [William] Davis, both indentured in 1676–7, reappear respec-tively as a vicar choral between 1689 and 1698, and as a probationary stipendiary whose place was declared void in July 1687 (C6/1/15/1/13; C6/1/7/3, 13 July 1687, 31 Oct. 1689, 12 July 1698). John Worrall, a choirboy at Christ Church from 1676/7, became a stipendiary and a vicar choral at St Patrick's in 1688 and at Christ Church in 1694 (by which time he was a clergyman), rising to dean's vicar in 1703, and eventually master of the boys at both cathedrals, positions he held until his retirement in 1746 (Barra Boydell, ed., *Music: Documents*, pp. 110, 137; C6/1/7/3, 23 Apr. 1688, 22 Oct. 1694; C6/1/26/16/13, 1702–3). Henry Swords, who left in 1697 having 'faithfully serv'd as a boye in the quier almost Eight yeares and his voice being broake', became a stipendiary at Christ Church and a vicar choral at St Patrick's the following year, and master of the boys from 1709 until 1714 (C6/1/7/3, 12 July 1698; C6/1/26/6/30; Cotton, *Fasti* ii, p. 207; Lawlor, *Fasti*, p. 232; Barra Boydell, ed., *Music: Documents*, p. 109). In addition to the above and the four boys noted in 1662 (see note 28 above), the other choirboys recorded at Christ Church between 1660 and 1700 are John Eagar (1676/7), [Master] Rathbone (1676/7), Walter Darsey (1676/7), [Thomas] Hunt (1678/9) and H. Hall ('one of the little boys', d.1688/9). Most of these are also documented as choirboys at St Patrick's. In addition, four boys at the King's Hospital School (the Thomas Hunt listed above, George Erwin, George Orr, and Nicholas Usher)

Randall Jewett's decision in 1638 noted in the previous chapter to remain as master of the boys after Benjamin Rogers had become organist marked the beginning of the separation of these two posts. Indeed, between the Restoration and Disestablishment the positions of master of the boys and organist were only held by the same person for a period of twenty years in the later eighteenth century.[76] Since the two cathedrals shared so many members of their choirs, including boys, it is not surprising to find that the same person often served as master of the boys in both cathedrals, but how the boys' education was divided between the two cathedrals when they were members of both choirs is not clear. The first master of the boys following the Restoration was Richard Hosier who was specifically mentioned at St Patrick's as 'master of the song and tutor of the boys', but clearly held the same position at Christ Church where he was paid on a regular basis for expenses in relation to the boys between 1662 and his death in 1677.[77] Nicholas Sanderson, who succeeded Hosier, was admonished in 1690/1 'for his ill management of the boys in not teaching them to sing according to art but by rote' as well as 'for not keeping them decently in apparel, and for not teaching them to write though he received allowance . . . for payment of a writing master to them'.[78] The boys continued to receive instrumental tuition as had been the case in the sixteenth and early seventeenth centuries: keyboard training on the organ is only specified when Robert Hodge was appointed master of the boys in 1698 but regular payments to Richard Hosier for lute strings after 1667 suggest that they were taught the lute at that period. A theorbo was purchased in 1668/9 on which the boys would have been trained in continuo for which keyboard instruments would later become more usual. Hosier was subsequently reimbursed for theorbo strings and a case for the instrument.[79] In all probability it was for the boys' musical education too that violins were bought between 1673 and 1680.[80] Evidence for choirboys learning or being encouraged to compose is provided by the Hosier MS which includes an anthem composed by Walter Hitchcock when he was still a choirboy at St Patrick's (and probably also at Christ Church), while other compositional sketches in the same manuscript could well have been done by other choirboys.[81]

State occasions and the use of instruments

While the regular morning and evening services on weekdays and Sundays formed the bulk of the choir's duties, there were occasions when more elaborate or additional services were held. As the state cathedral, Christ Church was the

were noted around this period as having 'gone to the choir', certainly referring to the combined choir of Christ Church and St Patrick's. I am grateful to Lesley Whiteside for this information.

76 See pp. 190, 193 below. In the nineteenth century the position of music master would become separated from that of master of the boys, who would no longer necessarily be a musician (see chs 4 and 5).

77 Barra Boydell, ed., *Music: Documents*, pp. 133–6; St Patrick's chapter acts, C2/1/3/3, p. 80.

78 Barra Boydell, ed., *Music: Documents*, pp. 102, 105, 137.

79 *Ibid.*, pp. 105, 135–6. On the theorbo in seventeenth-century England, see Sayce, 'Continuo lutes'.

80 Barra Boydell, ed., *Music: Documents*, pp. 136–7.

81 See pp. 89, 90 below.

venue for major commemorative and celebratory services at which the lord lieutenant and council and the lords justice attended 'in state'. Specific payments to
the choirmen occurred, for example, on St George's Day (23 April) in 1672 and
1676, the day on which the coronation of King Charles II in 1661 was celebrated.[82] During the deanery of William Moreton from 1677 payments also occur
to instrumentalists for participating on state days, providing clear evidence for
more elaborate music including symphony anthems on these occasions. Edward
Wetenhall again provides the authority for such practices when he wrote that

> As to *Instruments*, we generally content our selves with the *Organ* alone, that
> indeed being (as now it is perfected) deservedly to be preferred before, and
> supplying well the room of all other instruments . . . Notwithstanding we neither
> do, nor can condemn the grave use of *stringed instruments*, which therefore in
> the Kings Chappels, and perhaps in some other greater Quires, are upon some
> more solemn occasions imploied.[83]

In 1676/7 the musicians were paid 'for attendance at anthems' and two years
later 'the musicians at practice for encouragement', although in neither case is the
occasion specified.[84] The instruments used are not named, but would certainly
have included violins and bass viols, possibly also recorders and theorbo.[85] Musicians played again on 21 July 1681 (commemorating the defeat of the Armada in
1588), on St George's Day and on the king's birthday (29 May) in 1682, and on
unspecified occasions over the next two years. The proctor's accounts for 1685
and 1686 are particularly detailed in this regard.[86] In 1685, the year of Charles II's
death and the accession of James II, eight dates are cited on which the vicars
choral and/or the musicians received special payments:

12 March (celebration in Dublin of the accession of James II?, musicians
   only mentioned)
23 April (St George's day and James II's coronation; vicars choral only
   mentioned)
29 May (Charles II's Restoration; vicars choral only)
22 June (musicians only)[87]
23 August (a scribal error for 23 April? musicians only)
5 October (musicians only)
23 October (anniversary of the deliverance from the 1641 rebellion; both
   vicars choral and musicians)
5 November (deliverance from the Gunpowder Plot; both vicars choral and
   musicians)

Six special days are marked in 1686:

10 January (commemoration of Archbishop William Laud of Canterbury,
   beheaded 1645; musicians mentioned)

---

[82] Barra Boydell, ed., *Music: Documents*, pp. 136–7.
[83] Wetenhall, *Of Gifts and Offices*, pp. 533–4; cf. Barra Boydell, ed., *Music: Documents*, p. 162.
[84] Barra Boydell, ed., *Music: Documents*, pp. 136–7.
[85] Cf. Holman, *Four and Twenty Fiddlers*, pp. 405–11.
[86] Barra Boydell, ed., *Music: Documents*, pp. 138–9.
[87] The significance of 22 June 1685 is unclear: Trinity Sunday fell in that year on 14 June.

6 February (accession of James II; both vicars choral and musicians)
Easter Sunday (musicians)
23 April (both vicars choral and musicians)
29 May (both vicars choral and musicians)
Trinity Sunday (which fell on 6 June, musicians)

After the death of Charles II the musical style of the Chapel Royal under James II became more subdued, Thomas Tudway recording some years later that 'symphonies . . . with Instruments in the Chappell, were laid aside' and under William III the use of instruments in the Chapel Royal was discontinued, except on major state occasions.[88] Payments to musicians at Christ Church also decline rapidly, 1687 being the last year they are recorded when they played on 11 March (possibly a scribal error for 12 March to mark the accession of James II?), 23 April and 29 May, the vicars choral receiving additional payment on all occasions.[89] In 1687, as also in 1678/9, members of the Tollett family (four of whom served at one time or another in the Dublin city musicians between 1669 and 1688) are named as receiving payment for providing music, suggesting that it was the city musicians who accompanied the choir at Christ Church.[90] Musicians are not mentioned again at Christ Church until 1703 when the city music played on the occasion of the queen's birthday.[91]

The usual payment to the musicians on these state occasions was 15 shillings (£1 10s 0d paid in 1683/4 'To Mr Tallott' may thus have been for two separate visits by the city musicians), but in March 1685 a total of £4 10s 0d was paid on the one occasion, perhaps reflecting a larger than usual band of instrumentalists being employed for this service to mark the accession of James II, and on 22 June of the same year they received £2 5s 0d. On these occasions full 'symphony anthems' by composers of the Chapel Royal may have been performed, a repertoire for which the only direct evidence from Dublin is provided by the few such anthems (by Cooke, Humfrey, Taylor, and unattributed) included in the Hosier MS. A significant musical event in the late seventeenth century with which Christ Church was associated was the centenary celebration of Trinity College Dublin held on 9 January 1695 when Purcell's specially commissioned ode *Great Parent, Hail!* and Blow's anthem *I beheld and lo!* were performed. The choir of Christ Church took part in Purcell's ode but, although the title page proclaims it as a work first sung in Christ Church cathedral, doubt has been expressed as to whether the actual ceremony took place there rather than in the college, and the cathedral records make no mention of the event.[92]

---

88 Holman, *Four and Twenty Fiddlers*, pp. 411–14.

89 Barra Boydell, ed., *Music: Documents*, pp. 136–9.

90 The Tollett family also sold violins and 'anthems' to the cathedral (see note 80 above). Membership of the state musicians (attached to Dublin Castle) has not been established for this period, so the possibility that the Tolletts (or anyone else) served in both bodies cannot be ruled out. On the Tolletts see further Holman, 'Tollett'.

91 Barra Boydell, ed., *Music: Documents*, p. 143. The accounts of Archbishop William King of Dublin record a payment in October 1704 at St Patrick's cathedral 'for carrying the Musicall Instruments for the Choir All Saints night' (*IRL-Dtc*, MS 751/2, fol. 112).

92 Robinson-Hammerstein, 'With Great Solemnity'.

Organs and organists

The organ which had existed before 1647 must either have been removed during the Commonwealth or have fallen into a state of disrepair. Following the resumption of cathedral services in 1660 an organ apparently belonging to John Hawkshaw and which was small enough to be carried 'from church to church', probably between the two cathedrals, was set up by a Mr Parsons in November 1661 and tuned (a number of times) by a 'Mr Hollister'. Possibly the father of Robert Hollister who was appointed organist at St John's church, Fishamble Street in 1688, this establishes the presence in Dublin a generation earlier than previously recorded of this family of organists and organ makers so prominent in the eighteenth century.[93] Curtains and silken linings were provided for the organ, 'iron work' and other work carried out around it, and further repairs needed over the next two years, but it was clearly only a temporary measure. George Harris, who had carried out repairs in August 1663, was engaged to build a new instrument which he started in or around May 1664. Payments for painting the organ, for 'mending the wall by the organ', for iron stays (possibly for securing the front of the instrument) and for curtains mark progress in installing this organ which seems to have been completed before Michaelmas 1666.[94] Lancelot Pease, who had built an organ for King's College Cambridge in 1661 and a large organ for Canterbury in 1662–3, may have completed the installation of Harris's instrument: £20 paid to him 'for the organ' and 5 shillings for 'rectifying the organ' during 1665/6 mark his arrival in Dublin where he settled, becoming both a stipendiary in the choir of Christ Church and vicar choral of St Patrick's in 1667.[95]

In June 1667 Lancelot Pease signed a contract for the building of a chair organ at a total cost of £80, thus completing the provision of a full 'double' organ for the cathedral.[96] The contract specifies five stops: a principal of metal pipes in the front of the instrument down to *CC* ('double C fa ut') with 'the other seven basses within of wood to make up the stop', a stopped diapason (wood), a flute (wood), a recorder (wood), and a small principal (metal). The soundboard and roller were to be of well-seasoned oak 'with a set of keys suitable to the great organ'. As was the case earlier in the seventeenth century, the location of the organ at this period is not specified but a position on the choir screen is likely. Thomas Dineley referred in 1680–1 to 'the organ gallery' but in a manner which does not clarify the interior plan of the cathedral.[97] Pease was paid £2 a year for looking after the organs, which he continued to receive until 1682.[98] Care of the organ passed to Thomas

---

93 Barra Boydell, ed., *Music: Documents*, p. 132. Cf. *NG2* xi, p. 632.

94 Barra Boydell, ed., *Music: Documents*, pp. 132–4. The relationship of George Harris to the English organ maker Thomas Harris (father of Renatus Harris who built organs for Christ Church and St Patrick's in the 1690s – see p. 115 below) is uncertain.

95 Barra Boydell, ed., *Music: Documents*, p. 134; C6/1/7/2, fol. 150r; Cotton, *Fasti* ii, p. 205.

96 Barra Boydell, ed., *Music: Documents*, pp. 134, 159–61, pl. 7.

97 Ball, 'Extracts', pp. 289–90.

98 In 1670/1 he repaired both organs (i.e. the Harris organ and his own chair organ) and six years later the organ was 'taken down' and 'set up' at a time when the choir of the cathedral was being re-roofed (Barra Boydell, ed., *Music: Documents*, pp. 134–6; C6/1/15/1/4–18). In 1676–77 the

Finell in 1682/3, the salary increasing to £5 in 1684/5 and to £7 four years later.[99] By that stage the George Harris/Pease organ would be showing its age and a new instrument would be installed in 1698 (see next chapter).

In the same way that most choir members served in both Dublin cathedrals, and one person as master of the boys, so too the positions of organist at the two cathedrals were frequently (though not always) held by the one person.[100] The first organist at both cathedrals after 1660 was John Hawkshaw senior who was appointed at St Patrick's in October 1660 and must already have been serving at Christ Church as well, although he is not named as such before August 1661 (when he was threatened with dismissal for disobeying the dean's orders).[101] The one subsequent occasion when Hawkshaw was disciplined, when he was ordered in February 1664 to 'attend with the choir daily in his vicars stall, unless or until the service of the church doth require him to go to the organ', highlights his combined duties as both organist and equally as a member of the choir.[102]

Following the death of John Hawkshaw a period of nearly ten years ensued during which the post of organist at Christ Church was held by various people, none for very long. Thomas Godfrey, who had been organist at St Patrick's since 1685, held the post only between January and Michaelmas 1689. A chapter meeting the following month notes that Thomas Finell was to be paid for 'playing the organ in Christ Church' for the same half year.[103] What had become of Godfrey is not known, but his departure may well have been linked to this troubled period during the Williamite War when Christ Church was searched in 1689 for arms and temporarily closed on a number of occasions by soldiers loyal to James II, subsequently becoming a Roman Catholic cathedral for a period of seven months from late 1689 (James II attended mass in the cathedral on 17 November) up to the Williamite victory in 1690.[104] Despite Finell's apparently acting as organist, the chapter decided in January 1691 that Thomas Morgan was to 'serve as organist from Christmas last' but the following month Finell's salary as organist was confirmed 'till further order', suggesting that Morgan did not take up the post. Instead he appears to have gone to England, for at the end of March Walter Hitchcock was entrusted with £5 'to be transmitted into England to Thomas Morgan for his relief and encouragement to use his best endeavours to

---

organist John Hawkshaw was also paid 'for canvas to secure the organ case' (Barra Boydell, ed., *Music: Documents*, p. 136).

99   C6/1/15/1/15; Barra Boydell, ed., *Music: Documents*, pp. 102, 138–41. A stipendiary at least since 1678/9, Finell became a vicar choral in 1693 (C6/1/7/3, 12 Sept. 1693). He remained organ tuner and repairer until Cuvillie took over in 1697/8 (see p. 115 below) and also served as organist on a number of occasions between 1689 and 1699 (see pp. 86–7 below).

100   See appendix 1; cf. Grindle, *Cathedral Music*, pp. 223–4 but details for Christ Church are not always accurate.

101   The organist and organ blower are mentioned anonymously in March 1661 (C6/1/7/2, fols 95v, 96r; Barra Boydell, ed., *Music: Documents*, p. 96).

102   C6/1/7/2, fol. 124v.

103   Barra Boydell, ed., *Music: Documents*, pp. 102, 139.

104   On the historical background to this period and the Roman Catholic tenure of the cathedral see Milne, 'Restoration', pp. 269–75. There is no record of what music was performed during this period.

attain the perfection of an organist'.[105] Whither in England Morgan went is not known, he like Godfrey in 1689 also disappearing from the records.

After two years of unsuccessful appointments as organists, with Finell loyally but perhaps inadequately maintaining the post, the dean and chapter must have held their collective breath in November 1691 when they offered the position to Peter Isaack, organist and master of the choristers at Salisbury cathedral, 'if he should come over'.[106] Isaack was paid an additional gratuity on his appointment as both a vicar choral and organist of Christ Church on 31 March 1692, 'to both which places he was admitted on the account of his extraordinary skill in music'; a few days later he was also appointed organist and vicar choral at St Patrick's.[107] The dean and chapter's success in attracting Isaack was, however, to be short-lived: only two years later in August 1694 he died at Chester while on a visit to England. His widow was paid the balance of his due salary and, once again, Thomas Finell stepped into the breach, but this time on probation.[108] Probationer or no, Finell fulfilled the duties of organist for a further four years until the appointment of Daniel Roseingrave in November 1698, and he would continue to serve the cathedral as a vicar choral until his death in 1710.[109]

Music and repertoire

Two significant sources referred to earlier in this chapter provide detailed information about the anthem repertoire at the Restoration and over the following decade or so: the printed collection of anthem texts *Anthems to be Sung* published in 1662, and the Hosier MS. *Anthems to be Sung* is not only the earliest record of the Dublin cathedral repertoire but also the earliest such anthem text book known. It contains thirty-three pages of anthems preceded by an (incomplete) index, but there is no introduction or other prefatory information beyond what is given in the title. Published so soon after the resumption of cathedral services in 1660, it can reasonably be accepted as largely representing what had survived of the pre-Commonwealth anthem repertoire, most particularly since only seven of its fifty-one anthems also appear in Barnard's *The First Book of Selected Church Musick* (London, 1641) which was widely used in re-establishing cathedral

---

[105] Barra Boydell, ed., *Music: Documents*, pp. 102–3; cf. Shaw, *Organists*, p. 411. Grindle, *Cathedral Music*, p. 27 incorrectly stated that Morgan was to act as organist 'from Christmas 1689'; Finell is named as organist in the proctor's accounts throughout the period from Michaelmas 1689 to Michaelmas 1692 (C6/1/15/1/24–25).

[106] Barra Boydell, ed., *Music: Documents*, p. 103. A choirboy at the Chapel Royal until 1670, Peter Isaack had already spent fifteen years in Dublin as a vicar choral at St Patrick's from 1672 and a stipendiary choirman at Christ Church from 1676/7 before going to Salisbury in the autumn of 1687 (Holman, 'Bartholomew Isaack'; Barra Boydell, ed., *Music: Documents*, p. 136; C6/1/7/3, 23 Apr. 1688; Shaw, *Organists*, pp. 264, 419. See also Grindle, *Cathedral Music*, p. 27).

[107] Barra Boydell, ed., *Music: Documents*, p. 103. Shaw, *Organists*, p. 419.

[108] Shaw, *Organists*, p. 419; Barra Boydell, ed., *Music: Documents*, pp. 103–4.

[109] Grindle, *Cathedral Music*, p. 223 stated incorrectly that Robert Hodge is noted as organist in the chapter acts of 17 Mar. 1697. Peter Finell, probably a son of Thomas Finell, was to be a stipendiary and later a vicar choral at Christ Church between 1707 and his death in 1728 (see especially C6/1/8/4, pp. 20, 89; C6/1/8/5, p. 26).

repertoires following the Restoration.[110] Only one of the anthems in the collection can be shown with any certainty to post-date the Restoration: Richard Hosier's *Now that the Lord hath readvanc'd the crown* which, as was noted earlier, was composed for the consecration service on 27 January 1661.[111]

The Hosier manuscript

If *Anthems to be Sung* reflects the repertoire of the Dublin cathedrals immediately following the Restoration, the Hosier MS, which began to be compiled around the same time, demonstrates the introduction of anthems in a more contemporary, solo style. First brought to notice by Brian Crosby in 1974, the origins of this manuscript remained unknown until Ian Spink noted the presence of a number of composers associated with the Dublin cathedrals including Richard Hosier, alongside anthems by mainly contemporary English composers.[112] Comparison of Hosier's signature in this manuscript and in documents in the Christ Church archives has confirmed him as the main copyist, substantially fulfilling Peter Holman's comment that 'the least-known composer in a particular MS may, in the absence of other evidence, be a prime suspect as its copyist'.[113] The manuscript is leather bound and consists of 133 leaves. Most of the music was copied successively from the beginning of the volume (the 'forward pages'), but at some stage the volume was turned over and music began to be copied from the back ('reverse pages'). It is the earliest post-medieval music manuscript known to survive from Ireland and is of particular importance for the history of music at Christ Church and St Patrick's cathedrals since so little music has survived from before the eighteenth century.

The Hosier MS includes eight anthems by named local composers: six by Hosier himself, making him equally the most represented composer in the manuscript alongside Pelham Humfrey, and one anthem each by John Blett and Walter Hitchcock:

> Hosier: *Now that the Lord hath readvanc'd the crown* (Consecration anthem)[114]
> *O give thanks unto the Lord*
> *O love the Lord all ye saints*
> *Praise the Lord ye servants*

---

110 See pp. 59–60 above including outline of pre-Restoration repertoire. The following anthems are common to *Anthems to be Sung* and to Barnard: Bull, *Deliver me, O God*; Byrd, *Christ rising again*; *Hear my prayer O Lord*; *Teach me O Lord*; Ward, *Let God arise*. On the other hand Byrd's *Thou God that guidest* and Gibbons' *Behold thou hast made my days*, both in Barnard, appear as unattributed texts in *Anthems to be Sung*. There is no evidence that either Christ Church or St Patrick's purchased Barnard's collection which probably did not actually appear before 1660 when it was bought by a number of English cathedrals (Spink, *Restoration*, pp. 75–6).

111 On Holmes's *O God that art the well spring* see pp. 67–9 above.

112 Crosby, 'Early Restoration', including physical description and list of contents; see also Crosby, *Catalogue*, pp. 23–4. Spink, *Restoration*, pp. 225–6.

113 Holman, 'Bartholomew Isaack', pp. 381–5. On Hosier's signature see Barra Boydell, ed., *Music: Documents*, pp. 176–9 including pls 10, 11; cf. Crosby, 'Early Restoration', p. 462 and Crosby, *Catalogue*, p. 24.

114 See note 13 above.

> *Thou O God art praised in Sion*[115]
> *Unto thee do I cry*

Blett: *Ad te domine: Thou art O Lord my strength*[116]

Hitchcock: *Bow down thine ear*

The manuscript was copied between the early 1660s and the later 1670s. Hosier's *Now that the Lord*, composed in or shortly before January 1661, is the fifth of the thirty-eight anthems (or incomplete pieces) copied into the forward pages of the manuscript.[117] John Holmes's *O God that art the well spring*, which was noted above as very possibly having been sung at the consecration service in January 1661 or to mark the coronation of Charles II on 23 April 1661, is the ninth. Hosier's *Thou O God art praised* (no. 11) shares its final 'Hallelujah' with *Now that the Lord* (rather than copying out the music Hosier simply wrote at the end 'The same Hallelujah as in the Consecration Anthem'), implying that it dates from around the same period. Thus the first nine, possibly eleven, anthems appear to have been written down by (or not long after) 1661. The death in late 1665 or early 1666 of John Blett, one of eight stipendiaries elected at Christ Church in September 1661 and appointed a vicar choral at St Patrick's in 1664, provides a *terminus ante quem* for his anthem *Ad te Domine: Thou art O Lord my strength* (no. 15).[118] Walter Hitchcock's *Bow down thine ear*, which is present both in partial draft and complete form (nos 25 and 27) is dated [16]69. This unique inclusion of a date may reflect Hitchcock's (or his master Hosier's) pride in his youthful composition of an anthem: a choirboy at St Patrick's between 1664 and 1670 (and probably also Christ Church), he cannot have been aged much more than fifteen when he composed it (boys' voices typically breaking at the age of fifteen or sixteen at this time).[119]

The unattributed anthem *I beheld and lo* (no. 2) agrees quite closely in the chorus sections with the same anthem attributed to Benjamin Rogers in *GB-Lbl*, Add. MS 30,932[120] and could conceivably represent an earlier version dating from Rogers' years as organist of the Dublin cathedrals. On the other hand his *Magnificat* and *Nunc Dimittis* from the *Evening Service in Gamut* (no. 29), which follows shortly after Hitchcock's anthem, is ascribed to 'Dr. Rogers'. As Crosby pointed out, this places the copying of this part of the manuscript to no earlier than 1669, the year Rogers received his doctorate, which fits in with the date given with

---

[115] Music edited in Barra Boydell, ed., *Music: Documents*, pp. 200–5.

[116] Music edited in *ibid.*, pp. 207–11.

[117] The numbering of the anthems here follows Crosby 'Early Restoration'.

[118] Barra Boydell, ed., *Music: Documents*, pp. 97, 134. Note, however, that in April 1664 Blett is described as having been elected a stipendiary at Christ Church 'from Easter last' (C6/1/7/2, fol. 126r); Lawlor, *Fasti* ii, p. 214 gives his date of death as 'before 8 January 1666'.

[119] Crosby, 'Early Restoration', p. 462 notes that Hitchcock's anthem, Tallis's Short Service (reverse no. 3) and some miscellaneous fragments and oddments (e.g. nos 26, 38, reverse no. 17) are the only items not in Hosier's hand. Subsequently a vicar choral at St Patrick's from 1672 to 1692, Hitchcock is first mentioned at Christ Church in December 1674, is named as a stipendiary in 1676/7 and thereafter became a senior vicar choral (St Patrick's chapter acts C2/1/3/2, 14 Sept. 1664, 11 Jan. 1670; Lawlor, *Fasti* ii, pp. 215, 221, 239; C6/5/8/3; Barra Boydell, ed., *Music: Documents*, pp. 136, 139, 140). This is clearly not the same Hitchcock noted by Crosby, 'Early Restoration', p. 462 at Westminster in the years ending at Michaelmas 1689 and 1690.

[120] Crosby, 'Early Restoration', p. 458.

Hitchcock's anthem. Also unlikely to date from earlier than the later 1660s and occurring in the latter part of the forward pages, the first immediately preceding Hitchcock's 1669 anthem, are the three anthems by Michael Wise (c.1647–87).[121] Many of the twenty-four anthems (including fragments) copied into the reverse pages of the manuscript suggest a later date than those in the forward pages: here, alongside single anthems by Orlando Gibbons, Tallis and others, there is a preponderance of music by younger composers including five of the six anthems in the manuscript by Pelham Humfrey (c.1647–74)[122] and the one anthem by John Blow (1649–1708), *O sing unto the Lord a new song*, which is the final anthem in the reverse pages. It is in the reverse pages too that the majority of symphony anthems occur: two each by Humfrey and Cooke, one by Silas Taylor (?),[123] and the unattributed *Sing O daughters of Sion*. The two unattributed symphony anthems in the forward section of the manuscript, *The voice of my beloved* (no. 32) and *O sing praises* (no. 33), occur together towards the end of that section. As was noted above, evidence from Christ Church shows that symphony anthems were performed particularly in the late 1670s and early 1680s. The absence from the manuscript however of any music by Purcell, a composer who would otherwise surely have been represented, suggests that little if any of the manuscript was copied after Hosier's death in 1677.

In addition to the six anthems by Hosier and the single anthems by Blett and Hitchcock, a number of unattributed works, including short fragments, appear to have been composed in Dublin. At least some of these are compositional drafts, whether by Hosier or others (as master of the choristers he would have been involved in training the more promising boys in composition). For example, page 125 includes an untexted, two-part (treble and bass clefs) fragment of thirteen bars (no. 26, not in Hosier's hand); page 9 (reverse) includes thirteen bars of an untexted, four-voice 'I will magnifie thee' (reverse no. 7) containing many corrections suggesting that it was composed directly into the manuscript. On the same page there are also two canons (in the bass clef) which could have been written in connection with the boys' instrumental training (reverse no. 6). Judging by the length and correlation of verse/chorus indications, an unattributed organ part entitled *Hear my prayer O God* (reverse no. 1) appears to correspond to a third anthem text of the same title (also unattributed) in the 1662 collection.[124] One wonders if the presence of two anthems by John Ferrabosco, copied into the manuscript immediately after Blett's but before Hitchcock's anthems and thus

---

[121] *Have pity upon me* (no. 24), *Awake up my glory* (no. 30), and *I charge you O daughters* (no. 34). By 1676 one service and eleven anthems by Wise were in the repertory of the Chapel Royal which he joined in that year, having previously served there as a chorister (*NG2* xxvii, p. 447).

[122] *Have mercy upon me* (II); *Like as the hart*; *Lord teach us to number our days*; *O praise God* (known only from this source and considered doubtful, see Humfrey, *Church Music* ii, p. 120); *O praise the Lord. Haste thee O God* (the text of which had appeared in Clifford's *Divine Services*) is copied into the forward pages (no. 31) after the anthems by Hitchcock and 'Dr Rogers' discussed above.

[123] Humfrey, *O praise God* and *O praise the Lord*; Cooke, *Put me not to rebuke* and *O Lord thou hast searched me out. Lord let me know mine end* is attributed here to Silas Taylor but is elsewhere attributed to Matthew Locke (Crosby, 'Early Restoration', p. 460).

[124] *Anthems to be Sung*, p. 14; attributed by Crosby, 'Early Restoration', p. 459, to Thomas Wilkinson.

Ex. 3.2 Richard Hosier, *Unto thee do I cry*, bars 47–52

between c.1665 and 1669,[125] might be connected with the presence at Christ Church from August 1663 of a Henry Ferrabosco, subsequently appointed a vicar choral in March 1666.[126]

The anthems by Hosier and his colleagues, despite being musically and technically limited, are nevertheless progressive in their adoption of the solo Italianate style being introduced into English sacred music at this time by Matthew Locke, Henry Cooke and others.[127] They are all verse anthems in which the solos eschew the imitative style prevalent in pre-Commonwealth verse anthems in favour of a dramatic, declamatory style governed both by the meaning and the rhythms of the text and supported by an harmonic organ bass. Lines such as 'break them down' are typically set by Hosier in a direct, illustrative style (*Ex. 3.2*). The bass solos can be particularly dramatic, for example in Hosier's *Unto thee do I cry* where the words 'And in my song will I praise him' are enlivened by semiquaver flourishes, or in *Thou O God* in which a coloratura flourish on 'the raging of the seas' is immediately followed by a rising, largely chromatic line for the words 'and the madness of his people' before falling abruptly, perhaps 'madly', through an octave (*Ex. 3.3*). Clearly there was a fine bass singer in the Dublin cathedral choirs in the 1660s and 1670s. In view of the reluctance of many early Restoration composers to entrust solos to boys,[128] it is interesting to note that, without exception, all the anthems by Hosier, Blett and Hitchcock use boy soloists together with a bass (or a tenor in Blett's anthem).[129] In Hosier's case this surely reflects his own work as master of the choristers. The verses usually alternate sections for each soloist, although there are short duet passages, as in *Thou O God art praised in Sion*, in which the voices either move together or exchange short phrases. The two trebles in *Unto thee do I cry* sing consistently as a duet or as a trio with the bass. There is much use in the solo sections of ♪♪♪♩ rhythms. The bipartite division of solo vocal verses into a section in duple time followed by one in triple time, 'one of the most widely emulated of all Italian formal designs',[130] is only

---

[125] *I will sing a new song* and *By the waters of Babylon* (nos 16, 17).

[126] McEnery & Refaussé, *Deeds*, nos 1643, 1659, 1664, 1666, 1691; C6/1/7/2, fol. 143v. The relationship (if any) of this Henry Ferrabosco to John Ferrabosco has not been established. Cf. *NG2* viii, p. 692.

[127] Cooke is a notable absence from the earlier pages of the manuscript: his only anthems occur towards the end of the reverse pages (see Crosby, 'Early Restoration'). No music by Cooke survives at St Patrick's.

[128] Lewis, 'English Church Music', p. 497; Henry Cooke, as first master of the children in the Chapel Royal after the Restoration, did however frequently write for solo trebles.

[129] Hitchcock writes for 'meane' (C1 clef), Hosier and Blett for 'treble' (G2 clef).

[130] Dennison, *Humfrey*, p. 11.

Ex. 3.3 Richard Hosier, *Thou O God*, bars 59–67

found in Hosier's first anthem *Now that the Lord* in which the final solo verse couplet changes into triple time (this being repeated by the chorus) (*Ex. 3.4*). Each anthem starts with a brief organ introduction based on a variation of the same figure of either a rising (*c–d–e*) or descending (*g–f#–e–d*) bass line (*Ex. 3.5*).

The absence of contrapuntal textures is also a feature of the brief four-part choruses which only rarely depart from a homophonic, word-driven texture. Most of the choruses repeat the final phrases of the solo verses to the same music or a variation of it, but others are both musically and textually independent: in Blett's *Thou art O Lord* all three choruses are set to new text and music. Four of Hosier's anthems conclude with a 'Hallelujah' chorus, *Now that the Lord* and *Thou O God* sharing the same setting, while *O Give thanks* and *Praise the Lord* share a second setting. The harmonic language is limited and the organ bass unfigured except for twice in Hosier's *Thou O God* when the change of a chord from major to minor or vice versa is indicated (*Ex. 3.3*). Hosier's *Now that the Lord* remains in C major throughout with only passing references to A minor although his next anthem *Thou O God*, while also beginning and ending in C major, has internal cadences in A minor, D major (with passages in D minor), and F major, only returning to C major via A minor at the end of the final verse (which is repeated by the chorus before the concluding C major 'Hallelujah'). *O love the Lord*, copied into the reverse pages and thus assumed to be his latest anthem, is in C minor with internal cadences in G minor and E flat major. The minor mode and the use of a plaintive, plagal cadence for the final 'Amen' give this, the shortest of Hosier's anthems, an expressive quality not always present in his other works.

An orthographic feature of the anthems by Dublin composers in the Hosier manuscript is the presence of additions, corrections, or the re-writing of sections of the music, alongside blatant errors which must surely have been corrected in the performing parts before the music was performed. For example, the opening of Hosier's *O give thanks* was first written starting with a semibreve G in the organ, the bass soloist entering on the last crotchet. Subsequently Hosier inserted an organ introduction similar to that used in his anthem *Unto thee do I cry* later in the manuscript.[131] Walter Hitchcock's *Bow down thine ear* appears both as a draft

---

131 Illustrated in Barra Boydell, 'Now that the Lord', pl. 6.

Ex. 3.4 Richard Hosier, *Now that the Lord hath readvanc'd the crown*, bars 88–96

Ex. 3.5 Opening organ introductions in anthems by Dublin composers in Durham MS B.1

of the opening page (no. 25) and, starting two pages later, with the complete music incorporating changes (no. 27) suggesting that it was drafted and composed directly into the manuscript. Apart from this example, the anthem showing the most evidence of correction or recomposition is Holmes's *O God that art the well-spring* in which entire organ bass lines in solo verses have been crossed out and rewritten. This could be interpreted as evidence in support of its having been adapted for use in Dublin.[132] Hosier's *Now that the Lord* illustrates the occurrence of uncorrected 'wrong' notes showing that it is essentially a draft and certainly not a performing copy. For example, in bars 66–7 at the words 'still blossoms bear' both organ and bass soloist 'cadence' with *g–G*, leading not as expected to *c* but to another *G* (the organ also has *b*; *c* is very lightly indicated in the organ part, perhaps as a correction). In the penultimate bar of the same anthem the countertenor's two quavers *d' d'* sound against two Cs and an E in the other voices, while the tenor has a minim *g* against moving parts in the other voices outlining a first inversion D minor chord approaching the final cadence in C; in the final cadence the alto has a minum *e'* rather than the expected two crotchets *e'–d'* over the bass crotchets *g–G*. (*Plate 6*) Elsewhere in Hosier's anthems parallel fifths and unexplained discords occur, giving the impression of a careless if not inexperienced composer.

---

[132] See pp. 68–9 above.

Plate 6. The 'Hosier' MS (Durham, Dean and Chapter Library, MS B.1). Final page of Richard Hosier's anthem *Now that the Lord hath readvanc'd the crown*, with Hosier's autograph signature.

The conditions surrounding the composition of *Now that the Lord* may explain Hosier's at times crude compositional style, at least in this case. As the senior vicar choral and master of the choristers at both cathedrals the onus would have fallen either on him or on the organist John Hawkshaw to compose the music for the special anthem for the consecration service held at St Patrick's on 27 January 1661. But the absence of any anthems by John Hawkshaw in either this manuscript or in *Anthems to be Sung* suggests that he was not a composer. Thus Hosier may have found himself having to do his best to provide the music needed for the occasion even though he may have had little experience as a composer before this. The music of *Now that the Lord* as it stands appears to be essentially a draft rather than the final version. This view is supported not only by the presence of so many uncorrected 'grammatical' errors in the music which must have been ironed out before performance, but also by the fact that the verses as printed in *Anthems to be Sung* (1662) are indicated as being sung by treble and tenor soloists, whereas in the Hosier manuscript they are treble and bass. If *Anthems to be Sung* is to be believed, at some stage between writing the music into the manuscript in or before January 1661 and the publication of the text in 1662 Hosier made revisions (and, doubtless, corrections) which formed the basis for the (lost) parts copied for use by the choir. The very limited tonal structure of *Now that the Lord*, expanded in his later anthems, lends further support to the view that Hosier was not an experienced composer. The two anthems which precede *Now that the Lord* in the Hosier MS contain musical parallels and may have served Hosier as models. The fourth anthem is the unattributed *Look shepherds, look*, the text (without music) of which is found in *GB-Lbl*, MS Harl. 6346 attributed to Thomas Ford.[133] Apart from being in B flat rather than C major, it shares the same final 'Hallelujah' as Hosier used in *Now that the Lord* (and in *Thou O God*), while the organ introductions to all three anthems commence with variations of the same rising figure. Whether Hosier based his music on this model, or added the final 'Hallelujah' to this existing anthem, or possibly even adapted *Look shepherds* from another source, remains to be determined. Another version of the same opening organ figure is also found in *Rejoice in the Lord* (no. 3), unattributed but possibly by Richard Portman.[134] However, the final 'Hallelujah' in *Rejoice in the Lord*, while in a broadly similar style, is quite different from those by Hosier.

Richard Hosier must have been intimately involved in re-establishing and developing the choral repertoire following the Restoration. The Hosier MS may reflect his efforts both to develop as a composer and to collect anthems to add to the cathedral repertoire or to serve as teaching models for the choirboys under his care. Whatever the reasons for its having been compiled, the fortunate survival of this manuscript together with the printed volume of *Anthems to be Sung* provides a detailed view of the repertoire of anthems sung during the early Restoration period at Christ Church and St Patrick's cathedrals, Dublin. Taken together, these two sources reveal how concerned cathedral musicians in Dublin were to introduce an up-to-date repertoire and to provide often elaborate music including symphony anthems. The question remains as to how the manuscript came to be in

[133] Crosby, 'Early Restoration', p. 458.
[134] *Ibid.*, p. 458.

Durham. The inside cover of the 'Hosier' manuscript bears two signatures: 'John Blunderfild' and 'Thomas Blunderfild'. A John Blunderville was a vicar choral at St Patrick's between 1677 and 1680 and a 'Mr Blundervile' (presumably the same person) a stipendiary at Christ Church in 1678/9, not long after the death of Hosier.[135] Formerly at Ely (1669–74) and Lichfield (1676), John Blunderville left Dublin in 1682 for York (where he became master of the choristers), subsequently going to Durham where he died in 1721. It must surely be this John Blunderville who brought the Hosier MS from Dublin eventually to Durham.[136]

Later seventeenth-century Christ Church composers and the copying and provision of music

No musical sources or other anthem text books along the lines of *Anthems to be Sung* survive from Christ Church which can be firmly dated to the period between the Hosier MS and the early eighteenth century. The part, score and organ books dating from this later period and subsequently (which will be discussed in the next chapter) do however contain isolated examples of music composed by later seventeenth-century choir members, while a number of payments to choirmen suggest composition rather than merely the copying of music. Two incomplete verse anthems *God is our hope and strength* and *My song shall always* are attributed in the choir books to 'Mr Godfrey' , most of the surviving voice parts of these two anthems being in an unidentified hand probably dating from the early eighteenth century, while the style of the music suggests a late seventeenth-century date.[137] The composer can be identified with reasonable confidence as Thomas Godfrey, organist at Christ Church in 1689 and at St Patrick's 1685–9. In 1683/4 there is a payment to Peter Isaack for 'writing and setting' anthems, in other words for composing rather than just copying music.[138] Incomplete parts of an anthem *Let God arise* exist in the Christ Church choir books attributed to 'Isaac', the original of which could relate to this payment.[139] Another possibility is that this anthem is by Peter Isaack's brother Bartholomew, who was a stipendiary at Christ Church and vicar choral at St Patrick's between 1685 and 1687. Two anthems by Bartholomew Isaack are known from English sources but neither is thought to date from his Dublin years.[140] A payment in 1680/1 to Nicholas

135   Lawlor, *Fasti* ii, pp. 228, 244. Barra Boydell, ed., *Music: Documents*, p. 137.

136   Crosby, 'Early Restoration', pp. 463–4.

137   C6/1/24/3/1–6 (part books); C6/1/24/4/1, –/3, –/4, –/7 ('Old Loft Books'), treble and organ parts missing. Both anthems are also in the St Patrick's choir books, likewise missing treble and organ, and *God is our hope*, also in *GB-Ob*, Tenbury MS 1503, copied by John Phipps, who served in the choirs of both Dublin cathedrals from 1720 until his death in 1759 (see Houston, 'Music Manuscripts' and pp. 127–8 below).

138   Barra Boydell, ed., *Music: Documents*, p. 138; in the previous year Isaack had been paid 'for entering anthems in the books' (*ibid.*).

139   Treble, alto, tenor and bass voices but organ missing, C6/1/24/4/1, –/3, –/4, –/6 ('Old Loft Books'); this anthem is not present at St Patrick's. Also attributed to Purcell, sometimes in a later hand, but the music is not the same as Purcell's anthem of that name (Z. 23).

140   Spink, *Restoration*, pp. 226f. Bartholomew lost his position at both Dublin cathedrals in January 1687 having become a Catholic. He appears to have given different reasons for his conversion to the dean and chapters of the two Dublin cathedrals: at St Patrick's he pleaded that he had embraced Catholicism as being the faith of his sovereign James II, subsequently presenting a letter from the king in his support; the Christ Church chapter acts are missing for this period, but

Sanderson 'for full Anthems' could conceivably refer to composition although in other years he received payments which clearly refer to the copying of anthem books.[141] No music survives which is attributed to Sanderson.

Apart from music composed locally, the repertoire at Christ Church at this period as at other times can be assumed to have been essentially similar to that at any English cathedral given the constant coming and going of choirmen between Dublin and England. While certain unidentified copyists in the Christ Church choir books appear to date back to the early eighteenth century, just possibly even the later seventeenth,[142] only two further more-or-less specific references to music exist from the period covered by this chapter. In 1668/9 a payment was made as 'a gift to him that brought Mr Ren's anthem books'.[143] Charles Wren became organist at Rochester in 1672 and at Gloucester two years later, and from 1675 Robert Wren (possibly his brother) was organist of Canterbury Cathedral where both had been choirboys. Both composed anthems which survive in Canterbury, so the likelihood is that these anthems brought over to Christ Church were composed by either Charles or Robert Wren.[144] When Robert Hodge returned from a visit to England in 1697, the year before he became master of the boys, he brought back music for both Dublin cathedrals. At St Patrick's this music was listed and included verse anthems by Blow, Purcell and Tucker and services by Aldrich, Blow, Child and Purcell; at Christ Church the chapter subsequently recorded a gratuity to Hodge 'for his service in bringing over severall Anthems out of England for the service of this Church' but without giving further details.[145]

The need to rebuild the cathedral's music collection following the break in cathedral services during which much of it must have been mislaid or destroyed, and to introduce new repertoire in line with the changes in musical style associated with post-Restoration cathedral music, meant that the amount of copying and purchasing of music increased substantially following the Restoration.[146] Payment records tend to be vague, and it is often unclear whether a given payment

a letter to the dean survives in Isaack's hand in which he states that 'the only cause and motive was to save my poor soule' having 'made it my particular and dayly petition to Almighty God to direct me to the right way with a full Resignation to follow his Inspirations', no mention being made of the king's religion. Whatever the reason, he retained his salary for a short period afterwards although no longer serving either cathedral (Mason, *History and Antiquities*, pp. 203–5; C6/1/26/622 (letter 1 Jan. 1688 to the bishop of Kildare, dean of Christ Church); C6/1/7/3, 4 Jan., 26 Apr. 1687).

141 Barra Boydell, ed., *Music: Documents*, pp. 103, 137, 140.
142 For example, in C61/24/3/3 (Bass decani partbook) composers represented in the main hand (up to p. 181 representing the earliest layer of this volume) are (in order from the beginning) Child, Tallis, Farrant, Gibbons, Wise, Byrd, Rogers, Humfrey, Tucker, Blow, Aldrich and Priest (assumed to be Nathaniel Priest, organist at Bristol cathedral, 1710–34, and possibly Bangor cathedral, 1705–8; see Shaw, *Organists*, pp. 22, 38). Croft, widely represented in other hands, is not present in this layer.
143 Barra Boydell, ed., *Music: Documents*, p. 135.
144 Information on Canterbury kindly supplied by Denise Neary; see also Shaw, *Organists*, pp. 47, 235.
145 Barra Boydell, ed., *Music: Documents*, p. 105; for the gratuity paid by the chapter to Hodge in 1698–9, *ibid.*, p. 142. For details of anthems for St Patrick's, see Grindle, *Cathedral Music*, pp. 32–3.
146 To some extent this increase reflects the survival of more extensive and detailed records from after 1660.

refers to music bought for the cathedral or to the copying or even composing of music. This music copying activity provided an important means for choir members to supplement their incomes.[147] In 1664 Nicholas Seaward, one of the stipendiaries, received £6 for 'the anthems' and a deleted entry for a payment to John Tadpole (whether the father or the son is not clear) in March of the same year specifies the 'writing of anthems'. These payments could relate to the preparation of performing parts from anthems collected by Hosier in his manuscript and it may be these which were bound by the stationer Nathaniel Thomson later that same year.[148] In 1676/7 John Hawkshaw was paid 7s 6d for having the organ books bound.[149] The copying of music required the provision of ruled music paper, payments for which are recorded between 1676 and 1679, in the first instance specifically from London.[150] The production of ruled music paper during the late seventeenth century in England (and thus likely to apply to Ireland) appears to have been 'restricted to a small and highly centralised group of special-ised stationers' in London.[151] A comparison with contemporary records from England suggests that the total of £4 10s paid in the above instances might have accounted for up to eight or ten quires of paper.[152] Each quire consisted of twenty-four or twenty-five sheets, each sheet forming two leaves (i.e. four pages) of a folio book or four (eight pages) of quarto. The amount of music paper bought would therefore have provided up to ten 100-page folio books or (more probably) ten 200-page quarto books. It may be this same music paper which was used by John[?] Blundevile when he was paid £5 for 'writing' in the same year, as was Richard Hosier's widow who received £3 'for writing by her late husband'.[153] Nicholas Sanderson, chanter's vicar and master of the choristers, received a number of payments for 'full anthems' and 'anthem books' between 1679/80 and the year of his death in 1698. The chapter agreed in 1692 that he should

> make and perfect a new set of new Service anthem-books consisting of eight or more in number as shall be thought needful . . . and that when the books are finished he shall have four pounds per annum for keeping them in good repair and writing new anthems in them.

Sanderson completed the copying of these books two years later.[154] This marks the beginning of the practice of paying someone (usually the chanter's vicar) not only as the official copyist but also to look after the music books (for which the same amount, £4, was still being paid at the beginning of the nineteenth century).

Payments made to stationers and others outside the cathedral contribute to the scant information available on the music print trade in Dublin in the later seven-teenth century. There is no evidence for music printing in Dublin before 1685, so

---

[147] See in particular on John Matthews, pp. 129–31 below.
[148] Barra Boydell, ed., *Music: Documents*, p. 133. On Nathaniel Thompson see Pollard, *Book Trade*, pp. 564–5.
[149] Barra Boydell, ed., *Music: Documents*, p. 135.
[150] *Ibid.*, p. 137.
[151] Thompson, 'Manuscript Music'.
[152] *Ibid.*, pp. 606–7.
[153] Barra Boydell, ed., *Music: Documents*, p. 137.
[154] *Ibid.*, pp. 103, 140.

a payment 'for printing anthems and 2 books of common prayer' in 1665/6 must be for word books, possibly a reprint of the 1662 book of *Anthems to be Sung*.[155] 'Printed anthems' bought in 1664 from Nathaniel Thomson and 'anthem books' bought in 1667/8 from Samuel Dancer and from an unidentified 'Mr Robinson' are also likely to refer to word books, conceivably including Clifford's *Divine Services*.[156] While John Barnard's *The First Book of Selected Church Music* and Thomas Tomkins' *Musica Deo Sacrae et Ecclesiae Anglicanae* (published post-humously in 1668) were widely used as a basis for re-establishing cathedral repertoires following the Restoration, the paucity of anthems from Barnard in *Anthems to be Sung* noted above and the absence of any music by Tomkins in the (admittedly later) surviving repertoire of the cathedral suggest that this was not the case at Christ Church. In 1669/70 Richard Hawkshaw received £6 for 'anthem books' and in 1680/1 'new music books' were bought from an unnamed supplier.[157] Mary Crooke, John North, and William Winter are further Dublin stationers who sold 'music books', 'anthem books' and 'service books' to Christ Church between 1670 and 1672.[158] In 1681–82 an organ book was bought from the same John North who had already provided music books eleven years earlier.[159] Not all of these payments of course need necessarily have been for cathedral music: instrumental and other non-sacred music was doubtless also purchased to provide for the needs of the choirboys' musical education and instrumental training. This significant amount of music copying and purchasing during the latter part of the seventeenth century nevertheless reflects Christ Church's role as the religious flagship of Ireland's rulers. The dean and chapter were demonstrably concerned to enhance and expand the provision and practice of music as an element in the cathedral's public profile. The regret is that so little physical evidence of that activity survives today – unless further work on the extant, predominantly later eighteenth- and early nineteenth-century volumes of manuscript choir music from Christ Church identifies examples of music copied at this period.

By the close of the seventeenth century Anglo-Protestant rule in Ireland was securely established, being supported by legislation which deprived Irish Catho-lics of their land and prevented them from exercising any significant political influence. Ireland was entering an era of relative peace and prosperity which would be reflected in a period of unparalleled musical activity both in the cathe-dral and in the city of Dublin. The installation of a new organ in 1698 and the appointment in the same year of a new organist (Daniel Roseingrave) and a new

---

[155] Barra Boydell, 'Development of Music Print Trade', pp. 25–33; Barra Boydell, ed., *Music: Documents*, p. 134.

[156] *Ibid.*, pp. 134–5. On Dancer see Pollard, *Book Trade*, pp. 142–3.

[157] Barra Boydell, ed., *Music: Documents*, pp. 135, 137. The relationship of this Richard Hawkshaw to the organist John Hawkshaw is unknown. Nobody of this family name is listed as a stationer in Pollard, *Book Trade*.

[158] Barra Boydell, ed., *Music: Documents*, p. 135. See Pollard, *Book Trade*, pp. 134–6, 435–6, 631–2. A payment to the Tollett brothers in 1686–7 for '3 anthems' could refer either to music or to playing in three anthems, as they did on other occasions (see p. 84 above).

[159] Barra Boydell, ed., *Music: Documents*, p. 138.

master of the boys (Robert Hodge) can be seen together as marking both a renewal of three of the cardinal points of the cathedral's musical establishment and a change from the period of consolidation during the later seventeenth century to the eighteenth century, when Christ Church would enjoy arguably its greatest period of musical excellence.

FOUR

'The Increasing Excellence of
the Choir': the Eighteenth
and Early Nineteenth Centuries

The eighteenth century was a defining period in Dublin's cultural history, the physical appearance of the modern city being to a significant extent still dominated by the public and private buildings erected during that time. As a capital city and the second in size after London within Great Britain and Ireland, Dublin enjoyed a prolonged period of prosperity and at least superficial peace. Over the period covered by this chapter its population increased from nearly 60,000 in 1700, to about 140,000 in 1760, and approaching 250,000 by the 1820s, an increase which brought with it an ever larger number of people able to afford and patronise the arts, in particular music.[1] A vibrant musical life developed with public concerts forming an essential part of fashionable life. It was here that Handel's *Messiah* was first performed in 1742, an event with which the choir of Christ Church cathedral was closely involved. Handel's visit was not exceptional: musicians from all over Europe visited Dublin, some like Geminiani choosing to settle in the city for longer periods.[2] This vibrant musical life within the wider city was reflected in a period of notable musical activity at Christ Church, in particular during the century between Ralph Roseingrave's appointment as organist in 1727 and the death in 1833 of John Stevenson, vicar choral and composer of anthems and services which would remain amongst the most popular in the repertoires of the Dublin cathedrals throughout the nineteenth century. The music of these composers alongside that of leading later seventeenth- and eighteenth-century English cathedral composers survives in the extensive series of choir books from both cathedrals copied in the eighteenth and early nineteenth centuries.[3] Although prohibited by the dean and chapter from performing in public for personal gain, members of the cathedral choir (including choirboys) took an active part in Dublin's musical life including Handel's oratorio performances in 1741–2 and the concerts held for the benefit of the Rotunda hospital which took place during the summer months for nearly forty years up to 1791. The 'long' eighteenth

---

[1] Figures after *OCIH*, p. 170 and Brian Boydell, *Dublin Musical Calendar*, p. 11.

[2] Dublin's eighteenth-century musical life is documented in Brian Boydell, 'Music', *Dublin Musical Calendar* and *Rotunda Music*.

[3] On the Christ Church score-books see O'Keeffe, 'Score-Books'. On St Patrick's see Houston, 'Music Manuscripts'.

century, whose conclusion can be marked at Christ Church not only by the death of Stevenson and the passing in the same year (1833) of the Irish Church Tempo- ralities Act which reduced the autonomy and status of the cathedral, but in the wider context also by the end of the Georgian era with the death of George IV in 1830, marks a period of excellence for the cathedral's music.[4]

The social and political conditions which supported the development of musical life in eighteenth-century Dublin – the comparative peace and prosperity under the rule of a self-confident Anglo-Protestant elite representative of only a small minority of the country's population – were based on social inequality and repressive legislation. The prosperity was circumscribed by trade restrictions and limitations on the ownership of land by the majority Catholic population, while the growth of republican and egalitarian ideals would transform the political climate of Europe as the century drew to a close. The lifting of trade restrictions in 1779 allowing Ireland to trade freely with the British colonies and to export glass and wool, and the granting of a degree of legislative independence to the Irish parliament in 1782 were two important markers in the loosening of Britain's absolute control. But in response to the rise of the United Irishmen in the wake of the French Revolution and agitation for independence which culminated in the rebellion of 1798, the Act of Union was passed in 1800 making Ireland an integral part of the United Kingdom under direct rule from Westminster, with far-reaching effects on all aspects of Irish society. With Dublin no longer a capital city with its own parliament, however independent or not that may have been, most of the Anglo-Irish aristocracy ceased maintaining their Dublin residences and moved to London instead. Although the effects this had on the patronage of music and the arts were largely counterbalanced by the concurrent growth of a middle class eager to embrace the arts as a sign of gentility, aristocratic patronage of music in Dublin undoubtedly declined in the early years of the nineteenth century.

At the same time the fortunes of Christ Church cathedral were affected by other developments contributing to a decline in its status and wealth which would ultimately affect its musical life. In the course of the eighteenth century the devel- opment of fashionable squares to the north and east of the old city was gradually drawing commercial and fashionable life away from the former medieval heart of the city around the cathedral, a process which continued into the nineteenth century. In 1796 the law courts were moved from the precincts of Christ Church to the present Four Courts building on the north bank of the Liffey, while the Sessions, the Exchange, the Corn Market and the Custom House, all previously adjacent to or near the cathedral, were also relocated elsewhere in the developing city around this period.[5] In consequence the precincts of Christ Church ceased to be the important centre of civic life which they had been and the value of the

---

[4] In contrast a general decline of standards in English cathedral music arising out of a combination of the declining real incomes of choir members leading to disinterest and disaffection, and the prevalent stagnation of cathedral practice has been generally accepted, as articulated in Temperley, 'Music in Church', pp. 358–9 (but see also note 225 below).

[5] The Custom House (completed 1791), the Four Courts building (completed 1802) and the General Post Office (1815–18), the three major later Georgian public buildings of Dublin, are all situated on the north side of the river.

Plate 7. Christ Church cathedral from the south-west, c.1815. Watercolour by George Grattan. (Victoria and Albert Museum)

cathedral's properties and thus its income declined.[6] The cathedral's status would be further diminished after 1814 when a chapel royal at Dublin Castle was opened, the lord lieutenant no longer regularly attending Christ Church. However, despite this decline in its status and fortunes and although surrounded by decaying buildings (*Plate 7*), the cathedral itself was well cared for, and the musical establishment was to enjoy what at the time was widely considered an era of high musical standards. A description in 1818 commented that

> The interior of this cathedral evinces the unceasing attention of the dean and chapter; every part of it is kept in good repair, and is neat and clean, a circumstance not universally attended to in our places of worship: its exterior appearance announces its great antiquity, and it is to be lamented that its venerable features are disfigured and disgraced by the mean habitations and piles of disgusting ruins that not only environ, but press against it on the east and south.[7]

[6] See especially C6/1/7/9, pp. 76–80.
[7] Warburton *et al.*, *History* i, p. 497.

The conditions and duties of the choirmen

By the mid-eighteenth century the former vicars' lodgings within the precincts had decayed into a dangerous, crumbling tenement and the vicars were ordered to repair the building or pull it down.[8] The vicars choral themselves however were enjoying the high level of income accruing from their generous endowments of rents and tithes, while most choir men also received a double salary as members of the choirs of both Christ Church and St Patrick's cathedrals.[9] In 1800 the deans and chapters of the two cathedrals formally agreed to offer where possible a position in both choirs to new candidates 'whereby the inducement would be much stronger to procure persons of distinguish'd merit to fill the vacancies'.[10] A comparison of choirmen's salaries with English cathedrals in the second quarter of the nineteenth century is illuminating: a lay clerk in England might typically receive between £40 and £80 a year although at Durham, the most richly endowed cathedral, he could expect close to £115.[11] This is more or less what a stipendiary – the lowest-paid permanent position – received at Christ Church in 1835, the lay vicars choral receiving nearly £195. Furthermore when choirmen also served in the choir at St Patrick's this brought in at least an additional £156 6s 6¾d as a lay vicar.[12] As not only a vicar choral at St Patrick's (from 1816) and at Christ Church (from 1819, having come from England as a stipendiary in 1813) but also as vicars' steward, Robert Jager enjoyed a total annual income from both cathedrals of £468 11s 8d, up to ten times what a lay clerk at a less well-endowed English cathedral might receive, or about four times what he might receive at Durham. The dean and chapter exercised a paternalistic role towards their choir members who were helped during illness or when their families were sick, and the widows of deceased choirmen received financial support.[13] Nevertheless the vicars choral were as subject as the dean and chapter to the decline in property values in the early years of the nineteenth century, while their revenues from bequests and rents had been further depleted during the course of the later eighteenth century as a result of their appropriation by the dignitaries of the two cathedrals. John Spray, a vicar choral at both cathedrals from 1795, was largely responsible for retrieving these lost revenues which included a total of £238 12s 9d in 1808 for rents due to the vicars since 1794.[14]

[8] Barra Boydell, ed., *Music: Documents*, p. 112; C6/1/8/5, p. 164.
[9] See pp. 78–9 above.
[10] Barra Boydell, ed., *Music: Documents*, pp. 129–30.
[11] Barrett, *Barchester*, p. 188. The lay clerk's income at Durham in the 1840s comprised a basic salary of £60 which was augmented by attendance money and other allowances, producing a total of £114 (Crosby, 'Musical Scene', p. 74).
[12] Returns made to the ecclesiastical commissioners, cited after Grindle, *Cathedral Music*, pp. 61–2; however Bumpus, *Sir John Stevenson*, pp. 25–6 stated that a vicar choralship at Christ Church had been worth £222 per annum, a stipendiary £150.
[13] Barra Boydell, ed., *Music: Documents*, pp. 115, 127, 145, 149. Benefit concerts were also on occasion held for the 'widows and children of the vicars choral of the cathedrals' (Brian Boydell, *Dublin Musical Calendar*, p. 255).
[14] C6/1/7/8, p. 484; C6/1/15/2 (1808–9); Bumpus, 'Irish Church Composers', pp. 81, 117. Spray came to the notice of the Dublin cathedral authorities as a tenor at Lichfield cathedral and was persuaded to come over from England in 1795 as a vicar choral of both cathedrals. He opened a

While the incomes of the choirmen ensured a supply of the finest singers, their duties were, despite serving two cathedrals, not significantly more onerous than had they only served one. The pattern of services changed over time, demands on the choir varying as the relative fortunes of each cathedral fluctuated, but the choir's duties were generally shared between both in a manner which was neither too demanding nor contentious. In 1719 morning services were held at St Patrick's at nine o'clock and at Christ Church at ten o'clock (morning prayers were also read at Christ Church at six in the morning); evening prayer was held at three and four o'clock respectively in the two cathedrals, the same times being observed both on Sundays and weekdays.[15] In the absence of attendance records it is not clear whether the choir sang at both morning and evening services on all days of the week at this period, although the reiteration in 1703 of the 1662 choir orders which had specified attendance at both services suggests that this was the case, as does the staggering of both morning and evening service times at St Patrick's and Christ Church.[16] While the choir as a body may thus have attended twice daily in each of the two cathedrals, a reference at Christ Church in April 1710 to singers 'in waiting' suggests that during the weekdays one half attended each cathedral in rotation, week by week.[17]

By the 1760s the full choir normally attended on Sunday mornings (although sometimes only half were present), and typically half (but presumably with all the boys, whose attendance is not recorded) on Sunday evenings.[18] Half of the choir was usually present each weekday morning, but weekday evening services were typically attended by just one ordained vicar choral, with one or two other choirmen occasionally present. Only rarely was half the choir and exceptionally (for example on Good Friday) the full choir present on weekday evenings.[19] This is in marked contrast to the evidence from English cathedrals such as Exeter and Canterbury where attendance at weekday evening services remained fairly constant throughout the eighteenth and early nineteenth centuries with levels never falling as low as was the norm at Christ Church.[20] Services at this period were thus celebrated chorally on Sundays and weekday mornings. Even with only

musical academy in 1816 and was awarded an honorary Mus. D. by Dublin University in 1821 for his services to music in the city. An English contemporary described his voice as possessing 'a sort of oily liquidity of tone' and praised his exquisite diction; an obituary described him as 'one of the most distinguished members of the musical profession in this country, ornament of our cathedrals and animating spirit of social song in our highest circles of musical society' (William Gardiner of Leicester, cited after Bumpus, 'Irish Church Composers', p. 116) and he is described on his memorial in St Patrick's as 'the first tenor singer in the Empire' (*Freeman's Journal*, 23 Jan. 1827, cited after Hogan, *Anglo*-Irish Music, pp. 206–7). See further on Spray, *ibid.*, pp. 115–17.

15 'An Account of the Different Hours of Publick Prayer, as they are Observed in the Several Churches of this City . . .' from pamphlet *An Address to the Absenters from the Public Worship of God: with an Answer to their Pleas*, 3rd ed. (London and Dublin, 1719). There are many passing references in the Christ Church chapter acts to the reading of morning prayers at 6am.

16 Barra Boydell, ed., *Music: Documents*, p. 106.

17 *Ibid.*, p. 109.

18 Even when choir attendance records survive (a substantially complete run exists from 1762 (C6/1/23/1–12)) the attendance of the choirboys is not entered before the mid-nineteenth century.

19 C6/1/23/1. See also Barra Boydell, ed., *Music: Documents*, pp. 169–70.

20 Information on Exeter and Canterbury kindly provided by Denise Neary.

half the choir present (probably simpler) service settings and anthems were sung: while the organist George Walsh was frequently absent from weekday morning or Sunday evening services, a choirboy or one of his sons or his daughter substituted for him at the organ, the comment 'no anthem' which sometimes accompanies such substitutions indicating that the inclusion of an anthem represented the norm.[21]

By the late eighteenth century the full choir attended the services on Sunday evenings as well as in the mornings. Attendance on weekday mornings had however declined, typically being attended by one clerical vicar, the organist (or a deputy) and only one to three choir men (again, presumably also with the boys). None of the choir attended weekday evening services and there were even lengthy periods when no choirmen attended any weekday services either in the morning or the evening.[22] This change to full participation by the choir on Sunday evenings at the expense of weekday choral services may reflect the contemporary popularity of the solo, 'operatic' style of anthem which must have attracted an increasing congregation drawn to the cathedral as much for the opportunity to hear the leading singers of the day as for purely devotional reasons. The Irish cleric and reformer John Jebb later referred to the Sunday evening service which 'was discontinued about 1807' being 'greatly crowded'.[23]

Links between the choirs of the two cathedrals and Trinity College, three pillars of Protestant Dublin society, had long been close. Throughout the eighteenth century members of the cathedral choirs sang in Trinity College chapel on Trinity Sunday,[24] and from the 1760s they sang every Sunday in the college chapel, leaving the service there after the anthem and returning to Christ Church for morning service sung by the full choir.[25] The choir then sang an afternoon service at St Patrick's and an evening service again at Christ Church. In 1814, following the opening of the new Chapel Royal in Dublin Castle at which some of the choir now also sang on Sunday mornings, the Sunday evening service at Christ Church was discontinued and subsequent choir attendance books confirm that these were not held again (with exceptions such as on 19 August 1821 when King George IV was present, and thereafter for a period of three months) until St Patrick's was closed for renovation in 1862.[26] Choral weekday evening services

---

[21] E.g. C6/1/23/1, 24 Nov. 1762, 17 Apr. 1763, 8 Jan. 1764.

[22] C6/1/23/3–4. See for example between May 1786 and Sept. 1789.

[23] Jebb, *A Few Observations*, p. 13. The Sunday evening service at Christ Church was discontinued after 1814, not in 'about 1807' (see next paragraph). Cf. C.V. Stanford's comments on the 'audiences' (congregations) for solo anthems at Sunday evening services at St Patrick's in the 1850s, see p. 156 below.

[24] First noted in 1703, *IRL-Dtc*, MUN. V. 57. 1, p. 154.

[25] Whiteside, *Chapel*, p. 20; *IRL-Dtc*, MUN. V. 57. 4, p. 266; C6/1/15/2. The allowance paid by Trinity College for the cathedral choirboys' singing in the college chapel on Sundays was considered in 1777 to be insufficient and Christ Church considered withdrawing its services unless there was an increase (Barra Boydell, ed., *Music: Documents*, p. 122). In 1800 Trinity College offered to increase the amount they paid Christ Church for the provision of singers for their chapel service each week on condition that they could 'chuse Two Counter-Tenors, Two Tenors and Two Bass singers from the Choir at large' instead of being required to take six stipendiaries 'whatever their Voices may be' (*ibid.*, p. 129).

[26] C6/1/7/9, p. 279; choir attendance book 1819–25, C6/1/23/6; C6/1/7/13, pp. 129, 202. Bumpus's

were however resumed after 1814 with typically five or six singers together with a clerical vicar and the organist (and boys) attending three or four times a week.[27]

At the beginning of the eighteenth century the orders and statutes of the choir dating from 1662 were still enforced and, in order to comply with the requirement for choir members to improve their singing skills, weekly rehearsals were held at five o'clock on Saturdays in 1703, a practice which was reiterated twelve years later when those who were appointed to sing the anthem had to be reminded not to leave the church until the end of the service, while non-attendance at practices was punishable by a fine.[28] When Saturday morning rehearsals were again speci-fied in 1762 the chanter's vicar (or senior vicar present) was asked to leave a note of what was being performed in the chapter house before the service 'to prevent the confusion arising from the sending of Messages in the time of Divine service'.[29] A new set of choir orders drawn up in 1789 reiterated questions of attendance, punctuality, and the recording of such offences.[30] The practice was legitimised of half the choir attending weekly services alternately, week about, a practice reflected in the attendance books since the middle of the century. Rehearsals are confirmed as being held on Saturday mornings and, echoing views expressed by Wetenhall a century earlier, the music was to be appointed by the dean, sub-dean, chanter 'or other member of the chapter present' (or if no member of the chapter be present, by the chanter's or the dean's vicar). The music was probably actually selected by the organist or choir master, but the above require-ment ensured that the dean and chapter had the opportunity to approve his choice. The 'manner of playing the organ and performing the Service' at the Saturday practice, which was to be followed exactly on Sundays, was also nominally under the direction of the dean, sub-dean or senior member of the chapter. These rules of 1789 also reflect changes in the practice of psalm chanting when they specify that

all the Choristers Stipendiaries and Vicars do join in the Responses in such Musical Chords as are accustomed to be used in Cathedral Service and that in the Chaunting of the Psalms the Choristers Stipendiaries and Vicars each side join alternately with full Voice and both sides join with full Voice in the Gloria Patri.[31]

The standards of the cathedral choirs during the earlier eighteenth century are difficult to ascertain. Complaints of inattendance and misbehaviour, and the recording of fines or even (usually temporary) dismissal, recur with some regu-larity in the chapter acts as they do at most cathedrals. But are these the visible manifestation of a wider lack of commitment by the choirmen which would have had implications for their performance standards, or do they represent no more than an undue focussing of attention, through their being recorded at chapter

statement that 'at Christ Church, from 1807 to 1825 . . . there was evening service on Sunday at 7' is only partially correct ('Irish Church Composers', p. 146).

[27] C6/1/23/6.
[28] The imposition of fines for non-attendance at practices was raised again in 1717 (Barra Boydell, ed., *Music: Documents*, pp. 106, 110; C6/1/8/4, p. 81).
[29] Barra Boydell, ed., *Music: Documents*, p. 116.
[30] *Ibid.*, pp. 125–6.
[31] Cf. Temperley, 'Music in Church', p. 361.

level, on the exceptional behaviour of a small minority of individuals? Mrs
Delaney commented in 1731 on the 'good voices and a very sweet organ' at
Christ Church, and Handel expressed satisfaction at the singers in his oratorio
concerts who were largely members of the cathedral choirs.[32] On the other hand in
the 1730s Dean Swift expressed considerable concern, even exasperation, at the
levels of absence and general carelessness on the parts of some of his choirmen at
St Patrick's, most of them also members of Christ Church choir: John Smith, who
sang in both cathedral choirs, is described as 'very careless of his attendance,
either rambling abroad or idling at home . . . takes frolic to neglect his attendance
for two or three months together'; William Fox, also a member of both choirs,
was 'an infamous sot, who is daily losing his voice by intemperance . . . very
negligent in his attendance, scandalous in his behaviour and conversation'.[33]
Bishop Synge wrote to Swift comparing a Mr Hughes (not recorded at Christ
Church) to John Mason and William Lamb, both prominent members of the two
cathedral choirs and both of whom would sing solos in the first performance of
Messiah:

> His voice is not excellent, but will do; and if I mistake not, he has one good
> quality, not very common with the musical gentlemen i.e. he is desirous to
> improve himself. If Mason and Lambe were of his temper, they would be as fine
> fellows as they think themselves.[34]

Musical standards were considered good in the early nineteenth century, the
dean and chapter talking of the 'increasing excellence of the choir' in 1810 and
Monck Mason claiming in 1820 that 'there is not, at the present, a cathedral in
Great Britain wherein the choral service is better performed than in those of St.
Patrick's and Christ Church'.[35] Jebb later commented that Christ Church was
unusual in the earlier nineteenth century in that the members of the church
processed at every service into the choir with the organ playing, a practice more
usually reserved elsewhere for greater festivals and days of ceremony. This may
be a continuation of a practice possibly dating from before 1814 when the lord
lieutenant and dignitaries had regularly worshipped at Christ Church. Jebb also
stated that the canticles were always sung to services on Sundays, Wednesdays
and Fridays (the litany days, following the rubric in the Book of Common
Prayer), being chanted on other days with a full anthem sung. The playing of a
voluntary after the morning psalms on Sundays (except when communion was
held) had gone out of use by the 1840s, but a voluntary was played while the
preacher ascended the pulpit for the sermon, after which the anthem was sung.
The prayers and latter part of the litany were chanted by the dean's vicar with
harmonised responses peculiar to Dublin being sung up until 1826 or 1827, a
practice Jebb described as 'solemn and devotional in the highest degree'. The

[32] Llanover, *Mrs Delaney* i, pp. 294–5; Burrows, 'Dublin Performances', p. 56.

[33] Grindle, *Cathedral Music*, pp. 39–40.

[34] *Correspondence of Jonathan Swift* v, p. 124, cited after Grindle, *Cathedral Music*, p. 40. On
Mason and Lamb as soloists in *Messiah*, see p. 121 below.

[35] C6/1/7/9, p. 78; Mason, *History and Antiquities*, quoted after Bumpus, 'Irish Church
Composers', p. 81. See further Barra Boydell, 'Bright Exception'.

unison responses of Winchester were subsquently adopted at Christ Church, although the harmonised responses continued in use at St Patrick's.[36]

The choirboys and their master

Direct information on the choristers' lives and their contribution to the cathedral services continues to be sparse during most of the period covered by this chapter. In 1707 a standard wording for the indenture of apprenticeship was drawn up: each boy 'being desirous to be Instructed in singing and Musick, whereby he May be made Capable of serving in the Choire of the Cathedrall Church of the holy Trinity Dublin' was bound to the master of the boys 'freely voluntarily and with the consent of his parents' (from 1731 apprenticeship was to the proctor rather than the master of the boys).[37] The length of the apprenticeship was not predetermined, but 'meat, drink, lodging, washing and clothing' as well as the teaching of 'singing and music' are specified. In 1725 it was agreed that boys should be presented to the dean and chapter 'to be tried, examined and approved of' before being apprenticed to the cathedral.[38] Boys could be admitted as choristers on a trial basis, and in special cases a boy with exceptional talent was admitted as a supernumerary member, enjoying the same level of maintenance and instruction as the regular choirboys, as when Henry Lemon was admitted in 1789 because of his 'remarkable fine voice'.[39] At a combined meeting of the deans and chapters of the two Dublin cathedrals held in November 1777 following the sudden death of the organist and master of the boys Richard Woodward the younger it was agreed to apprentice the choirboys simultaneously to both cathedrals.[40] This created its own problems when boys were preferred for vacancies at one or other cathedral: in 1783 Edward Kingsley was apprenticed by the chapter of Christ Church on the recommendation of their chancellor but without consulting the dean and chapter of St Patrick's who had previously recommended another boy, John Malley, for the vacancy, a conflict which was resolved by agreeing that Malley would be given the next vacancy due to fall some five months later.[41] Relatively few choirboys failed to fulfil their service, but there were always exceptions as in 1779 when one boy was discharged for bad behaviour and his apprenticeship indentures cancelled, while a second who absented himself from the choir had to enter into a bond for his future attendance and performance.[42]

There were normally six choirboys in the earlier eighteenth century, four on the foundation plus a further two. But there must also have been other boys in the school being trained for the choir, although direct evidence is lacking at this

---

36 Jebb, *Choral Service*, pp. 229, 232, 249, 487, 494; Jebb, *A Few Observations*, p. 14. On Jebb's comments on the performance of the solo anthem after the sermon, see pp. 141, 167 below.

37 Barra Boydell, ed., *Music: Documents*, pp. 106, 112. Cf. also C6/1/8/5, p. 69 (17 April 1732).

38 Barra Boydell, ed., *Music: Documents*, p. 111.

39 C6/1/8/6, pp. 31–2; Barra Boydell, ed., *Music: Documents*, p. 114; C6/1/7/7, pp. 140, 260; Henry Lemon subsequently became a full choirboy, being apprenticed out on leaving the choir in 1794–95 (C6/1/15/2), and eventually an organ builder (see Henry Leaman, p. 117 below).

40 Barra Boydell, ed., *Music: Documents*, p. 122.

41 C6/1/7/7, pp. 162, 164, 165.

42 C6/1/7/7, p. 120.

period.[43] In 1809 however one boy aged eight was described as having been 'for some time past . . . prepared with the other boys of the choir for the church service' and was deemed fit to join the choir.[44] In 1761 it was decided to increase the number of boys by two 'to make up the whole Number Eight', St Patrick's contributing a quarter of the cost 'for their Maintenance Education and Cloathing'.[45] Like their adult choir colleagues, choirboys tended to belong to both cathedral choirs: in 1709 the boys were noted as singing in both cathedral choirs, while at least four of the six choirboys listed at the dean's visitation at St Patrick's in January 1744 can be identified at Christ Church around the same period, and typically five or six of the (usually) eight boys named each year at St Patrick's between 1768 and 1777 can also be traced at Christ Church.[46] However by the 1830s (and possibly earlier) the choirboys were attached exclusively to one cathedral rather than both.[47] The number of choirboys at Christ Church appears to have risen in the nineteenth century but, in the absence of definitive listings, the difficulties in assessing their numbers can be illustrated by the case in February 1815 when the writing master Francis Robinson (father of four sons who were all associated with both cathedrals as singers and organists, including the younger Francis who would be assistant organist of Christ Church from 1815 to 1833)[48] made a proposal to look after and instruct the boys. Robinson referred to the dieting and washing of 'the four young gentlemen of the choir' (the foundation choirboys) but also to the education of six boys.[49] The accounts for the previous two years however (those for the same year are not specific as to numbers) record payments for the maintenance of ten boys, a number which is repeated in 1819.[50] However, in the following year the costs of looking after no more than five boys are recorded (this number increases to six in subsequent years and to seven in 1827).[51]

Up to the mid-eighteenth century the master of the boys was usually (but not always) either the dean's vicar or chanter's (precentor's) vicar, in other words one of the senior vicars choral.[52] Thereafter, however, the post was typically given to lay choir members (not necessarily vicars choral) who were prominent as

---

[43] Cf. Barra Boydell, ed., *Music: Documents*, pp. 108, 109; C6/1/8/4, p. 91; C6/1/26/16/14–22.

[44] C6/1/7/9, p. 36.

[45] Barra Boydell, ed., *Music: Documents*, p. 116. That this increase was effected is confirmed in 1768 when Richard Woodward the elder was appointed master of the boys and his allowance increased to 'One hundred and five pounds, eighteen Shillings for eight Boys' (Barra Boydell, ed., *Music: Documents*, p. 118). The contribution by St Patrick's of only one quarter of the choirboys' costs reflects the fact that weekday choral services were not held at St Patrick's at this period.

[46] See note 43 above; cf. St Patrick's chapter acts (C2/1/3/8–9, *passim*) and C6/1/7/6–7, *passim*. The larger number of choirboys at St Patrick's reflects the larger size of its foundation.

[47] See ch. 5.

[48] See ch. 5, note 18.

[49] C6/1/7/9, pp. 285f.

[50] C6/1/15/3; C6/1/7/10, p. 101.

[51] C6/1/15/3.

[52] Although a priest, Henry Swords (master of the boys from 1709 to 1714) appears unusually at this period to have been a stipendiary but not a vicar choral at Christ Church, a position he did however hold at St Patrick's (see ch. 3, note 75). Cotton, *Fasti*, ii, p. 207 incorrectly gives Sword's death as 1710 but notes that he was buried at St Werburgh's church.

musicians. The master of the boys continued up to the end of the eighteenth century to be responsible for their food, accommodation and clothing as well as for their musical education, a 'writing master', normally paid out of the master's salary and thus not usually separately recorded, looking after their non-musical education.[53] The duties of Robert Hodge, appointed master of the boys and chanter's vicar in November 1698 on the same day that Daniel Roseingrave was appointed organist, were defined as 'teaching and Instructing the Boys in singing and in the Knowledge of the Organ' as well as 'finding them with sufficient meat drink clothing lodging and washing'.[54] The Revd John Worrall, who held the post from 1714 to 1746, was also master of the boys and dean's vicar at St Patrick's.[55] As master of the boys at both cathedrals he received a total income of £111 out of a potential maximum of £120 in 1726 when Dean Swift urged he be granted an increase.[56] In July 1746, by which time he would have been in his late seventies and master of the boys for over thirty years, Worrall expressed his desire to retire from the position. The chapter not only agreed to find a replacement for him but also made a presentation of silver worth 20 guineas in gratitude for his 'past services as master of the boys'.[57] William Lamb, who succeeded Worrall as master of the boys following the latter's death in 1751, and as a vicar choral, was the first master of the boys who was not ordained.[58] Samuel Murphy, a former choirboy, is unusual for having been master of the boys for two separate periods, the first of ten years from 1758 until 1768, the second from 1777 following the early death of Richard Woodward the younger until his own death in 1780.[59] It is a measure of the regard in which Samuel Murphy was held that his widow was to receive an annual bounty of 10 guineas for the rest of her life (she outlived her husband by more than twenty years).[60]

A number of events during Richard Woodward the elder's incumbency reflect typical aspects of the duties of the master of the boys at this time: in December

---

[53] Barra Boydell, ed., *Music: Documents*, pp. 135, 138; C6/1/7/4, 24 Nov. 1713. Payments to John Worrall, master of the boys, in 1716–17 (signed receipts, C6/1/26/16/[17c]) and between 1733 and 1738 (C6/1/26/16/21), specifically for 'teaching the boys to write', do not necessarily mean that he taught them himself rather than marking reimbursements for having paid the writing master himself.

[54] Barra Boydell, ed., *Music: Documents*, p. 105.

[55] See ch. 3, note 75.

[56] Copy of letter from Dean Swift to the trustees of the augmentation fund, 4 Feb. 1726, PRONI, Pakenham papers, TD 5777, Y/12/15 (temporary shelfmark).

[57] C6/1/8/6, pp. 35–6.

[58] Barra Boydell, ed., *Music: Documents*, pp. 113, 114; C6/1/8/6, p. 77. John Worrall's death was reported in the *Dublin Journal* of 9 July 1751.

[59] Barra Boydell, ed., *Music: Documents*, pp. 116, 118, 122, 123. Baptised at St Werburgh's in Dublin on 3 January 1725 (O'Keeffe, 'Score-Books', p. 74), Murphy was a choirboy at Christ Church until his voice broke in 1744. He was made a stipendiary in 1758 when he was appointed master of the boys (C6/1/8/6, p. 21). Samuel Murphy seems to disprove the widely repeated claim that, prior to John Stevenson's being admitted as a choir boy in 1771, no boys of Irish parentage were admitted to the cathedral choir school (cf. chapter 3, note 69). Murphy was also organist at Trinity College Chapel in 1750 and a vicar choral at St Patrick's from 1759. On Murphy as cathedral organist see p. 118 below.

[60] C6/1/7/7, p. 136; C6/1/15/2, 1780–81 to 1805–6. Murphy's widow also received a pension of 6 guineas from St Patrick's cathedral (C2/1/3/9, fol. 117v).

1770 arrangements were made for Robert Tuke, a sick chorister whose illness Woodward feared might spread to the others, to be lodged in another house and properly cared for.[61] Four months later Woodward was reminded not to permit any of the choirboys to sing at public concerts without the permission of the dean or sub-dean.[62] By 1775 Woodward was being assisted by his son and a year later they were given a special payment for their 'extraordinary good care and attention to the Choir Boys'.[63] Langrish Doyle, master of the boys at both cathedrals and organist at Christ Church from 1780, was a prominent figure in Dublin's musical life, being active as a conductor of public concerts and oratorio performances including the Handel commemoration concerts held at Christ Church in April 1788 and the Rotunda concerts for the 1791 season.[64]

An unsettled period followed Doyle's resignation as master of the boys in 1797 (although he continued to care for them for a further six months and remained on as organist at Christ Church until 1814)[65] which suggests that the financial benefits of the position of master of the boys were no longer considered sufficient to compensate for the duties and responsibilities involved. Having previously been organist at Armagh since 1794, John Clarke (known after 1814 as John Clarke-Whitfeld) served as master of the choirboys at both Dublin cathedrals for less than six months (his departure to England in 1798 was reportedly as result of the outbreak of rebellion) and, even though he continued at Christ Church as a vicar choral until his death in 1827, John Spray subsequently held the position for only eighteen months.[66] Following Spray's resignation the temporary division of responsibility for the boys between the verger James Hewitt who looked after their maintenance, and the Revd Charles G. Osborne who instructed them in

[61] Barra Boydell, ed., *Music: Documents*, p. 118. Robert Tuke was a soloist in the Rotunda concerts in 1772–3 (see p. 123 below), ceased as a choirboy when his voice broke in 1775, became a stipendiary, suffered a 'paralytic stroke' in 1792 and died five years later (C6/1/7/7, pp. 55f, 99, 271f, 324; C/6/1/7/8, p. 76).

[62] Barra Boydell, ed., *Music: Documents*, p. 118. On choirboys as soloists in the Rotunda concerts see p. 123 below.

[63] *Ibid.*, pp. 116, 117, 121, 122; C6/1/7/7, pp. 64f, 67f, 89. Richard Woodward the younger became a choirboy at Christ Church following his father's arrival in Dublin from Salisbury in 1751, subsequently continuing as a member of the choir. He was appointed organist in succession to George Walsh in 1765 and a vicar choral at St Patrick's in 1770. It was probably on the basis of the publication of his *Cathedral Music* in 1771 (which led to his music becoming known in England) that he was awarded a Mus. D. from Dublin University in the same year. His father resigned as master of the boys in his favour in October 1776 but he died unexpectedly in November 1777.

[64] Doyle had been a choirboy at both cathedrals up to 1768, subsequently becoming a stipendiary choirman before being appointed organist of Armagh cathedral in 1776. When he returned to Dublin in 1780 he was also appointed organist of Trinity College chapel. C6/1/7/6, fol. 117v; C2/1/3/9; C6/1/7/7, pp. 76, 77, 92; Barra Boydell, ed., *Music: Documents*, pp. 123–4.

[65] Barra Boydell, ed., *Music: Documents*, p. 127; C6/1/7/8, p. 123.

[66] Barra Boydell, ed., *Music: Documents*, pp. 128, 129, 130, 154; Seymour, *Christ Church*, p. 76. Shortly after Clarke's departure it transpired that he had left owing the cathedral approximately £110. The ancient right of the liberty of Christ Church was invoked when, the dean and chapter having secured Clarke's belongings remaining in his residence as surety for his debt, they demanded and received an apology from the high sheriff's agent for entering the liberty of Christ Church to recover Clarke's goods without the dean and chapter's permission (Barra Boydell, ed., *Music: Documents*, pp. 128–9; C6/1/7/8, pp. 108–110).

music, anticipated future developments.[67] Charles Osborne was the last master of the boys who combined overall responsibility with teaching music. When complaints were made in March 1806 about Osborne's neglect of duty in the education of the boys the post of a master to teach the boys 'reading, writing and arithmetic' was advertised, to which Francis Robinson was appointed.[68]

The change from the earlier position of the master of the boys having overall responsibility for the boys' care and education, under whom a 'writing master' might be engaged in a subordinate role, to the nineteenth-century position where responsibility for the musical and for the general education of the boys would be in separate hands, reflects the growing attention being paid in the early nineteenth century to the education of choirboys: the national school movement and the pioneering work of reformers like Maria Hackett contributed to a climate in which greater emphasis was now given to their general education. However the cathedral's declining revenues also affected the choir school during the first third of the nineteenth century, the costs of looking after and educating the choirboys coming under scrutiny as economies within the cathedral's finances were called for.[69] Approaches were made to the dean and chapter of St Patrick's in 1801, and again in 1806, to discuss 'an arrangement for the support of the school of their common choir', and by 1814 Christ Church was claiming it carried a disproportionate share of the cost.[70] Increases in the contributions from Trinity College and St Patrick's were sought, St Patrick's agreeing to support one of the Christ Church boys provided its own boys could assist at the services in Christ Church.[71] A proposal that boys should no longer board within the precincts of Christ Church but live with their parents who would be paid an allowance, while an additional senior boy who could already play the organ would be maintained at the expense of the organist, was rejected by the parents in 1815. Over the next eighteen years a variety of solutions concerning the boys' accommodation were explored. In some years they were boarded out with people appointed by the chapter but living beyond the precincts (including the writing master, Francis Robinson). At other times it was considered more appropriate to have the boys back within the

---

67 *Ibid.*, pp. 130–1; C6/1/7/8, p. 149. In August 1800 Osborne submitted a lengthy complaint to the chapter relating how Spray had called him 'impertinent and a puppy' after he, as choirmaster, had objected to Spray's interrupting a rehearsal of Handel's *Dettingen Te Deum* in St Patrick's when a boy soloist was having difficulty singing a demanding solo part. Spray eventually apologised to Osborne (Barra Boydell, ed., *Music: Documents*, pp. 131–2).

68 C6/1/7/8, pp. 373, 381; C6/1/15/2–3. Francis Robinson (the elder) continued in this position until 1820, being succeeded by Charles V. Kelly ('tutor to the children of the choir', 1820–21) and Charles Osborne (the younger, referred to from 1827 as 'The Revd') (1821–33). For subsequent masters of the choir school, all of whom after 1833 were senior clergy of the cathedral, see ch. 5, note 41.

69 Around the turn of the century the school house and other aspects of the boys' care were nevertheless improved. The accounts for 1799 to 1801 include payments for papering, painting, white-washing, glazing and upholstery in the 'school house', in addition to more detailed payments than usual for clothing, footwear and other sundries for the boys (Barra Boydell, ed., *Music: Documents*, pp. 144–5).

70 C6/1/7/8, pp. 158, 390, 391; C6/1/7/9, pp. 257, 265–6, 271–4, 278–9.

71 The implications of this comment in regard to the sharing of choirboys between the two cathedrals are unclear. St Patrick's 'own choristers' may be a reference to the additional choirboys on its foundation, St Patrick's having always had a larger statutory choir.

precincts in the dean's or the verger's lodgings.[72] In 1833 the proctor's proposal for reorganising the choirboys' accommodation and schooling in view of the state of the church's finances following the recent passing of the Church Temporalities Act would be adopted and the arrangement which had been tried out unsuccessfully in the past of paying the boys' parents an allowance for their accommodation would be reintroduced successfully.[73]

The instrumental training which the choirboys had received in the later seventeenth century on lute and violin gave way in the eighteenth to a more exclusive emphasis on keyboard instruments. In 1707–8 £2 10s 0d was paid for a spinet, an instrument which was repaired by John Worrall in 1714 when it is referred to as being 'for the use of the boys'.[74] By 1781 the cathedral owned two fortepianos specifically for the use of the choirboys,[75] a harpsichord costing £11 7s 6d was bought from William Castles Hollister in 1797–98, and as late as 1816–17 a harpsichord by Kirkman was bought for £31 8s 4d.[76] Pianos were bought in the early nineteenth century when the boys' keyboard training included Cramer's studies and Corfe's *Principles of Harmony and Thorough-Bass Explained* purchased in 1817 and 1818, the boys continuing as before to learn organ and occasionally to act as deputies.[77]

Organs and organists

The provision of a new cathedral organ marks the beginning of the period covered by this chapter. By 1694 the Harris/Pease organ dating from 1665–7 needed to be replaced but the process of acquiring a new instrument turned out to be somewhat tortuous. In April £50 was paid to Richard Battell, sub-dean of the Chapel Royal, for an organ which was 'to be brought out of England'. This is possibly a first payment towards a new instrument to be built by Bernard Smith, the king's organ maker. The following month the chapter authorised the dean 'to Treat and Conclude for a new Organ' and an agreement with Bernard Smith was confirmed and sealed on 23 November.[78] The dean and chapter must have assumed that their new organ was nearing completion, for in March 1697 £100 was to be paid to the 'dean in London for the organ for the church when it is ready to be brought over',

---

72 C6/1/12/1, 30 Oct. 1818; C6/1/7/10, pp. 96, 101. There was some opposition to this new plan and two boys were re-bound according to the old indentures (C6/1/7/10, p. 105).
73 *Ibid.*, p. 248; C6/1/15/3f. See also ch. 5.
74 Barra Boydell, ed., *Music: Documents*, pp. 105, 110, 144.
75 *Ibid.*, pp. 151, 152. The earlier payment is to Ferdinand Weber for repairs. Weber was the leading organ and harpsichord maker in Ireland at the time and very possibly also made these fortepianos. The later payment is for repairs carried out under Weber's widow who continued her husband's business after his death in 1784.
76 Barra Boydell, ed., *Music: Documents*, p. 153; C6/1/15/3, 1816–17; C6/1/21/1, 5 Sept. 1819. A secondhand Kirkman harpsichord had been sought in 1802 (C6/1/7/8, p. 226) which may be the same instrument for which 13 guineas was paid in 1803–4 (C6/1/15/2).
77 C6/1/7/8, p. 346; C6/1/7/9, p. 273; C6/1/7/10, p. 43; C6/1/15/2, 1804–5; C6/1/15/3, 1820–1, 1829–30; C6/1/12/1, 15 May 1817, 6 Mar., 30 Oct. 1818.
78 Barra Boydell, ed., *Music: Documents*, pp. 103, 140.

a payment confirmed at a meeting the following month.[79] But at the eleventh hour Smith did not fulfil his part of the agreement (Grindle suggests that this may have been due to pressure of work, Smith being the foremost builder in England) for in May 1697, barely seven weeks after the dean and chapter had agreed a payment of £100 to be sent to Smith, a contract to provide a new organ costing £1200 was agreed with Renatus Harris who had just completed an instrument for St Patrick's cathedral and was currently installing one at Limerick cathedral.[80] The new organ for Christ Church was the one Harris had built for the 'battle of the organs', a direct competition between himself and Smith to build the better instrument at the Temple Church in London in 1688 from which Smith had emerged triumphant. It was to be ready at Chester for transporting to Dublin by 10 August and installed by 25 March of the following year. Harris was liable either to repair it or to replace it in the event of its being lost or damaged *en route* and he also agreed to indemnify the dean and chapter against any claims which Bernard Smith might make in respect of their earlier agreement. Harris was further empowered to recover £100 from Smith and was also to be paid forthwith a further £100 which was to have been paid to Smith when the new instrument arrived in Dublin. Perhaps wary of being let down by Harris as they were by Smith, the dean and chapter demanded that Harris pay them £200 as security out of the money he had just received for the new organ at St Patrick's.[81] Dublin city council contributed £50 towards the cost of the new instrument, with lesser contributions coming from individuals including the bishop of Kilmore (the former precentor Edward Wetenhall).[82]

Renatus Harris's organ was probably installed by John Baptist Cuvillie who had come to Dublin as his assistant and who was to become the leading organ builder in Ireland during the first quarter of the eighteenth century.[83] Cuvillie was engaged in September 1698 as organ tuner and repairer for the next twenty years at a fee of £10 a year and carried out more substantial work costing £30 in 1703.[84] An undated note by Cuvillie claimed that these repairs and improvements would make it 'thoroughly as full, and compleate, as any Organ beyond Sea, and for advantage to the Organist For all manner of Voluntaryes, French or Italian grounds whatsoever'.[85] The changes included replacing a wooden flute with a metal flute, moving the cromorne from the great to the chair and the vox humane from the chair to the great, and providing the vox humane with a tremulant 'which no organ in England can show the like, For they have not found out to make a Tramblan [sic] stop'. Apart from repairing some damage to the organ when part of the ceiling fell on it in 1724–25 (the roof above the organ had been giving

[79] *Ibid.*, p. 104.
[80] *Ibid.*, p. 104; McEnery & Refaussé, *Deeds*, no. 1932; Grindle, *Cathedral Music*, pp. 134, 140. On Harris see also *NG2* xxiii, pp. 568–71.
[81] Barra Boydell, ed., *Music: Documents*, pp. 104–5. Work on the new organ and payment in bonds agreed in November 1698 are reflected in the proctor's accounts 1696–1701 (*ibid.*, pp. 141–3).
[82] *Ibid.*, pp. 142–3.
[83] For more on Cuvillie see Barra Boydell, 'John Baptiste Cuvillie'; Neary, 'Cuvillie'.
[84] Barra Boydell, ed., *Music: Documents*, pp. 104–5, 106–7, 143, 144; McEnery & Refaussé, *Deeds*, no. 1941.
[85] Barra Boydell, ed., *Music: Documents*, pp. 167–9. This note is an eighteenth-century copy not in Cuvillie's hand.

trouble for a few years, slaters and carpenters having been busy 'over the organ' in 1719–20), Cuvillie only had to attend to the regular tuning and maintenance of the instrument up to his death in 1728 when John Byfield was appointed to look after the organ.[86] Although based in England, Byfield spent a number of years in Dublin at this time adding stops to the organs in St Patrick's cathedral and St Michan's church.[87] However, in 1733 Philip Hollister, one of a dynasty of Dublin organists and organ builders, took over responsibility for the organ at the usual salary of £10 per annum.[88]

By 1750 the Renatus Harris/Cuvillie organ needed replacement and the cathedral turned back to Byfield of London for a new instrument.[89] The *Dublin Journal* reported in May 1752 that 'a very fine new organ' for Christ Church had arrived in the port from England and in July that 'Mr Byfield is now taking down the old organ in Christ Church in order to erect a new one in its stead, which though it cost but £800 is allowed to equal any in England'.[90] The new organ was inaugurated on the occasion of the annual remembrance service on 23 October 1752 to mark the 1641 rebellion. The old organ was offered for sale but Byfield ended up taking it back with him to England. On his way home he died and his widow sold it for £500 to St John's, Wolverhampton, where it remains today, rebuilt and enlarged.[91] By 1766, but in all probability some years earlier (he had maintained the organ of Trinity College since c.1760) Ferdinand Weber was looking after the Christ Church organ, still at an annual salary of £10, and making unspecified improvements at a cost of £103 15s 0d in 1781–82.[92] When William Castles Hollister (son of Philip Hollister) was appointed to look after the organ following Weber's death in 1784, one of his first jobs was to repair the organ bellows, while in 1786 repairs to the cathedral resulted in damage to the organ.[93] William Castles Hollister continued to look after the organ until his death in 1802 when his son Frederick took over.[94]

Prior to 1791 the organ was sited on a side gallery towards the north-east end of the choir with a curved projection in front (for the solo anthem singers). In that year it was moved to the choir screen which had formerly been occupied by the lord lieutenant's seat.[95] The Byfield organ of 1752 was showing its age by the early years of the nineteenth century: following an inspection in 1810 it was described as 'imperfect and ruinous' and insufficient for the needs of the choir.

---

[86] *Ibid.*, pp. 111, 145, 146.

[87] Barra Boydell, 'St Michan's', p. 88.

[88] Barra Boydell, ed., *Music: Documents*, p. 112.

[89] *Ibid.*, p. 115. This could refer either to John Byfield the elder, who had maintained the instrument in 1728–33, or to his son.

[90] Brian Boydell, *Dublin Musical Calendar*, pp. 166, 168.

[91] Brian Boydell, 'Organs', pp. 59–60; see also Hickman, *History*.

[92] Barra Boydell, 'John Baptiste Cuvillie', p. 22; Barra Boydell, ed., *Music: Documents*, pp. 147, 151.

[93] Barra Boydell, ed., *Music: Documents*, pp. 124, 151, 152. On the latter occasion payment for repairing the bellows was made to James Hollister.

[94] C6/1/7/8, p. 209.

[95] Jebb, *A Few Observations*, pp. 10, 11; C6/1/7/7, pp. 310–11. When Hollister presented his bill for this work it was questioned by the chapter who engaged the controller of tradesmen's bills to inspect Hollister's work and report on it. The accounts note a subsequent payment to Hollister of £113 4s 0d (Barra Boydell, ed., *Music: Documents*, pp. 126–7, 152).

An appeal was made to the lord lieutenant seeking government funding as part of a broader appeal towards improving the dilapidated condition of the cathedral.[96] Hollister was replaced as organ tuner by William Hull who carried out repairs and additions the following year.[97] But by 1814 it was reported that Hull had 'totally neglected the organ' and Timothy Lawless had to spend more than ten days tuning it. A mere two years later Henry Leaman presented an estimate for further repairs and additions costing 188 guineas. An expenditure of 100 guineas was approved with a further 100 guineas should somebody be forthcoming with the money.[98] Leaman's estimate included new bellows, cleaning the whole instrument, renewing the trumpet stop the pipes of which had been cut down in the course of tuning, adding a 'cojoin' (sic: possibly a coupler; the word is inserted in a second hand, neither scribe evidently understanding Leaman's original which is now lost), adding 'handles' to the stop diapason, and increasing the range of the double stop diapason down to *GG*. In the event Dean Charles Lindsey himself offered to pay the additional expense except that, instead of extending the double stop diapason downwards, an overall increase of the upper range by three notes from *d′′′* to *f′′′* was to be carried out at a cost of 84 guineas since the current range meant that the organist was obliged 'to omit or transpose many fine passages for want of three notes'.[99] When he started work on the organ Leaman uncovered examples of poor quality work carried out by Hull six years earlier. Again, the dean came to the rescue by offering to pay not only for the additional work, which included replacing the open diapason and repairing the double bassoon in the great organ and the bassoon in the chair organ 'which have been silent for many years', but also for a downward extension of the open diapason agreed some months later.[100] Apart from regular tuning and minor repairs, Leaman's work seems to have proved satisfactory up until the renovation of the long choir of the cathedral in the early 1830s.

The completion of Renatus Harris's organ in 1698 had coincided with the appointment of (and was probably also a factor in attracting) Daniel Roseingrave as organist. Roseingrave was also encouraged to come to Dublin from Salisbury (where he had succeeded Peter Isaack as organist in 1692) by the very real financial inducements of being offered the posts of organist at both Christ Church and St Patrick's cathedrals as well as those of vicar choral at St Patrick's and a stipendiary at Christ Church (the latter of which was effectively a sinecure since, a year after his appointment, he was allowed 'not to do any other duty belonging to the Church as a stipendiary thereof but only attend the organist place').[101] Although he had been organist at Salisbury and before that at Gloucester and Winchester cathedrals, Roseingrave may originally have come from Dublin: a Ralph Roseingrave (the same first name as Daniel's youngest son) was a leaseholder of

[96]   C6/1/7/9, pp. 72, 76f.
[97]   *Ibid.*, p. 141; C6/1/15/2, 1809–10, 1810–11.
[98]   C6/1/7/9, pp. 281, 342f. This Henry Leaman is probably the same as the former choirboy referred to as Henry Lemon.
[99]   C6/1/7/9, pp. 344f.
[100] *Ibid.*, pp. 348f, 373f; C6/1/15/3, 1815–17.
[101] Barra Boydell, ed., *Music: Documents*, pp. 104, 105, 106; Grindle, *Cathedral Music*, p. 28.

Christ Church in the 1660s.[102] Although Roseingrave continued as organist at Christ Church until his death in 1727, he had resigned at St Patrick's in 1719 in favour of his son Ralph who was formally appointed organist at Christ Church at an increased salary of £50 in October 1727.[103] Shortly after George Walsh, himself a choirboy at Christ Church up to 1735, succeeded as organist in 1747 he took on as an apprentice a former choirboy, John Marsh, but assistant organists were not otherwise appointed at this period.[104]

When Richard Woodward the younger (who had become organist in 1765 at the age of about twenty one)[105] died in 1777 Samuel Murphy was elected organist (a position he already held since 1769 at St Patrick's) as well as master of the boys for a second time (see page 111). The two unsuccessful candidates for organist on this occasion were the former choirboy and apprentice organist John Marsh (by now organist of St Peter's church) and Lewis Gibson, subsequently organist of Cloyne cathedral.[106] The post of assistant organist was first recognised in 1805 when Langrish Doyle requested that due to his 'age and long services' his nephew William Warren (a former choirboy) should be appointed as assistant organist. Warren formally succeeded Doyle as organist in 1814.[107] The organist's salary was increased to £80 from December 1814 (reflecting the decision at that time that one senior choirboy who could already play the organ be maintained at the cost of the organist), at which level it remained (with a change in 1825 to £73 17s 0d sterling resulting from the unification of the British and Irish currencies) until it was increased to £100 in 1845 and £125 in 1865.[108] Francis Robinson the younger, who became assistant organist following Warren's appointment as full organist, was then aged only fifteen.[109] The fact that the post of organist, as was the case with choir positions, was held for life could have clear implications for musical standards: by the 1830s Dr Warren's age was proving a liability but, although the dean urged him to retire in 1833, he refused to recognise the need.

---

[102] Shaw, *Organists*, p. 421. On the earlier Ralph Roseingrave see ch. 3, note 57 above. Daniel Roseingrave seems to have had a somewhat belligerent nature: in 1699 he was involved in a tavern brawl with Richard Hodge for which he was fined by the dean and chapter of St Patrick's £3 as the 'first and chief aggressor', and the following year he was involved in an argument with Thomas Finell resulting in their both losing three weeks' pay, the chapter of Christ Church passing a resolution that 'henceforth no vicar or stipendiary of this church do wear a sword under the penalty of expulsion'. It is perhaps significant that in both these cases he was involved in arguments with his predecessors as organist in the respective cathedrals (Grindle, *Cathedral Music*, p. 28; Barra Boydell, ed., *Music: Documents*, p. 106).

[103] Barra Boydell, ed., *Music: Documents*, p. 111.

[104] *Ibid.*, pp. 114, 147. Marsh had been a chorister up to January 1746.

[105] Barra Boydell, ed., *Music: Documents*, p. 117.

[106] *Ibid.*, p. 122. An incomplete evening service by Gibson survives in the Cloyne and Cashel cathedral music books (see Barra Boydell, 'Manuscript Sources').

[107] Warren had been paid as such (rather than as assistant) from Michaelmas 1812, both men receiving the full salary of £60. C6/1/7/8, p. 347; C6/1/7/9, p. 187; C6/1/15/3, 1812–13.

[108] C6/1/7/9, p. 273; C6/1/7/12, p. 225; C6/1/15/3, 1814–15; C6/1/15/4, 1865–6.

[109] This was not the Francis Robinson who was acting as the boys' schoolmaster but his eldest son: the proctor's accounts specifically record payment 'To Mr Robinson Junior three quarter years Salary as Deputy Organist ending 29 September [1815]' (C6/1/15/3, 1814–15). Although Robinson resigned and was asked to find a substitute following his becoming a stipendiary singer in 1829, he continued to be paid as deputy organist until September 1833 (C6/1/15/3, 1814–15, 1833–4; C6/1/7/11, p. 164).

An agreement was finally reached whereby he was offered retirement on full salary, which he continued to receive until 1841.[110]

The state cathedral

The cathedral remained the venue for official celebrations including state anniversaries, the formal first visits to the cathedral by newly appointed lords lieutenant, or to mark English military victories and peace celebrations when *Te Deums*, *Jubilates* and celebratory anthems were performed.[111] Although direct evidence is lacking, settings by Purcell were doubtless often performed at Christ Church on such occasions as was common in England.[112] Local composers were however also represented: the *Te Deum* sung at the celebration of the Treaty of Utrecht on 9 June 1713 was prepared by Johann Sigismund Cousser (Küsser) who, although he did not succeed William Viner as 'composer of state music' until 1716, had composed the annual Birthday Ode performed at Dublin Castle since 1708, and the anthem was by 'Mr Rosengrave' (presumably Daniel Roseingrave).[113] At a thanksgiving in 1749 to mark the Peace of Aix-la-Chapelle of the previous year, Lord Mornington conducted Handel's *Te Deum* and *Jubilate* and *Coronation Anthem*, the parts having been borrowed from Mercer's Hospital,[114] and a *Te Deum* and *Jubilate* by the then organist George Walsh was performed on 23 October 1752 at the annual remembrance of the 1641 rebellion.[115] In 1759 the capture of Quebec was celebrated with a new *Te Deum* and *Jubilate* 'accompanied with a Grand Band of Musick', the *Dublin Journal* referring to 'fine Anthems . . . set to music and performed by the best voices and instruments in Christ Church, conducted by Mr Dubourg, Master of H[is] M[ajesty]'s Band of Musick'.[116] Some idea of the ceremonial associated with state occasions is provided by an 'order of procession' for a general thanksgiving in December

---

[110] C6/1/7/11, pp. 263, 277, 285; C6/1/15/3, 1841–2.

[111] E.g. when the proctor was instructed on 7 June 1711 to 'prepare Musick for the Te Deum to be performed on the first Day of his Grace the Lord Lieutenant's comeing to this church' (Barra Boydell, ed., *Music: Documents*, p. 109). James, second duke of Ormond, was sworn in as lord lieutenant on 3 July 1711.

[112] On the use of Purcell's music see comments in Weber, *Musical Classics*, pp. 111, 116–17. *Te Deum* and *Jubilate* settings specifically by Purcell featured in the St Cecilia's day celebration at St Patrick's in 1731 and at a benefit for Mercer's hospital held in St Anne's church in December 1749 (Brian Boydell, *Dublin Musical Calendar*, pp. 48, 132).

[113] Brian Boydell, *Dublin Musical Calendar*, p. 35 suggested that the anthem might have been *Arise, Shine* by Daniel's son Thomas Roseingrave, but no copies of this anthem survive in Dublin, and Gifford and Platt state that it was composed in Venice in 1713 to mark the same occasion (Gifford & Platt, 'Thomas Roseingrave').

[114] Brian Boydell, *Dublin Musical Calendar*, p. 126. These same works were regularly performed at the annual benefit concert held from 1736 for Mercer's Hospital, usually in St Andrew's Round Church (*ibid.*, p. 15).

[115] *Ibid.*, pp. 35, 126, 170, 253. The service on 23 October 1752 was also the occasion on which the new Byfield organ was officially opened by Walsh. This *Te Deum* and *Jubilate* by Walsh is probably the setting which survives in the Christ Church cathedral choir books (see p. 134 below).

[116] Brian Boydell, *Dublin Musical Calendar*, p. 253.

1805 to mark the Battle of Trafalgar, which describes the lord lieutenant being preceded by the choirboys, stipendiaries and vicars choral and the prebendaries, dignitaries and dean processing from the chapter room (at that period sited within the south aisle of the nave) to the choir. Following the service the lord lieutenant was again accompanied by the same procession to the great west door, outside which the choir and clergy ranged themselves on either side to form a passage through which the lord lieutenant was escorted to his carriage by the archbishops, bishops, dean and chapter. On this occasion a temporary stage ('orchestra') was erected within the choir of the cathedral, possibly to accommodate additional musicians.[117] In addition to these state celebrations held within the cathedral, the participation of the choir in official ceremonies held elsewhere marks a continuation of a practice noted since the later sixteenth century. In the early years of the eighteenth century members of the choir were regularly involved in the annual birthday odes performed in honour of the monarch in Dublin Castle, for example in 1712 when 'Mr Sword's five boys' (Henry Swords being master of the boys at the time) took part in a *Serenata Theatrale* composed by Cousser.[118]

Cathedral musicians and public performance

While major religious and state occasions had been marked at Christ Church at least since the sixteenth century, the cathedral choirs constituted a body of trained singers, including boys, who increasingly took part in musical events outside the cathedral, whether individually or as a body, thereby establishing a new dimension in the choir's musical life which would be a frequent cause of tension between choir members and the dean and chapter. Participation in concerts of a charitable nature (which were becoming an increasingly important part of Dublin's musical life) was approved of in principle by the deans and chapters of the two cathedrals provided permission was sought in advance and choir members offered their services for free. But theatres provided the venues for much of the city's concert life and the deans and chapters viewed any association with the theatre or other secular venues with the utmost suspicion.[119] Towards the end of 1741 Dean Jonathan Swift learned that three of his choir at St Patrick's cathedral, two of whom (John Phipps and John Church) were also members of the Christ Church choir,[120] had 'presumed to sing and fiddle at a Club of Fiddlers in Fishamble-street' without his leave (Neal's Music Hall in Fishamble Street, at which Handel would give the first performance of *Messiah* some months later, had recently been opened). He asked his sub-dean and chapter

---

117 C6/1/7/8, pp. 349–50, 354. A proposal a week later to use the cathedral for a performance of a 'grand selection of sacred music' as a civic celebration of the Battle of Trafalgar and to raise funds for a memorial to Lord Nelson was rejected by the lord mayor (C6/1/7/8, pp. 351, 354).

118 Walsh, *Opera 1705–1797*, p. 26. The published text (but not the music) of this *Serenata Theatrale* is in *IRL-CAb*.

119 In 1764 an English gentleman resident in Dublin complained about the habit of cathedral choristers being forbidden to sing oratorios on stage (*Freeman's Journal*, 7–10 Apr. 1764).

120 Church was one of the principal singers in the first benefit concert for Mercer's hospital in 1736, subsequently appearing in a number of later years (Brian Boydell, *Dublin Musical Calendar*, p. 274).

to punish such vicars as shall ever appear there as songsters, fiddlers, pipers, trumpeters, drummers, drummajors or in any sonal quality, according to the flagitious aggravations of their respective disobedience, rebellion, perfidy and ingratitude.[121]

The dean and chapter of Christ Church consequently, but somewhat more prosaically, passed their own resolution

forbidding all persons employd in the Choir of this Cathedral from assisting at any Musical performance, without the Special leave of the Chapter first had and obtained, and that the Said Chapter are resolved to proceed with the Utmost Severity against any Vicar and to discharge the Organist and any Stipendiary or Chorister, who shall presume to disobey this order, and the Choir being Calld in, the Deane acquainted them with the Said Order.[122]

These injunctions, which would be reiterated when the question of choir members performing outside the cathedral recurred in the 1770s,[123] came after the choir members had participated in at least some of Handel's first series of six subscription concerts held in late 1741 to early 1742. In a letter to Charles Jennens written after the first concert of that series Handel wrote that

I have form'd an other Tenor Voice which gives great Satisfaction, the Basses and Counter Tenors are very good, and the rest of the chorus Singers (by my Direction) do exceeding well.[124]

In January 1742 permission was requested by Mercer's Hospital for the two cathedral choirs to assist the Philharmonick Society in charity performances directed by Handel. A similar request the following March relating to an unspecified performance in aid of three charities refers to the forthcoming first performance of *Messiah* on 13 April 1742 at which members of the combined choirs of the two cathedrals largely formed the choir (although it would seem that the choirboys did not take part, the top line being sung by female sopranos).[125] Five members of the Christ Church choir (all also members of St Patrick's) were soloists on this occasion: William Lamb and Joseph Ward (countertenors, both stipendiaries), James Bayly (tenor, a stipendiary), and John Hill and John Mason (basses, a stipendiary and a vicar choral respectively).[126] The public success of this occasion seems to have emboldened Ward and Hill to risk appearing in

[121] *The Correspondence of Jonathan Swift* v, pp. 267f, quoted after Brian Boydell, *Dublin Musical Calendar*, p. 76.

[122] Barra Boydell, ed., *Music: Documents*, pp. 112–13.

[123] *Ibid.*, p. 118.

[124] 'An other Tenor Voice' probably refers to the cathedral choirman James Bayly (Bayleys, Bailey) who sang in a number of Handel's performances including this first concert. Widely quoted, e.g. Burrows, *Handel: Messiah*, p. 15 and Burrows, 'Handel's Dublin Performances', pp. 56, 69.

[125] Brian Boydell, *Dublin Musical Calendar*, p. 17; Burrows, 'Handel's Dublin Performances', pp. 49, 56.

[126] Burrows, *Handel: Messiah*, pp. 15, 16, 19; Burrows, 'Handel's Dublin Performances', pp. 56, 67, 70. The status within the choir of each given here is as of April 1742, Ward later becoming a vicar choral and Lamb a vicar choral and master of the boys.

subsequent concerts of Handel's series for which, not being specifically charitable occasions, the dean and chapter had not given permission: they were each fined 40 shillings (subsequently remitted) specifically for 'singing at a public musical performance in Neal's Music Room in Fishamble Street on Friday the 21st of [May]', this date corresponding to a public rehearsal of *Saul*, Handel's penultimate concert in Dublin.[127]

When the Revd Thomas Mosse, chaplain of the Lying-In Hospital (subsequently to be known as the Rotunda), sought permission for the boys and 'some few others belonging to the choir' to take part in a performance of *Messiah* on 16 April 1772 for the benefit of the hospital, permission was granted 'during Passion week only but at no other time' on the basis that these were charitable sacred performance and with assurances that, despite the performances taking place in a theatre, 'an Orchestra [i.e. stage] is intended to be erected to Separate the Choir from any Stage Players'.[128] A similar occasion recurred in 1777, this time in aid of Mercer's Hospital, when one of the dean and chapter's conditions (alongside the erection once again of a stage to separate choir from 'stage players') was that the organist (Richard Woodward the younger) should prevail on Anthony Webster, a visiting vocal soloist from London, to give his services free.[129] The annual concerts held during holy week between 1794 and 1819 by the Irish Musical Fund Society for the benefit of 'distressed musicians and their families' were supported by the choir of Christ Church (the dean, as bishop of Kildare, was a patron of this charity). These concerts, modelled on the Westminster Handel commemoration concerts of 1784 and held in the Rotunda (except for 1799 in St Mark's church and 1800–1 in the Theatre Royal, Crow Street), became an important part of Dublin's musical life.[130] However, as late as in 1822 permission for the choir to sing at a concert in a theatre 'for the relief of the peasantry in the distressed parts of Ireland' was only given because it was to be 'unmingled with any theatrical performance' and the musicians were performing *gratis*.[131] In contrast, requests

---

127 Barra Boydell, ed., *Music: Documents*, p. 113; C6/1/8/6, p. 14; Brian Boydell, *Dublin Musical Calendar*, p. 82.

128 Barra Boydell, ed., *Music: Documents*, p. 119; Brian Boydell, *Rotunda Music*, p. 93.

129 Barra Boydell, ed., *Music: Documents*, pp. 121–2; Brian Boydell, *Rotunda Music*, pp. 109, 226.

130 C6/1/7/8, pp. 158, 209, 377 etc. Founded in 1787, the Irish Musical Fund Society was also known after 1794 as the Incorporated Musical Fund Society. In 1818 its annual request to Christ Church for the participation of its choir members was noted as being irregular because the seal was not attached (C6/1/7/10, pp. 16–17). For a sample programme of these concerts with details of patrons and performers (including 'the gentlemen of the [cathedral] choir', soloists from the cathedrals, including John Spray and David Weymann, 'several amateurs, and all the principal instrumental performers in this city' and conducted by Philip Cogan, organist of St Patrick's) see *Freeman's Journal*, 9 April 1805. Information kindly supplied by Derek Collins from an unpublished paper read at the annual conference of the RMA (Irish Chapter), University College Dublin, 3–4 May 2002. Another example of a charity concert is provided by a 'Grand Commemorative [Charity] Concert' for the Mendicity Association on 8 December 1818 in the Great Room of the Rotunda at which the soloists included the cathedral singers John Spray, Robert Jager and David Weyman 'assisted by the choirs of Christ Church and of St Patricks and of the College Chapel' (*Freeman's Journal*, 1 Dec. 1818).

131 C6/1/7/10, p. 167. The situation could be reversed: in 1835 the organiser of an oratorio performance would not accept the conditions laid down by the dean and chapter for the participation of some of the choir (C6/1/7/12, p. 3).

for a limited number of boys and men to assist at charity sermons held in parish churches were readily agreed to.[132]

Three Handel commemoration concerts held in Christ Church cathedral itself in April 1788 in aid of Decayed Musicians, the Meath Hospital and the Lying-In Hospital mark the first recorded occasion on which charitable concerts were held within the cathedral itself.[133] However these concerts, which must have been large-scale affairs and were inspired by the Westminster Abbey Handel commemorations, pass by unmentioned in the cathedral records. It is also within the context of demonstrably charitable concerts that boy soloists from both cathedrals performed in the frequent concerts organised by the Rotunda Hospital during the later eighteenth century which provided the main venue for public concerts in Dublin. In 1766 William Brett (the younger), who completed his apprenticeship as a choirboy at Christ Church in 1768,[134] received a fee of 40 guineas, and 50 guineas during the following two seasons, for singing at the Rotunda. In his *Recollections* John O'Keeffe related how Brett

> belonging to the choir of Christ Church Cathedral . . . [was] so blundering a boy, that one day, in a sacred oratorio at St. Andrew's Church, he sang a tender amorous love-song; but the choir being very fine, and he singing it admirable, the great impropriety was overlooked.[135]

Other choirboys of Christ Church (and like Brett also of St Patrick's) to appear as soloists at the Rotunda were Robert Tuke in 1772 and 1773 and John Andrew Stevenson in 1779.[136] Despite his clerical status the Revd Samuel Murphy (then organist at St Patrick's although not yet at Christ Church) appeared as an organist at the Rotunda in 1771 and is presumed to have been in charge of the Rotunda music in 1773, and Langrish Doyle, organist and master of the boys, conducted the Rotunda concerts in 1790.[137] In the early years of the nineteenth century the choir began to be asked to perform outside the city of Dublin. In 1802 Lord Sunderlin asked for the Dublin-born bass soloist David Weyman (a stipendiary at Christ Church and vicar choral at St Patrick's from 1802 until his death in 1823) and three boys to sing at the opening of a new church in County Westmeath.[138] Members of the cathedral choir even travelled to Belfast in October 1813 following a request to sing in concerts organised by Edward Bunting to benefit the Poor House, including the first Belfast performance of *Messiah*.[139]

---

[132] E.g. Barra Boydell, ed., *Music: Documents*, pp. 124 (St Anne's church, Feb. 1786), 132 (St Mary's church and the Rotunda chapel, Dec. 1800).

[133] *Freeman's Journal*, 1–3 Mar. 1788.

[134] C6/1/7/6, fol. 117v.

[135] Brian Boydell, *Rotunda Music*, p. 68. Not associated with the cathedral as an adult, Brett subsequently appeared in a number of opera productions including the first performance in Dublin of Grétry's *Richard Coeur de Lion* (in Thomas Linley's English adaptation) at the Smock Alley theatre in March 1787 (Walsh, *Opera 1705–1797*, pp. 261, 288).

[136] Brian Boydell, *Rotunda Music*, pp. 68, 94–5, 117–18.

[137] *Ibid.*, pp. 215, 221.

[138] C6/1/7/8, p. 231. Bumpus, 'Irish Church Composers', p. 124 states that Weyman died in August 1822, but the proctor's accounts at Christ Church include a posthumous payment to the 'late David Weyman as stipendiary from 25 March 1822 to 8 February 1823' (C6/1/15/3, 1822–3).

[139] C6/1/7/9, p. 208; *Belfast Newsletter*, 15 Oct. 1813; Johnston, *Bunting*, pp. 78–80.

The growing prominence of individual choir members as soloists in public concerts in the early years of the nineteenth century, most notably the tenor John Spray and the basses David Weyman and Robert Jager, was a continued source of friction with the cathedral authorities.[140] In 1819, for example, the dean reported seeing an advertisement in the newspaper of a concert to be held in Townsend Street Roman Catholic church in which Spray, Weyman, Jager and John Smith were named as performers, which they were reminded was not 'consistent with their canonical duty'.[141] Spray and Smith became involved in a prolonged dispute with the dean and chapter in 1823 arising out of a public oratorio performance in St Patrick's for which they had received payment, a dispute which eventually had to be settled by appeal to the archbishop of Dublin.[142] This growing emphasis on the profile of choirmen as individual soloists is evidenced in their singing in music festivals at English cathedrals, Simeon Pinto Buggine at York in 1823 and William Hamerton at Worcester in 1824.[143] Within their own private circle as cathedral musicians the choirmen sang glees and catches, often of a ribald nature quite foreign to their daily professional duties. The Hibernian Catch Club, still in existence, is reputed to have been founded by the vicars choral of the two cathedrals in c.1680, although surviving records only date back to 1770 when membership was opened to others.[144] It was for convivial men's clubs such as this, not only in Dublin but elsewhere in Ireland and England, that Richard Woodward (the younger) composed his catches which appeared in his *Songs, Canons and Catches*, opus 1, published in 1761.

Less prominent than public musical performance but also forbidden by the chapter in 1763 was the acceptance by choirmen of positions as parish clerks in any parish church, a position which involved leading the congregation in the singing of metrical psalms and the prohibition of which must have been related to the conflict of duties at times when the choirmen's attendance was required in the cathedral.[145] Nevertheless a number of the cathedral's organists and choirmen do appear to have held positions as organists in various parish churches in the city. George Walsh, organist at Christ Church from 1747, was also organist at St Mary's church from 1750 to 1760 when he became organist at St Patrick's

---

[140] C6/1/7/9, p. 41; C6/1/7/10, p. 29. Spray and Weyman are cited on a number of occasions as soloists in public concerts in Walsh, *Opera 1798–1820*, pp. 33–4, 114, 134, 250–2. As late as 1843 when Thomas Yeokley was appointed a vicar choral he was specifically told 'to renounce singing in all public places except by the special leave of the dean and chapter' (C6/1/7/12, p. 160).

[141] C6/1/7/10, p. 65. Smith was a native of Cambridge and nephew of John Spray who came to Dublin in 1815 as a stipendiary at Christ Church, becoming a vicar choral at St Patrick's in 1817, organist of the Chapel Royal in Dublin Castle in 1833 and professor of music at Trinity College, Dublin, from 1845 to 1865. C6/1/7/9, p. 311; Lawlor, *Fasti*, ii, p. 230.

[142] C6/1/7/10, pp. 224–33, 275f, 286; Erck, *Ecclesiastical Establishment*, pp. 293f. John Smith's quarrel with the dean ensured that he was never to become a vicar choral, a position he did however hold at St Patrick's.

[143] C6/1/7/10, pp. 206, 251. Buggine, born Simon Peter Buggins, was a native of Birmingham who joined the Dublin cathedral choirs in 1819. He was a noted countertenor who adopted an Italianate version of his name following a period of study in Italy. See further Bumpus 'Irish Church Composers', pp. 124f.

[144] Brian Boydell, *Dublin Musical Calendar*, p. 267.

[145] Barra Boydell, ed., *Music: Documents*, pp. 116–17.

cathedral as well as at Christ Church.[146] John Colgan, at the time a vicar choral at St Patrick's although he was not to join the choir at Christ Church until 1760 as a stipendiary and 'overseer of the bells', was organist at St Peter's church from 1740–54.[147] Although there is some uncertainty whether or not this was the same person, John Mathews appears to have been organist of St Mary's church from 1790 until his death in 1799 in addition to his choir duties and activities as a copyist at both cathedrals (see below).[148] The next organist at St Mary's until 1812 however certainly was the same John Mathews' brother Thomas who continued to serve as chanter's vicar at Christ Church until 1830.[149]

The purchase and copying of music

Evidence for the activities of choir members as composers and in the purchase and copying of music survives from the eighteenth and early nineteenth centuries not only from documentary records but also from the extensive surviving collection of manuscript and printed music of the period. During the course of the eighteenth century printed editions of cathedral music began to be published in England in significant numbers, to many of which Christ Church subscribed. Especially in the earlier part of the century however unspecific payments for 'church music', 'choir books' etc. must most often have been for music in manuscript,[150] but a subscription for 'a book of Anthems' (paid to Daniel Roseingrave) in 1724 was most probably for William Croft's *Musica Sacra* published in that year.[151] Subsequent purchases of printed editions of English cathedral music during the period covered by this chapter, copies of most of which survive in the cathedral, include eight sets of Maurice Greene's *Forty Select Anthems* (1743),[152] twelve of William Boyce's *Cathedral Music* (3 vols, London, 1760–73), seven of John Alcock's *Six and Twenty Select Anthems in Score* (1771), nine copies of

---

[146] Walsh had previously been organist at St Catherine's and St Ann's churches before being appointed to Christ Church (Neary, 'Music' (1995), pp. 154, 156; O'Keeffe, 'Score-Books', p. 79; Grindle, *Cathedral Music*, p. 224); Walsh appears also to have performed organ concertos on a number of occasions in public concerts (Brian Boydell, *Dublin Musical Calendar*, pp. 158 (Dec. 1751), 194 (May 1754)), although mention here and elsewhere is to a 'Mr Walsh' could equally refer to George Walsh's son Henry (who succeeded him as organist at St Patrick's following his death in 1765).

[147] Neary, 'Music' (1995), p. 155; Brian Boydell, *Dublin Musical Calendar*, p. 275; C6/1/7/6, fol. 71v. The John Smith who was organist of St Werburgh's church from 1733–50 should not be confused with the John Eusebius Smith who was a vicar choral at Christ Church from 1729 and a half-vicar at St Patrick's from 1737 until his death in 1744 (*pace* Brian Boydell, *Dublin Musical Calendar*, p. 290).

[148] Neary, 'Music' (1995), p. 156. However Bernard, *Registers*, p. 96 records the death in April 1797 of 'William Mathews, organist of St Mary's Church . . . aged 28 years'.

[149] Neary, 'Music' (1995), p. 156.

[150] E.g. '2 Quire books' in 1697–8, 'church music and binding' (paid to the dean, the bishop of Kildare) in 1702–3, 'a New sett of Quire Books' in 1703–4, and a payment to a stipendiary John Phipps in 1722–3 'for an Anthem brought out of England' (Barra Boydell, ed., *Music: Documents*, pp. 142–4, 146).

[151] *Ibid.*, p. 146. See further p. 128 below.

[152] The subscription list in Greene indicates nine sets bought by Christ Church rather than the eight noted in the chapter acts of 26 Apr. 1742.

James Nares' *Twenty Anthems in Score* (1778), seven of Thomas Ebdon's *Sacred Music . . .* volume one (1790) and six of volume two (1810),[153] six sets of John Stafford Smith's *Anthems, Composed for the Choir-Service of the Church of England* (c.1793) and two copies of his *Musica Antiqua* (referred to as 'John Stafford's Antient Music') published in 1812, nine copies of James Kent's *Twelve Anthems* (first published in 1773) bought in 1797, nine of William Hayes' *Cathedral Music in Score . . .* ([1795]), seven sets of volume one of John Clarke-Whitfeld's *Cathedral Music* (1800),[154] four copies of John Page's 'selection of Handel anthems' in 1808, two of Samuel Porter's *Cathedral Music* published posthumously by his son William James Porter (c.1815), and an edition of Croft's anthems in 1820.[155] The dean and chapter of Christ Church are listed as subscribers to many of the above collections, in most cases purchasing as many copies or more than any other subscribers including major English cathedrals, a fact which reflects the comparative wealth at the time of Christ Church cathedral. Also surviving in the cathedral but whose purchase is not itemised in the records is a single copy of James Power's *Service and Anthems* (1825). To the above publications can be added editions of Handel oratorios and of chants and metrical psalms bought in the early nineteenth century.[156]

Two Christ Church cathedral composers who published volumes of cathedral music during this period were Richard Woodward and John Stevenson.[157] Woodward's *Cathedral Music* of 1771 contains nine anthems, a *Veni Creator Spiritus* (composed for the consecration of the bishop of Cloyne in 1767, published in Dublin as his opus 2 in the same year and in a revised form in *Cathedral Music*), a Service in B flat and a number of chants. A subscription was taken out in 1771/2 and Woodward was paid a further £23 2s 0d in 1774.[158] In 1811 the chapter agreed to subscribe to twenty copies of Stevenson's 'intended publication of anthems'.[159] This could refer to his *A Series of Sacred Songs* selected from Mozart and others and published in London between 1816 and 1824, or it may be a response to an initial announcement by Stevenson of what would eventually appear as his *Morning and Evening Services and Anthems* in 1825. Christ Church was however well served by manuscript copies of Stevenson's sacred music

153 The seven copies of Ebdon's *Sacred Music* were purchased from the Dublin music seller John McCalley, both McCalley ('music seller, Dublin') and the dean and chapter of Christ Church being listed amongst the subscribers. On McCalley see Pollard, *Book Trade*, pp. 376–7.
154 The relevant entry reads 'Cash paid for Doctor Clark's Musick'. 'Dean & Chapter of Christ Church Dublin 7 sets' has been added in ink to the subscription list of at least one of the six volumes surviving in the cathedral.
155 Barra Boydell, ed., *Music: Documents*, pp. 113, 115, 123, 125, 127, 146, 148–9, 150, 152, 153; C6/1/15/2, 1804–5, 1810/11; C6/1/7/8, p. 447; C6/1/7/9, pp. 48, 55, 200; C6/1/7/10, p. 124.
156 'Dr Clark's chants' in 1808 (presumably John Clarke-Whitfeld's *A Selection of Single and Double Chants*, i–ii published in 1810), C6/1/7/8, p. 457; 'Dr Beckwith's Chants' (*The First Verse of every Psalm of David, with an Ancient or Modern Chant*, 1808), C6/1/15/2, 1809–10; *Messiah* and *Israel in Egypt* in 1817, C6/1/7/9, p. 368; and Clarke-Whitfeld's edition of *Messiah* in 1820, C6/1/7/10, p. 124.
157 Clarke-Whitfeld's *Cathedral Music* i–iv (London, 1800–37) post-dates his brief period at Christ Church between 1797 and 1798.
158 Barra Boydell, ed., *Music: Documents*, p. 149. *Veni Creator Spiritus* edited in *ibid.*, pp. 229–33.
159 C6/1/7/9, p. 131.

which would continue to form the backbone of the cathedral's repertoire throughout much of the nineteenth century.

These purchases of published collections enlarged the repertoire and ensured that it remained up to date, but for the most part the choir continued at least into the later nineteenth century to sing from manuscript volumes. One choir member, most often though not always the chanter's vicar, was appointed to look after these manuscript volumes, often being referred to as 'keeper and pricker of the anthem books' or as 'keeper of the choir books'. The surviving collection of these manuscript choir books from Christ Church comprises thirty-four score books, seventy-seven part books (including twelve 'loft books' used by soloists probably singing from the organ loft), twenty-five organ books and seven organ and solo books dating from the earlier eighteenth into the nineteenth centuries. The manuscript part books have been labelled as sets, possibly since their creation but certainly since the choir books were catalogued in the early 1820s.[160] The repertoire within each set is more or less consistent, but in some cases individual part books from a given set must have been lost or otherwise become unusable, in which cases later copies were substituted which can be distinguished through the different copyists' hands and the use of later paper. Many of the books have also been rebound at a later period, sometimes involving trimming of the pages and, possibly, the insertion or rearrangement of some of the contents. Unfortunately, with the exception of John Mathews in the late eighteenth century (see below), copyists seldom if ever signed their work so that identification of individual scribes is often not possible.

The flyleaf of one of the 'old loft books' is inscribed 'Christ Church 1730'.[161] This book corresponds in paper type and copyists with five of the first set of part books, along with at least two of the other old loft books'.[162] This first set most probably corresponds to a series of payments recorded in the 1720s for the purchase of music paper and for copying. Twenty-one quires of ruled paper were bought for £5 5s 0d in 1722/3 from the stationer Robert Thornton (who had been the first person to print and publish music in Ireland in 1686) and in the course of the same and the following year Thomas Hill, one of the stipendiaries, was paid for copying a total of four choir books. These were then bound by Robert Thornton's brother Charles and fitted with brass bosses (against wear and tear) by Philip Bullock. Another stipendiary, John Phipps, copied eight books in 1724/5, four of which were again bound and fitted with brass.[163] Thus a total of twelve choir

---

160 There are two almost identical catalogue lists (one is C6/1/24/1/36, the other remains to be catalogued) both on paper made in 1820 and in the hand of John Grey, the main copyist of the early nineteenth century (see p. 131 below). One is dated 1821. I am indebted to Sue Hemmens for information relating to the scribes and dating of the choir books, in particular her unpublished paper ' "Paid to this Place": Copyists and Repertoire Development in Christ Church Cathedral, Dublin, during the Eighteenth Century' read at the annual conference of the RMA (Irish Chapter), University College Dublin, 3–4 May 2002.

161 Counter tenor 1 (old loft books), C6/1/24/4/1.

162 Part books C6/1/24/3/1, –/3–6; old loft books C6/1/24/4/1, –/3. Tenor *Decani* 1 part book of this set (C6/1/24/3/2) uses a completely different paper and is copied in a different hand – possibly a later replacement following some accident to the original part book.

163 Barra Boydell, ed., *Music: Documents*, p. 146. On Robert and Charles Thornton see Pollard,

books were copied over a period of two years, a number which may reasonably be assumed to correspond to the eight part-books of the first set, plus four of the 'Old loft books' for the soloists.[164] John Phipps' hand can be identified from his signature and music copying in MS Tenbury 1503, albeit dating from some twenty years before the Christ Church books, and is preceded in the Christ Church part-books by two other hands, one of which must be Thomas Hill's. A feature of one of these earlier hands (referred to by Sue Hemmens as the 'epsilon hand') is its use of archaic features including the time signature 3/1, usually considered a seventeenth-century feature although apparently still used here in the 1720s. The bulk of the music copied by both the epsilon hand and the other pre-Phipps hand is by composers of the late seventeenth century or earlier. On the other hand, most of the music copied by Phipps is by Croft, almost certainly copied by him from Croft's *Music Sacra* which was noted above as having apparently been purchased by Christ Church in 1724, the year of its publication. This suggests that, the decision having been taken sometime around 1722 or 1723 to compile a new set of choir books, possibly on the initiative of Charles Taylor following his appointment as keeper of the choir books in 1718, the existing predominantly late seventeenth-century repertoire was first transferred into the new part-books.[165] Then in 1724 anthems from Croft's *Musica Sacra* became available and were added to the books over the following years. At various later stages other repertoire was further added into these part books both by Phipps and by others.

A further, unspecified number of choir books were bound in 1733/4 by James Kelburn, stationer, at a cost of £2 10s 0d.[166] If the four books bound ten years earlier cost £1 4s 0d, this amount suggests that there may have been eight books in 1733–4 (costing slightly more each), a number which would correspond to a second full set of choir part books, one for each voice part *decani* and *cantoris*. No payments for copying music are recorded in the years between those noted above in the mid-1720s and the binding of these books in 1733/4, but a number of payments are noted in succeeding years. Charles Taylor was paid for 'copying Dr Greene's anthems' in 1735, and again 'for Music' in 1737–8. The anthems by Maurice Greene must have been circulating in hand-written copies since he is not known to have published any collections before 1743.[167] The following year John Church was paid for 'New Anthems' and Ralph Roseingrave for 'making organ parts', the latter payment including two surviving organ books which can be positively identified as being in Roseingrave's hand thanks to a comparison with his signature in the St Patrick's account books.[168] On being appointed chanter's vicar in 1743 John Church was asked to 'examine and collect the Scores of such good

---

Book Trade, pp. 566–7. On music printing see Barra Boydell, 'Development of Music Print Trade'.

[164] The original eight part-books and four old loft books do not however all survive, some having been replaced at a later date.

[165] The decision to compile a new set of choir books may correspond to the entry in the chapter acts of 27 May 1723 'Ordered that Dr Travers the Proctor do provide Musicke books for the Choire' (Barra Boydell, ed., *Music: Documents*, p. 111).

[166] *Ibid.*, p. 146. On Kelburn see Pollard, *Book Trade*, p. 334.

[167] Barra Boydell, ed., *Music: Documents*, pp. 146–7.

[168] *Ibid.*, p. 147. Organ books 1 and 2 (C6/1/24/7/1, –/1a), both of which include works by Ralph Roseingrave. I am indebted to Sue Hemmens and Dr Kerry Houston for this information.

Musick as are to be met with in The Old Choir books' and to 'examine and consider the music lately copied and transcribed by Mr Mason and make his Report thereupon'.[169] The copying of music for the choir features prominently from when the surviving accounts recommence in 1766 after a break of twenty-eight years. John Mason is confirmed as a major copyist by his being paid a total of £23 15s 11½d for anthems and services between 1766 and 1767, including copying what are designated as 'Loft' books, and in the latter year Richard Woodward (the younger) also copied organ music including 'sundry books of anthems' for use in the loft.[170] In 1775 the widow of John Arnold, a former stipendiary, received payment for copying done by her husband. Langrish Doyle, at that time a stipendiary, was paid the following year for 'writing music' and again in 1781 by which date he had become master of the boys.[171]

Music copying at Christ Church (and St Patrick's) in the late eighteenth century is dominated by the work of John Mathews. Formerly at Winchester, Salisbury and Durham, Mathews came to Dublin as a choir member of both cathedrals in 1776. He had already established a reputation for himself as a copyist, particularly at Durham where his work is well represented in the cathedral music library.[172] He became the sole music copyist at St Patrick's from about 1778 until his death in 1799, earning a total of close to £100.[173] Other copyists were also active to a lesser extent at Christ Church during Mathews' first few years, but after 1781 he was sole copyist there too, earning a total of £134 1s 8½d over a period of about twenty years. The reasons for Mathews' extensive activity as a copyist may be twofold: on the one hand his manuscripts are of a clarity and elegance which must have recommended his work to the authorities in Christ Church and St Patrick's and encouraged the preparation of new choir books both to update the repertoire and to replace earlier, worn copies (*Plate 8*); on the other hand Mathews actively solicited work. In a letter to Durham cathedral dated 30 October 1777, some five or six months after he had come to Dublin, he outlined some of the music available in Dublin which was not represented at Durham and openly invited to be commissioned to prepare and send over copies of these.[174] In December 1779 he put a proposal to the dean and chapter of Christ Church for 'Transcribing certain Services and Anthems necessary for the Service of the Choir of this Church', having already received £22 17s 6½d for copying music up to 25 June 1779, that is, in the first two years since his arrival.[175] Varying payments to Mathews are recorded in the accounts in most years between 1778/9 and his death (a six-year gap in payments after 1784/5 is followed by a cumulative sum in 1791/2), his annual income from copying averaging a little over £6 a year during his twenty-two years at Christ Church.[176] In 1797 he was directed to copy the remaining choir books from a list prepared by the chanter's vicar and keeper

169 Barra Boydell, ed., *Music: Documents*, p. 113.
170 *Ibid.*, pp. 117, 147, 148.
171 *Ibid.*, pp. 121, 150, 151.
172 See Crosby, *Catalogue*.
173 Information from Kerry Houston.
174 *GB-DRc*, Mus. MS A. 18, inside front cover.
175 Barra Boydell, ed., *Music: Documents*, p. 123.
176 *Ibid.*, pp. 150–4.

Plate 8. Opening of Ralph Roseingrave, *Bow down thine ear, O Lord*, copied by John Mathews, c.1795. (Christ Church Cathedral, Score Book 24. Representative Church Body Library, Dublin, C6/1/24/1/24)

of the choir books, his brother Thomas Mathews, who would be paid 20 guineas the following year for making an index of all the music in the church and who on occasions had acted as a copyist himself.[177] A reference in March 1797 to 'the Sixteen Musick Books written by Mr John Mathews for the use of the Choir for which he has been paid Fourteen pounds Eleven Shillings and four pence' represents an average payment of 18s 2½d per book. The size of different music books can vary considerably and Mathews often added to the contents of an existing book rather than copying an entire volume himself; furthermore, the rate at which Mathews was paid may also have varied over his two decades at Christ Church. But using the above figure as an approximate guide, Mathews must have copied the equivalent of well over one hundred choir books for Christ Church, about twenty-five of which (or the equivalent) seem to have been completed during his first two years in Dublin. Certainly there is no doubt that he was the major single scribe of the eighteenth-century choir books which survive in Christ Church, and he holds a similar position in regard to the (less extensive) collection of surviving choir books from St Patrick's as well as being represented in the collections of Trinity College Dublin and Cashel cathedral.[178] Kerry Houston suggests that

[177] *Ibid.*, pp. 127, 128, 150; C6/1/15/2, 1803–4.
[178] *IRL-Dtc*; *IRL-CAb* (uncatalogued). See further Barra Boydell, 'Manuscript Sources'.

Mathews' personal taste had an important influence on the repertoire in the Dublin cathedrals and draws attention to the presence in his hand of music by contemporary composers which he imported from Winchester, Salisbury and Durham, including the works of minor composers like Edward Blake of Salisbury, the dissemination of whose two known anthems can be directly linked with Mathews.[179] Between c.1811 and 1833–4 regular payments for music copying were made to John Grey, not apparently a member of the choir.[180] Like Mathews he served as copyist for over twenty years, but it is probably a measure of the monetary inflation which followed the Napoleonic era that his income of £274 3s 11d from copying was more than twice what Mathews received over a similar period.

Music composed by Christ Church musicians

The eighteenth and early nineteenth centuries mark a particularly rich period for the composition of anthems and service settings by musicians working at the Dublin cathedrals, a substantial repertoire of which survives in the Christ Church cathedral choir books. In addition, a number of ambiguous references could refer either to music copying or to compositional activity by choir members who are not represented by surviving music. In 1704, for example, George Rogers (a stipendiary since 1700 but subsequently a vicar choral) was paid £5 'on account of his Service in giveing some Anthems for the use of the Church'.[181] In 1708 the stipendiary singer John Harris was paid for 'furnishing the Church with an Anthem' and another stipendiary, Josias Bouchier 'for anthems' in 1715–16; unspecific payments in the 1730s to John Church and Charles Taylor for 'new anthems' and 'music' were noted above in the context of music copying. Other payment records are either less ambiguous or can be substantiated by the presence of music by that person in the choir books: in addition to preparing new organ books Daniel Roseingrave was paid shortly after his appointment as organist in 1698 specifically for 'writeing Services' and again in 1699 for 'three services and two Creeds for the use of the Church'.[182] Although the choir books contain no music attributed to Daniel Roseingrave and his surviving anthems and a service predate his Dublin years,[183] it is possible that some of the music attributed to his son Ralph Roseingrave may turn out to be by Daniel. The one anthem by Daniel Roseingrave which has been edited in a modern edition reveals him 'to be a no less able composer than the best of his contemporaries'.[184] Robert Hodge is also known to have composed anthems but these date from before he came to Dublin

---

179 Kerry Houston, unpubl. paper 'John Mathews – A Specimen of Georgian Ignorance?' read at the annual conference of the RMA (Irish Chapter), University College Dublin, 3–4 May 2002; see also Houston, 'Music Manuscripts'. Edward Blake's *I have set God always before me* is also present at Cashel in Mathews' hand.

180 C6/1/15/2–3, *passim*. On Gray's index of the music books see note 160 above.

181 Barra Boydell, ed., *Music: Documents*, p. 107.

182 *Ibid.*, pp. 106, 142.

183 Grindle, *Cathedral Music*, pp. 165f; Spink, *Restoration*, p. 228; Gillen & Johnstone, *Anthology*, pp. 94–5.

184 *Ibid.*, pp. 73–93 (edition of *Lord, thou art become gracious*), 96.

Ex. 4.1 Ralph Roseingrave, *O how amiable*, bars 21–42

in 1693 as organist of St Patrick's and a stipendiary at Christ Church and nothing by him survives in the Dublin cathedrals.[185]

The most prolific Dublin cathedral composer of the first half of the eighteenth century was Daniel Roseingrave's son Ralph. He was paid for writing anthems in 1736/7 and the Christ Church choir books contain a total of twenty-four anthems and two services attributed either specifically to him or to 'Mr Roseingrave'.[186] While some of the anthems may have been composed by Daniel Roseingrave, two

---

[185] Shaw, *Organists*, p. 288; C6/1/7/3, 21 Apr. 1693, 4 June 1695; Barra Boydell, ed., *Music: Documents*, p. 105. Two anthems in Durham part books (Spink, *Restoration*, p. 233).

[186] Barra Boydell, ed., *Music: Documents*, p. 147. For a list of works see Gillen & Johnstone, *Anthology*, p. 97.

Ex. 4.2 Ralph Roseingrave, *O give thanks*, bars 89–101

organ books include four of Ralph Roseingrave's anthems and his Services in C
and F in the composer's own hand, thus establishing their attribution beyond
doubt.[187] Many of the solo anthems (including those in Ralph Roseingrave's
hand) display characteristics more readily associated with the later seventeenth
century, including ground basses in *It is a good thing* and *O how amiable*, occasional uses of 'Scotch snap' rhythms, and a preponderance of 3/2 time signatures
(*Ex. 4.1*). Elsewhere, florid semiquaver passages for both soloist and organ, the
latter sometimes with indications for registration, suggest a more up-to-date
idiom (*Ex. 4.2*). The full anthem *Bow down thine ear* and *I will cry unto God* in the
'full with verse' style are representative of Roseingrave's choral anthems: both

187 See note 168 above. Organ Book 1a (C6/1/24/2/1a) contains the following anthems by Ralph
Roseingrave: *O give thanks* (verse, countertenor and bass solos), *Rejoice in the Lord* (full
anthem – there are also two other settings attributed to Roseingrave, see Gillen & Johnstone,
Anthology, p. 97), *O how amiable* (verse, tenor and bass solos), *It is a good thing* (bass solo), and
his Service in F. Organ Book 1 (C6/1/24/2/1) contains his Services in C and F. Gillen & Johnstone, *Anthology*, p. 96 comment that 'while some of [the works attributed to 'Roseingrave' or
'Mr Ralph Roseingrave'] must surely have been composed by Ralph, the items bearing his name
are bewilderingly variable in style and competence . . . Though it is tempting to make speculative
attributions, an acceptable degree of conclusiveness would depend on a technical and stylistic
critique based on a complete edition.'

Ex. 4.3 Ralph Roseingrave, *Bow down thine ear*, bars 42–55

open imitatively with a musical phrase which starts with a longer note tied across the barline, a feature common to a number of his full anthems (*Plate 8*).[188] The writing balances imitative with homophonic sections, with rising chromatic melodic lines and an often rich though essentially conservative harmonic idiom serving to heighten the expressive content. (*Ex. 4.3*) As Grindle has pointed out, Purcell is recalled in the frequent use of general rests and the repetition of text for emphasis.[189]

A morning Service in D by George Walsh is in a solid, predominantly homophonic style but with some imitative entries and culminating at the conclusion of the *Jubilate* with *divisi* voices in a rich, eight-part texture.[190] It remained in the repertoire throughout the nineteenth century, being commented on favourably

[188] *Bow down thine ear*, ed. Simon Hill (Dorchester: Cathedral Music, 1980), *I will cry unto God* in Barra Boydell, ed., *Music: Documents*, pp. 212–17, both ed. Douglas Gunn (Melrose Music, 2001); see also Cunningham, 'Eighteenth Century Anthems'; Moran, 'Eighteenth Century Anthems'. Gillen and Johnstone unfairly dismiss these two anthems as 'the work of a tiro' (Gillen & Johnstone, *Anthology*, p. 96).

[189] Grindle, *Cathedral Music*, pp. 170–1.

[190] C6/1/24/1/15, –/21 (score books); C6/1/24/3/7–16, –/55–56, C6/1/24/8. The index to C6/1/24/1/21 (in John Mathews' hand) indicates a communion service (which is also adverted to in a later hand in pencil in C6/1/24/1/15), but the corresponding pages at the end of the volume are now missing; a *Kyrie* and *Sanctus* to Walsh's service composed by Robert Prescott Stewart is present in some of the part books. The music of Walsh's service in the two score books, copied by John Mathews and dated 13 and 14 Aug. 1798 (towards the conclusion of the *Jubilate* in C6/1/24/1/21, pp. 174–82) was liberally annotated in pencil by R.P. Stewart in the later nineteenth century. For example, below the index of contents inside the front cover of C6/1/24/1/21 Stewart has written 'This clever service (which only exists in ms in this Cathedral) has been meddled with by the horrid old vandal John Mathews, whose cooking has been struck out by my pencil as far as possible. (RPS) Any good musician can readily trace the tinkerings of this besotted old copyist, and the restoration of the true text as written by Geo Walsh would be a *good & worthy work* [original emphasis]. Extra parts, silly shakes, graceless graces are here to be found in wild profusion.' Stewart has deleted the second treble part in the doxology of Walsh's *Jubilate*, describing it as largely 'a forgery'.

not only by Bumpus, who described it as 'really fine and scholarly', but also by Robert Prescott Stewart (despite his negative comments on the reliability of John Mathews' score of the work), and it was also in the repertoire of a number of English cathedrals.[191] There is a single anthem *Oh praise the Lord ye that fear Him* by Samuel Murphy. 'Notable for its inordinate length', it is a verse anthem in seven sections concluding with an eight-voice 'Hallelujah' which may have been written as his exercise for the degree of Doctor of Music at Trinity College Dublin which was conferred on him in 1768.[192] John Mathews mentioned in his letter to Durham in October 1777 that 'Dr Murphy is Composing a Service in 8 Parts which is expected to be a very fine one', but this service appears to have remained unfinished at Murphy's death three years later.[193] Edward Higgens, a vicar choral from 1765 until his death four years later, is represented by a total of five services,[194] while an anthem *O Lord who has taught us* of which only the treble part survives and which is only attributed by surname was probably written by John Marsh.[195] The surviving treble part, which includes both chorus and some verses, suggests a simple, homophonic style possibly influenced by Ralph Roseingrave under whom he would have served as a choirboy.

The precise attribution of five anthems and one service attributed to 'Carter' in the Christ Church choir books (a second service is contained in the music books of Trinity College Dublin) remains problematic but there may be a Christ Church connection.[196] Kerry Houston comments that the *Jubilate* from the Service in C 'in terms of both rhythm and imitation is clearly a work from the early eighteenth century', adding that it 'is one of the better examples of post-Restoration writing in Dublin'. He also points to the fact that the copying of this service into part books at St Patrick's cathedral was completed before 1760 on paper purchased in 1738, while two anthems *Hear my prayer* (published in 1751) and *I cried unto the Lord* are included in the book of anthem texts from Christ Church published in 1745.[197] It seems therefore that the Service in C and at least some of the five anthems attributed to 'Carter' in the Christ Church books may have been composed by Timothy Carter (son of Arnold Carter who completed his term as a choirboy at Christ Church in 1702 but who subsequently took up an apprenticeship as a barber and wig maker)[198] who was a choirboy at Christ Church up to

191 Walsh's service was performed once at Christ Church during the period April to October 1846 (see 'Christ Church Cathedral. Course of Services and Anthems . . . 26 April 1846 [to] 24 Oct. 1846', uncatalogued handwritten ledger held in Christ Church) and five times during the two years between 1878 and 1880 (Seymour, *Choral Services*). See also Bumpus, 'Irish Church Composers', p. 93; Grindle, *Cathedral Music*, p. 179.
192 C6/1/24/1/22 (score book); commentary in Cunningham 'Eighteenth Century Anthems', pp. 50–7; Grindle, *Cathedral Music*, p. 191. There is a reference in the chapter acts of St Patrick's in 1768 to Murphy's having 'composed a piece of music' (Shaw, *Organists*, p. 422).
193 *GB-DRc*, Mus. MS A. 18, inside front cover.
194 C6/1/24/1/20 (score book); twenty-two various part-books, C6/1/24/3/7–.
195 C6/1/24/3/21, –/25; C6/1/8/6, p. 31; Barra Boydell, ed., *Music: Documents*, pp. 114, 122; Neary, 'Music' (1995), p. 155. On Marsh see p. 118 above.
196 On the possible (and confusing) identities of the various members of the Carter family in eighteenth-century Dublin see Barra Boydell & Klein, 'Carter', and Gillen & Johnstone, *Anthology*, pp. 124–6.
197 Gillen & Johnstone, *Anthology*, p. 125. On the 1745 anthem book see p. 147 below.
198 C6/1/7/3, 18 Feb. 1703.

1730, was paid for singing in the choir in 1739, became a stipendiary in 1740 and is present in the choir attendance lists which survive between 1762 and 1769.[199]

The Revd Robert Shenton (1730–1798), a chorister and lay clerk at Magdalen College, Oxford, and vicar choral at Hereford before becoming dean's vicar at Christ Church from 1757 until his death and a vicar choral rising to dean's vicar at St Patrick's over the same period, was the most prolific Dublin cathedral composer of the period. The Christ Church choir books contain twenty anthems and four services by Shenton (including one anthem in which he set new words to music by Handel and Beretti and another by Boyce to which he added a final chorus). The Service in E flat includes settings of the *Sanctus, Sursum corda* (responses) and *Gloria* which Shenton wrote specially for the use of Durham cathedral at the time when John Mathews was corresponding with Durham in 1777. Shenton favoured anthems in the multi-movement, solo-cantata style popularised by Greene and influenced by Handel, which comprises recitatives, short arias and the relatively restrained use of chorus. While certainly no unrecognised genius, Grindle's dismissal of Shenton as a composer whose 'output was as considerable as his lack of inspiration' is perhaps a little harsh.[200] Verse anthems such as *The beauty of Israel* or *Behold how good and joyful* and full anthems like *O God my heart is ready* are not without merit, although he does tend to over-repeat individual musical ideas, often attractive in themselves, with little variation or modulation.[201] Scored for five voices (two trebles, alto, tenor, bass) and organ, with solos for all voices, *The beauty of Israel* (a setting of David's lament for Saul and Jonathan) provides many opportunities for expressive writing in minor keys. The chorus sections are short and homophonic, although elsewhere Shenton does write more extended fugal choruses.

Richard Woodward the younger, a talented musician whose death at the age of thirty-three in 1777 deprived Irish music of one of its most promising talents, was the first Irish-based composer to publish a collection of cathedral music, his *Cathedral Music* published in London in 1771 which was referred to earlier. The majority of Woodward's anthems are in the extended solo style in which the advanced keyboard writing in the organ accompaniments and the often demanding solo parts for all voices including trebles give some indication not only of his abilities as an organist and his success in training the choirboys, but also of the musical standards expected at Christ Church in the later eighteenth century. *They that go down to the sea in ships* and *O be joyful in God all ye lands* (subtitled *A Thanksgiving Anthem*) are the most extended and virtuosic of his anthems, the former with verses for countertenor, tenor and bass soloists, the latter for two trebles, alto and tenor (*Ex. 4.4*).[202] In contrast, 'full with verse'

---

[199] C6/1/8/5, pp. 48, 161, 164; C6/1/23/1. Grindle's attribution (*Cathedral Music*, pp. 180f) of these anthems and the Service in C to either of the later Thomas Carters born c.1735/40 and 1769 is clearly no longer tenable.

[200] Grindle, *Cathedral Music*, p. 178.

[201] *The Beauty of Israel* edited in Barra Boydell, ed., *Music: Documents*, pp. 219–28; *Behold how good and joyful* in Cunningham, 'Eighteenth Century Anthems'. These and *O God my heart is ready* in C6/1/24/1/26.

[202] *Veni Creator Spiritus* edited in Barra Boydell, ed., *Music: Documents*, pp. 229–33; *O be joyful in God all ye lands* in Cunningham, 'Eighteenth Century Anthems'; *O praise God in his holiness,*

anthems such as *Veni Creator Spiritus* and *Sing O ye heavens* are written in a simpler, more restrained style.

John Andrew Stevenson, born in Dublin probably in 1767, became the dominant figure in the musical life not only of the Dublin cathedrals at the time but also of the city at large.[203] A composer of theatre music, songs and glees as well as cathedral music, he mixed freely with the highest levels of fashionable society and has the distinction of being the first person anywhere to be knighted for his services to music. Son of a violinist from Scotland who had settled in Dublin as a member of the state band and attached to various theatres, he joined Christ Church as a choirboy in 1773 and may have been one of the trebles for whom Woodward wrote his sometimes demanding solo anthems.[204] Appointed a stipendiary choirman at Christ Church in 1781, he succeeded to the position of vicar choral at St Patrick's (where he had been a choirboy from 1775 to 1780 and subsequently an adult choir member) in 1783 although frequent absences from duty – his facility at writing glees, catches, and songs for stage and drawing room had endeared him to fashionable society – may have contributed to his not being appointed a vicar choral at Christ Church until 1800.[205] He received an honorary Mus. D. from Dublin University in 1791. Stevenson is perhaps best known for his 'symphonies and accompaniments' to Thomas Moore's *Irish Melodies* which remained enormously popular throughout the nineteenth century. He was essentially self-taught, modelling his style largely on the music of Haydn as well as on the prevailing eighteenth-century cathedral repertoire.

In his role as a cathedral musician Stevenson composed eight services and twenty-six anthems which survive in manuscript in the choir books of Christ Church, St Patrick's, the chapel royal of Dublin Castle, and Trinity College chapel.[206] A selection of four services and twelve anthems, together with twelve

Sing O ye heavens, the *Magnificat* and *Nunc Dimittis* from the Service in B flat edited in Donnelly, 'Woodward', pp. 103–12, 118–37; *O praise God* and *Sing O ye heavens*, ed. Douglas Gunn (Melrose Music, 2001). For commentaries on Woodward's music see especially Donnelly, 'Woodward' and Grindle, *Cathedral Music*, pp. 187–91.

[203] There is some doubt as to Stevenson's date of birth. A memorial erected in his memory at Christ Church in 1843 gives his date of birth as 1767 but 1761 has also been suggested (Brian Boydell, *Rotunda Music*, p. 225).

[204] Bumpus, 'Irish Church Composers', p. 96 stated that Stevenson became a choirboy in 1771 and this date has been widely repeated, together with a birth date of 1761 (sometimes 1762). The earliest record I can find is in May 1773 when 'Stephenson' was one of a number of boys for whom it was 'ordered that indentures be prepared in the usual form' for apprenticing them 'to serve as choristers in the choir'. If he was born in 1767 he would then have been aged 6, young but a more likely age to commence as a choir boy than 11 to 13 as he would have been had he been born in 1761 or 1762 (C6/1/7/7, p. 48).

[205] C6/1/7/7, p. 140; Lawlor, *Fasti*, p. 233; C6/1/7/8, pp. 136f. For absences from Christ Church see C/6/1/7/7, pp. 191–2, 271f; on Stevenson as a composer of theatre music see Walsh, *Opera 1798–1820*, *passim*, and the work list in *NG2* xxiv, p. 378.

[206] C6/1/24/1/29, C6/1/24/2–5; St Patrick's part books and organ books and Chapel Royal part books (in St Patrick's cathedral). Other contemporary copies in *IRL-CAb* (from Cashel cathedral). In addition to the anthems published during the nineteenth century (see following note) *The Lord is my shepherd, By the waters of Babylon, Lord how are they increased* and *Grant to us O Lord* have been edited in Sherwin, 'Stevenson'. The responses and three chants from his 1825 publication are in Gillen & Johnstone, *Anthology*, pp. 127–39.

Ex. 4.4 Richard Woodward, *O be joyful*, bars 108–52

double chants, was published during his lifetime,[207] while a small number of individual anthems appeared in other editions later during the nineteenth century including three from the 1825 collection plus the previously unpublished *By the waters of Babylon* in an edition by Joseph Robinson.[208] Stevenson remained one of the most popular composers in the repertoire of Christ Church throughout the nineteenth century.[209] His facility as a composer at times lends his music a certain predictability although his use of harmonic colour can be most effective, as in his use of an almost Schubertian shift to the flattened submediant in *I looked and behold* (*Ex. 4.5*). Stevenson only wrote one full anthem, *Grant to us, Lord*, most of his anthems consisting of often lengthy and dramatic solos, usually for alto, tenor and bass either individually or in various combinations, but with relatively infrequent choral sections. Less often, as in *By the waters of Babylon* and *I looked and behold*,[210] a larger number of shorter verses typically for ensembles of four or

207 *Morning and Evening Services and Anthems* (London, 1825). The anthems contained in this collection were: *O Lord our Governor; There were shepherds; I looked and behold; Bow down thine ear; Lord, how are they increased; I am well pleased; Rejoice in the Lord; Blessed be the Lord, my strength; I looked, and lo!; Blessed is he that considereth; The earth is the Lord's; I will magnify thee.*

208 *Sacred Music by the late Sir John Stevenson*, ed. Joseph Robinson (Dublin, [c.1840]). Robinson made a number of sometimes significant alterations beyond the addition of expression marks and other performance indications. Most notably in *By the waters of Babylon* he deleted Stevenson's final section (bars 207–85) comprising a verse and chorus to the words 'Yea, happy shall he be that rewardeth thee as thou hast served us', replacing it with an adapted reprise of the opening section of the anthem.

209 In 1849 (the earliest complete year for which service lists survive at Christ Church) six anthems by Stevenson were performed a total of twelve times making him the sixth most popular composer (out of fifty-four) in terms of numbers of anthems and the eleventh in frequency of performance; with thirteen anthems he is the fifth most popular composer in terms of numbers of anthems listed in 1852 in Finlayson, *Anthems*; in *Cathedral Anthems* (1880) he is represented by twenty anthems making him the eighth most represented composer out of 168 listed; a more accurate measure of the same period is provided by Seymour, *Choral Services* which lists all anthems and services sung (and how often) on Sundays and festivals over two years between 1878 and 1880: six anthems by Stevenson were sung a total of forty times, making him the most-performed anthem composer at Sunday and festival services at that time (the next most-performed were Handel with thirty-seven performances of fifteen anthems and Boyce with twenty-nine performances of eight anthems), while three services by Stevenson were sung a total of fifteen times in the same two years making him the equal fifth most-performed composer of services alongside Boyce and Nares.

210 Both recorded on *Sing* (CD), the former in the somewhat altered later edition of Joseph Robinson (see note 208 above), the latter in the version contained in Score Book 29 (C6/1/24/1/29) in

Ex. 4.5 John Stevenson, *I looked, and behold*, bars 129–42

five solo voices are interspersed with more frequent but still relatively brief choruses. His solo parts, which seldom call for exceptional vocal technique, are notable for their melodiousness and were written specially for the singers of the Dublin cathedrals including John Spray who was a close friend of Stevenson. An interesting feature is the exceptionally high tessitura of some of the solo bass writing, particularly in the anthem *I am well pleased* which frequently rises to *f′* or even *g′* (*Ex. 4.6*). While Stevenson was himself a bass and often sang duets with Spray, these high bass solos must have been written for Robert Jager who is reputed to have 'possessed a fine bass voice with an admirable falsetto in addition'.[211] In contrast to Woodward, Stevenson rarely wrote treble solos but when he does so the music, while not demanding the same agility as in some of Woodward's anthems of a generation earlier, nevertheless suggests considerable confidence in the ability of at least some of the choirboys. *The Lord is my shepherd*, which comprises solos exclusively for one or two trebles before the chorus concludes the anthem, is of particular interest for the amount of ornamentation indicated in the music, mainly in the form of appoggiaturas and mordents (*Ex. 4.7*). Stevenson appears to have been something of a pioneer in his practice of writing independent and fully written-out organ accompaniments at a time when

which, amongst other detailed differences, the organ part is somewhat less elaborate than that in Score Book 31 (C6/1/24/1/31).

[211] C6/1/15/3, 1814–15; Cotton, *Fasti* ii, p. 88; Bumpus, 'Irish Church Composers', p. 124.

Ex. 4.6 John Stevenson, *I am well pleased*, bars 38–45

Ex. 4.7 John Stevenson, *The Lord is my shepherd*, bars 34–40

a doubling of the vocal lines in choruses was the norm. The organ accompaniment to the words 'out of the throne proceedeth lightnings and thunderings' from *I looked, and behold*, especially in the more elaborate of the two versions in the Christ Church score books,[212] illustrates his keen sense of the dramatic (*Ex. 4.8*).

There can be little doubt that Stevenson was consciously writing music of a style which would appeal directly to the congregation and which suited the fine singers available. These lengthy verse anthems were sung following the sermon, the soloists singing from the elevated position of the balcony (or 'loft') adjacent to the organ while the rest of the choir remained below in their stalls. Writing in the 1840s, John Jebb was thankful that this practice had gone out of use because it interrupted the service and only left the weaker choir members to sing the responses.[213] The influence of Haydn on Stevenson's music contributed to growing criticism of his sacred music later in the nineteenth century when Haydn's style was considered too secular for church music. Despite such

---

[212] Score Book 31 (C6/1/24/1/31).
[213] Jebb, *Choral Service*, pp. 373f.

Ex. 4.8 John Stevenson, *I looked, and behold*, bars 79–105

criticisms, however, Jebb commented in 1843 that 'with all his faults . . . this composer is far superior to many trashy and flimsy contemporaries, who have in England obtained a much wider fame'.[214] Bumpus also acknowledged his limitations but praised his church music as such that 'the world will not willingly let die – music which will ever reach the heart, and surely no more legitimate test could be applied'. He reserved particular praise for the solo verse movements, 'several of [which], for melodious grace and harmonious expression rank among the best things of the kind with which I am acquainted'.[215] During the twentieth century, however, Stevenson's church music went out of favour both because of the preference for a choral rather than solo style of cathedral music, and because of a growing disdain for the music of 'lesser' composers, a view summarised by Grindle's comment that 'the most serious deficiency in Stevenson's music is the

---

214 *Ibid.*, p. 392; compare Bumpus, *Sir John Stevenson*, p. 29: 'Whatever grammatical faults he may have possessed he was immeasurably superior to many a feeble and flimsy English contemporary.'
215 Bumpus, 'Irish Church Composers', pp. 100–1.

Ex. 4.8 *cont.*

absence of that genuine originality without which no composer can expect to capture the attention and win the esteem of a discriminating audience'.[216]

While Stevenson was outstandingly the most popular Irish composer of cathedral music in the early nineteenth century, a number of other Christ Church musicians were also active as composers. Some of the services and anthems published in the earliest of John Clarke-Whitfeld's four volumes of *Cathedral Music* (London, 1800–37) must surely date from his years in Ireland prior to 1798, but he is more properly associated with his subsequent career as organist at Trinity and St John's colleges, Cambridge and subsequently Hereford cathedral, and as professor of music at Cambridge from 1821.[217] The words of a verse anthem *O Lord my God* by John Spray is included in Jellett, *Anthems* (1821) but the music is not present in the Christ Church choir books. His colleague Simeon Pinto Buggine is however represented by one anthem, *By the waters of Babylon*.[218] The organist William Warren has left a verse Service in E flat containing canticles for morning service and communion.[219] John Smith published a volume of *Cathedral Music* in London in 1837 containing services in B flat and C, a *Veni Creator Spiritus* and twelve chants, but a further Service in A and ten anthems also exist in

[216] Grindle, *Cathedral Music*, p. 195.
[217] Clarke-Whitfeld's cathedral music is extensively represented in the Christ Church part books. On Clarke-Whitfeld see further *NG2* v, p. 922.
[218] C6/1/24/3/37–44.
[219] C6/1/24/1/27; C6/1/24/3/18, –/20, –/29–36, –/59–60; C6/1/24/7/7. Bumpus was only familiar with a double chant by Warren ('Irish Church Composers', p. 123).

Ex. 4.8 *cont.*

manuscript in the Christ Church and the Trinity College chapel choir-books.[220] It is fair to say that, although maintaining a foothold in the Dublin cathedral repertoires throughout the nineteenth century, Smith's music has generally received a less than enthusiastic reception.[221] To these composers might be added Richard Gaudry (1800–24), not apparently linked to Christ Church (unless possibly as a choirboy) but who served as organist at St Ann's church, Dublin and whose anthem *O Lord thou art my God*, an arrangement after Haydn, is included in the choir books and maintained a presence in the repertoire throughout the century.[222] Although not known to have written any anthems or service music, David Weyman published the collection *Melodia Sacra*, which first appeared in 1812, containing arrangements of the psalms for between one and four voices and was widely used in parish churches throughout Ireland before the first Irish church

220 Gillen & Johnstone, *Anthology*, p. 23, where the Service in B flat is listed as two services in order to take account of two settings of the *Te Deum*, one 'long', one 'short'.

221 Bumpus, 'Irish Church Composers', p. 125 states that his Service in B flat 'if not characterized by profundity, is, it must be confessed, most melodious, telling, and effective . . . constant repetition is, however, its fault'. Grindle, *Cathedral Music*, p. 196 echoed Stewart's opinion when he wrote that 'of the twelve anthems . . . little can or need be said, since their quality rarely rises above mediocrity'.

222 C6/1/24/1/34; C6/1/24/3/37–46; 'Christ Church Cathedral. Course of Services and Anthems . . . 7 Jan 1849 [to] 6 Jan. 1850' (uncatalogued handwritten ledger held in Christ Church); Seymour, *Choral Services*.

Ex. 4.8 *cont.*

hymnal appeared in 1864.[223] Weyman was also active in other contexts as an arranger, for example of an edition of 'the celebrated Grand Funeral Anthem' performed at the Rotunda and in both cathedrals following the death of Queen Charlotte in December 1818.[224] The presence of some of the cathedral's most active composers during the century between Ralph Roseingrave's appointment as organist in 1727 and the death of John Stevenson in 1833, the extensive evidence for the purchasing and copying of music, and the often demanding solo writing in anthems for the cathedral choir demonstrate that this was a period during which musical activity at Christ Church cathedral was certainly not depressed: public interest in the performance of solo anthems in the early nineteenth century must have contributed to the relative buoyancy of music at Christ Church even while other aspects of the cathedral began to sink into neglect.[225]

---

[223] Grindle, *Cathedral music*, p. 66.

[224] *Freeman's Journal*, 7 Dec. 1818.

[225] John Alcock's statement in the preface to his anthems published in 1771 that Anglican cathedral music was 'never at so low an ebb' has been widely quoted in support of the view that English cathedral music in the late eighteenth and early nineteenth centuries had largely stagnated (cf. *NG2* i, p. 724; Gatens, *Victorian Cathedral Music*, p. 6). However, Alcock should perhaps be taken with a pinch of salt since his argumentative and disruptive behaviour at Lichfield cathedral, where he was organist from 1750–60 and lay vicar from 1750 until his death in 1806,

Ex. 4.8 *cont.*

The choral repertoire

The repertoire of anthems and services sung at Christ Church during the eighteenth and early nineteenth centuries is essentially contained in the choir books described above. However a detailed analysis of this extensive repertoire to determine when particular works were copied, whether this represents their introduction into the cathedral repertoire or a re-copying of existing repertoire, and how long individual works may have remained current in the repertoire, remains to be undertaken. Some general observations are nevertheless pertinent, bearing in mind that these choir books were copied over a period of a century or more, broadly (but not exclusively) falling within the period covered by this chapter. Composers range from those of the sixteenth century, for example Byrd and Tallis, up to the time when the books were copied. As a representative cross-section, an analysis of the anthems and services by a total of sixty-nine composers represented in the score books shows that the three most popular composers of anthems (based on the number of works by each composer) are

suggests that he was not the most reliable of commentators and may have made the above comment in order to promote his own publications. I am grateful to Denise Neary for the above comments.

Boyce with thirty anthems, Greene with twenty-seven, and Handel with twenty-one (including choruses from oratorios, etc.), all composers of the earlier to mid-eighteenth century. The next most frequently represented composers are Stevenson with nineteen anthems, Shenton and James Kent with seventeen, and Blow with fifteen: on the one hand two local composers, on the other hand English composers of the mid-eighteenth and later seventeenth centuries. Perhaps reflecting the more conservative approach to service settings, the most popular composers of services represented in the score books are Aldrich, Charles King and Stevenson with five services each, and Child, Dupuis and Shenton with four each, a group with a slightly stronger emphasis on the seventeenth and early eighteenth centuries represented by Child and Aldrich.

More precise indications of the choral repertoire at Christ Church are provided by two published books of texts of anthems sung in the cathedral, one from the mid-eighteenth century, the other from the 1820s. Like the equivalent volume dating from 1662 discussed in the previous chapter, these provide no information on the frequency with which any of these anthems were sung, nor does the presence of a given anthem necessarily mean that it was in actual fact sung at all, but they do nevertheless provide a view of what was considered at the time of publication to be a useable or appropriate repertoire. A *Collection of Anthems, as the Same are Now Performed in the Cathedral Church of the Holy and Undivided Trinity, Dublin* was published in Dublin in 1745.[226] Of 186 anthems listed, nearly 70 per cent (130 in all) are verse anthems and contemporary or recent composers predominate: Greene is by far the most popular composer with forty-eight anthems, Croft following with thirty-nine and Boyce with fifteen anthems. The music of the later seventeenth century is less well represented, Blow and Purcell having thirteen anthems each, and Aldrich and Humfrey seven each. Composers of the sixteenth and early seventeenth centuries are barely represented: [Richard] Farrant and Gibbons each have two anthems, and Byrd, Hooper and Tallis one each.[227] A puzzling omission from the composers represented in this 1745 collection is Ralph Roseingrave, organist at Christ Church at the time and, as was noted earlier, composer of a number of anthems and two services represented in the cathedral music books, some dating from this same period. A contemporary bound, handwritten copy of this 1745 collection also exists, prepared by the Dublin bookseller John Watson and 'put into a ready method of finding the anthem . . . for his own use that he may have the pleasure of understanding the words, whenever he hears the performance'.[228]

---

[226] *GB-Lbl*, shelf mark: 3438. i. 3. Gillen & Johnstone, *Anthology*, p. 20 point out the invalidity of my earlier supposition (Barra Boydell, ed., *Music: Documents*, p. 180, prompted by the inclusion in this book of two anthems by 'Carter') that the publication date might be a misprint.

[227] Farrant, *Call to remembrance* and *Hide not thou thy face*; Gibbons, *Hosanna to the son of David*; Byrd, *Be not wroth very sore* (an arrangement of *Civitas Sancti Tui*, probably by Aldrich; see *NG2*, iv, p. 726); Hooper, *Behold it is*; Tallis, *I call and cry to thee*. Attributed to Gibbons in this collection (and also in the Christ Church part books) is a setting of *O Lord God, to whom vengeance belongeth*.

[228] *IRL-Dtc*, MS 3179 which omits Wise's *Thy beauty, O Israel* but also includes, after the index at the end, an 'Easter Hymn' starting 'Christ Our Lord is Risen this Day. Hallelujah', and the text of Handel's *Messiah*.

In 1821 the Revd Morgan Jellett published a volume of anthem texts in Dublin which provides a comparable cross-section of the repertoire three quarters of a century later.[229] Solo verse anthems again predominate with 72 per cent (188) of the 261 anthems, 19 per cent (fifty anthems) are full with verse, and only twenty-three (8 per cent) are full. The development over the intervening period of a largely retrospective, canon-forming approach to repertoire is reflected in the fact that Greene, Croft and Boyce remain the most popular composers, as they had been in 1745, although Boyce has now overtaken Croft: there are twenty-five anthems by Greene, twenty-four by Boyce and twenty-one by Croft. Stevenson, at the height of his fame in 1821 as a singer and composer in Dublin, is the next most popular with twenty anthems, followed by Handel, Nares and Kent. Shenton has nine anthems and Woodward five, but the other local composers present (John Spray, John Smith and Samuel Murphy) have only one each. Apart from Purcell (seven) and Blow (five), earlier composers are again poorly represented, Gibbons, Farrant and Byrd being the only renaissance composers although Palestrina makes an appearance in the form of one arrangement by Aldrich.[230]

The 'long eighteenth century' covered by this chapter represents not only a period of excellence for the cathedral's music but also one of significant transition. At the beginning of the eighteenth century Christ Church enjoyed a position of unchallenged authority as the state cathedral of a confident, Anglo-Protestant administration and the civic cathedral of a city entering a period of dramatic economic and population growth. Religious opposition was contained by repressive legislation which protected the interests of the country's ruling Protestant minority, and the cathedral's finances were securely based on tithes and revenues from its extensive properties both in Dublin and beyond. By the end of this period, however, Dublin was no longer a centre of government but merely a provincial capital within the United Kingdom. The status of Christ Church as the state cathedral had been further diminished by the opening of a private chapel royal within Dublin Castle, and the cathedral's revenues (not to mention its location in relation to the city's civic and economic life) had been adversely affected by the physical development of the city. The relaxing of anti-Catholic legislation, culminating in Catholic emancipation in 1829, removed Christ Church's status as a cathedral which could claim to represent the people of Dublin, the majority of whom were by now Catholic. Furthermore, the Irish Church Temporalities Act of 1833 would significantly reduce the cathedral's income. The deanery of Christ Church had long been held by successive bishops of Kildare, the revenues of the deanery coming to be regarded as belonging to the bishop. On the death of the current bishop the diocese of Kildare was to be united with those of Dublin and

---

229 Jellett, *Anthems*. The spine bears the title *Anthems as used at Christ Church and St Patrick's cathedrals, Dublin*. I am grateful to Stuart Kinsella for making available his copy which bears the inscription 'John S. Bumpus. From Sir Robert Stewart at Christ Church Cathedral, Dublin. Sunday August 16 1891'. The purchase by the cathedral of copies of this publication (referred to as 'anthem books') is recorded in the accounts for 1822/3 (C6/1/15/3).

230 Gibbons, *Hosanna to the Son of David*; *Lift Up Your Heads*; *O clap Your Hands*; Farrant, as in 1745 (see note 227); Byrd, *Bow Thine Ear*. Aldrich, *We Have Heard* (after Palestrina, *Doctor Bonus et Amicus Dei*). On the latter anthem see Blezzard, *Borrowings*, p. 46.

Glendalough and, when Bishop Charles Lindsay of Kildare, dean of Christ Church, died in office in 1846 the dean's revenue no longer accrued to Christ Church. Following the separation of the see of Kildare from the deanery of Christ Church, the latter was united with that of St Patrick's.[231] Within the first three or four decades of the nineteenth century Christ Church was effectively transformed from being a wealthy state cathedral supported by the highest ranks of society into a provincial cathedral serving the predominantly middle-class Protestants of Dublin who now formed a minority of the city's population and whose loyalties were divided between the city's two cathedrals. This very changed background would create new conditions and challenges for the cathedral's musical establishment through the middle of the nineteenth century.

---

[231] For more on the Irish Church Temporalities Act see Milne, 'Stripping of the Assets', pp. 315–18. See also Seymour, *Christ Church*, p. 69.

FIVE

'A More Efficient Performance of the Duties of the Choir': the Mid-Nineteenth Century

If the opening decades of the nineteenth century had witnessed a decline in the status and fortunes of Christ Church cathedral, those following the passing of the Church Temporalities Act in 1833 would see that process continued to the point where the cathedral's very survival would be cast into doubt. The Protestant domination of politics was on the decline and Ireland's Anglican cathedrals now occupied an increasingly marginal place within the country as a whole. Freed from the repressive legislation of previous centuries, the majority of the population could now openly express its Catholic identity and new cathedrals were built throughout the country to serve the re-established, Catholic diocesan system. Although a significant proportion of Dublin's wealth remained in the hands of the Protestant minority, the presence of two cathedrals within the city began to be called into question. But it is to the credit of Dean Henry Pakenham of St Patrick's (who assumed the deanery of Christ Church in 1846 under the terms of the Church Temporalities Act) that he proved assiduous in carrying out his additional duties as dean of Christ Church and maintained its independent role where otherwise it might have been subsumed under the shadow of its sister cathedral.[1] The recommendation in a report of the royal commissioners in 1868 that Christ Church be reduced to the status of a parish church, a move which might have brought with it an end to Christ Church cathedral's musical tradition, was not carried out, but growing political pressure for the Church of Ireland to be disestablished culminated in the Irish Church Act of 1869.[2] Not only was the Church of Ireland's privileged (but by now quite anomalous) position as the established church removed but it was also largely disendowed: from the point of view of music at Christ Church this would mean that the vicars choral would no longer constitute a corporate body owning properties which, together with the 'augmentation estate' established by Charles II (now also to be annulled), had provided the exceptional salaries that had attracted leading singers to the choir.

The radical changes which were to take place in the organisation of the

---

1 Milne, 'Stripping of the Assets', pp. 317–18.
2 The Irish Church Act, commonly referred to as Disestablishment, became law on 26 July 1869 but did not come into effect until 1 January 1871. See *OCIH*, p. 158 and (with specific reference to Christ Church) Milne, 'Stripping of the Assets', pp. 319ff.

cathedral during the nineteenth century were paralleled by equally profound changes in its physical structure. The structural conditions of both Christ Church and St Patrick's cathedrals had been a cause of concern to their respective chapters since the eighteenth century and by the nineteenth century both buildings needed significant repairs or renovation. In 1821 the cathedral architect at Christ Church had warned that the building was 'in a state of so much decay that although it will be safe for the present resort after no long time it must be rebuilt or fall into utter ruin'.[3] During divine service on Sunday 9 November 1828 'strange noises' were heard, apparently coming from the fabric of the building and causing 'extraordinary alarm' amongst the congregation and throwing the canons into panic. A programme of partial repair and restoration was undertaken which was largely cosmetic but resulted in the 'restoration' of much of the fourteenth-century long choir, nearly as long as the nave and in which all services were held (*Plate 9*).[4] As a result very few of the original medieval features of the long choir now remained. This programme of restoration carried out in 1830–33 would not however prove to be a long-term solution: in 1852 the cathedral was described as 'a worn and dingy building, grimed with smoke and dirt, and disfigured by modern mutilations and barbarous repairs'.[5] In 1868 the chapter invited the architect George Edmund Street to report on the condition of the building and to make proposals for its restoration. Thanks to the generous offer to fund Street's ambitious plans made in 1871 by Henry Roe, a wealthy distillery owner, the cathedral was closed for rebuilding between the end of July 1872 and 1878, resulting in the total transformation of the crumbling edifice into the building we know today (*Plate 1*).[6] The period of less than four decades between 1833 and 1871 would thus effectively mark a final chapter in both the cathedral's constitution and its physical appearance as these had effectively existed since the Reformation. No longer the acknowledged cathedral of city and state, Christ Church would become a largely superfluous cathedral serving a dwindling Protestant population but about to boast a magnificent, partially medieval but largely new, neo-Gothic building.

The reduced finances of the cathedral after 1833 became a recurring theme over the ensuing decades as the dean and chapter repeatedly sought to effect economies, an atmosphere of 'fire fighting' being discernable in many of the chapter acts of this period which contrasts with the administrative and financial certainties of earlier periods. However the independent income of the vicars choral and stipendiaries, which was not affected by the Church Temporalities Act, to a large

---

[3] On the condition of the cathedral and the 1830–33 restoration see Stalley, 'George . . . Restoration', pp. 354–6.

[4] On the long choir see Stalley, 'Architecture', pp. 95–102.

[5] *Ecclesiologist* xiii (1852), p. 169.

[6] On Street's restoration see Stalley, 'George . . . Restoration' and Stalley, *George Edmund Street*. The nave and roof of St Patrick's had been propped up with timber supports since the late eighteenth century and the whole building subject to periodic flooding. Benjamin Lee Guinness (of the brewing family) offered to fund the complete restoration of the cathedral which was closed for reconstruction between 1862 and 1865. The fact that St Patrick's cathedral was restored through the generosity of a brewery owner and Christ Church through that of Henry Roe, a distillery owner, gave rise to the comment that of Dublin's two Protestant cathedrals one was built on Guinness, the other on whiskey!

Plate 9. The fourteenth-century 'long choir' (demolished c.1872) as remodelled 1830–33, looking west. The view into the nave is blocked off by Telford's organ of 1856–7. (Photograph: National Library of Ireland, Dublin)

extent insulated the individual choir members from the full effects of the changed economic climate: within the musical context the cathedral's reduced circumstances manifested themselves above all in the education and care of the choirboys, the costs of which came directly from cathedral funds. The middle decades of the nineteenth century were marked by a recurring concern for the 'efficiency' of the choir and of the arrangements for the choirboys, while the reforms initiated by the Oxford movement would begin to be reflected in the repertoire and in concerns for musical standards. Indeed, despite what he described as the 'headless condition of the cathedral' (a reference to its deanery having been combined with that of St Patrick's), Canon Edward Seymour commented in 1869 that 'never before were the choir and whole cathedral staff so thoroughly everything that they ought to be' and that the choir 'can fairly challenge the history of the past to show a more efficient or effective body . . . or one whose tone could bear comparison'.[7] Charles Villiers Stanford also recalled that in the early 1860s music at Christ Church 'was as good as, often better than that at St Patrick's, but there was no theatrical crowd there. Something in the noble atmosphere made it unthinkable'.[8] Comments such as these stand in marked contrast not only to the declining status of the cathedral and its circumstances, but also to the often depressed situation within the English cathedral tradition around the same period.[9] On the one hand therefore the mid-nineteenth century was an era of uncertainty and retrenchment. On the other hand the cathedral's strong musical tradition would see it continue to flourish through this demanding period.

The conditions, standards and duties of the choir

The vicars choral and stipendiaries continued to enjoy exceptional salaries for the period, a situation which, in a plea for the proper funding of cathedral music in order to ensure high standards, Seymour later acknowledged to be 'a bright exception to the general rule'.[10] By the 1860s the vicars each received £222 per annum, the stipendiaries £140.[11] The vicars were nonetheless vigilant in guarding their rights and incomes: in 1855 they challenged the legality of the decision to transfer the rights and revenues of dean's vicar and chanter's (or precentor's) vicar from the vicars choral to the prebendaries of St Michael's and St Michan's respectively, a move which they rightly claimed was in contravention of the 1604 charter of James I.[12] Vacancies for boys had been advertised in the Dublin newspapers from at least 1814, but improvements in transport between the two countries following the introduction of steamships in the 1820s encouraged the advertising of positions for both boys and adult choir members in English as well as Irish newspapers from 1831.[13] An advertisement in 1858 elicited a total of twenty-six applications all of whom, with the exception of George Bilbrough, principal alto and choirmaster at Limerick cathedral, were from England.[14]

Steps were taken in 1840 and 1841 to obtain 'a more efficient performance of the duties of the choir', matters of attendance receiving particular attention. Fines for absence were increased, the problem of aging or infirm choir members addressed by the appointment of substitutes to be paid out of the vicar's or stipendiary's salary, and attendance at weekday services (or the provision by choirmen

[7]   Seymour, *Christ Church*, pp. 71, 83.
[8]   Stanford, *Pages*, p. 39.
[9]   See for example comments on Westminster abbey cited in Knight, 'Westminster Abbey', pp. 80–81.
[10] Seymour, *Cathedral System*, p. 22.
[11] Seymour, *Christ Church*, p. 73.
[12] Letter from vicars choral to the dean and chapter, 6 June 1855, PRONI, Pakenham papers, TD 5777, Y/12/3 (temporary shelfmark).
[13] C6/1/7/8, p. 381; C6/1/7/9, p. 280; C6/1/7/11, p. 226.
[14] PRONI, Pakenham papers, TD 5777, Y/12/5 (temporary shelfmark).

of appropriate deputies) insisted upon.[15] A year later, while recording regular and satisfactory attendance at services over the previous year, the chapter took the opportunity to remind choirmen to appoint a deputy whenever they were granted leave of absence.[16] It was around this time that the deans of the two cathedrals supposedly agreed not to promote any choirman to one cathedral who already held a post at the other, a decision which is reported to have had a deleterious effect on the choirs since singers of high quality were no longer attracted from England, and which was consequently revoked.[17] Although there is no reference to this decision in the chapter acts of either cathedral (nor by Seymour in 1869), Joseph, the youngest of the Robinson brothers,[18] did resign as a stipendiary at Christ Church at the time he was elected a full vicar at St Patrick's in 1843 and new singers appointed to each choir after c.1840 do not appear already to have been members of the other cathedral choir before 1865 when Samuel Dobbin, a vicar choral at Christ Church, was appointed to the same position at St Patrick's.[19]

The Revd John Jebb, a central figure in the high church revival of choral practices which had been developing in England in the wake of the Oxford and High Church movements, wrote of the lay vicars of St Patrick's cathedral in 1843 that 'nothing can surpass their musical skill, great pains having been taken in the selection of qualified singers'. Jebb's praise must be equally applicable to the choir of Christ Church, which he referred to as 'this noble choir' and of which most of these singers were members too.[20] The evidence suggests that musical standards at Christ Church were, at least on Sundays, anything but 'incompetent and careless' as the music in many English cathedrals at the time has been described.[21] The situation during weekdays appears however to have been quite another matter. In 1843 Jebb commented that

It is to be regretted, that the service, so full on Sundays, should on week days be attended by so few vicars: but one priest and three laymen being required to be present. It is strange indeed that this should be the case in a choir so richly endowed. In some of the very poorest [cathedrals] the week-day service is far more efficiently performed.[22]

15 C6/1/7/12, pp. 92, 103, 112–13.
16 *Ibid.*, p. 123.
17 *The Dublin University Magazine* xxxvii (April 1851), p. 500; Bumpus, *Sir John Stevenson*, p. 26; Bumpus 'Irish Church Composers', p. 82.
18 Francis (1799–1872), William (1805–81), John (1810–44) and Joseph (1816–98) Robinson were noted singers and musicians who played a central role both in the cathedrals and in nineteenth-century Dublin musical life. Joseph was a choirboy at St Patrick's before becoming a stipendiary and vicar choral at Christ Church from 1836 and a vicar choral at St Patrick's from 1843. In 1834 he founded the Antient Concerts Society, the city's leading orchestral and choral society which he conducted until 1863 and which hosted visits by soloists including Thalberg, Rubenstein and Joachim. He was also the first conductor of the University of Dublin Choral Society (1837–47). On Joseph Robinson's church music see pp. 163–4 below. See further Bumpus 'Irish Church Composers', pp. 130f; Grindle, *Cathedral Music*, pp. 70, 196f; Doran, 'Robinsons'; Gillen & Johnstone, *Anthology*, pp. 177–9.
19 Seymour, *Christ Church*; C6/1/7/12, p. 162; Lawlor, *Fasti*, p. 243.
20 Jebb, *Choral Service*, pp. 104, 121. Jebb acted as consultant to Revd Walter Farquar Hook, vicar of Leeds parish church where ground-breaking reforms in church music were initiated in 1841 (Gatens, *Victorian Cathedral Music*, p. 8).
21 Rainbow, *Choral Revival*, p. 257, but cf. ch. 4, note 225, above.
22 Jebb, *Choral Service*, p. 121.

Full attendance at weekday services was only required on rare occasions, morning weekday services continuing to be attended by at most half the choirmen in rotation as well as the organist (or more often a deputy) and the choirboys. An evening service was not usually held on Saturdays or Sundays and, as earlier in the century, the pattern on other days varied considerably: by the mid-1840s choral evening services were often only held between the end of March and the end of June, and in September, although at other times morning and evening weekday services appear to have been held regularly. It was not unusual however for weekday evening services to be attended only by the reader and the organist (probably with the choirboys).[23] A visitor in the early 1860s wrote of the 'dreary service' at Christ Church on weekday mornings performed by 'an "army of six" irregular forces, namely, one singing man and five small boys'.[24] In 1889 Robert Prescott Stewart, organist from 1844 to 1894 and one of the leading figures in Dublin's musical establishment, recalled how conditions were before 1865:

> The cathedral was not at that time in a flourishing state either chorally or as to its fabric. The weekday services were starved, sometimes trebles only were present, and rarely more than one man for each of the other parts, and that only on Thursdays and Fridays when the Dean (Bishop of Kildare) used to attend.[25]

Changes aimed at raising the quality and efficiency of the cathedral's music were introduced following the appointment of John West as dean in January 1864. The appointment to the chapter in 1865 of Canon Edward Seymour, a strong supporter of the cathedral's music who would later become precentor, and Revd John Finlayson who became precentor's assistant (or succentor) in November of the same year may also be seen as part of this movement of renewal within the cathedral's music. Previously master of the choir school, Finlayson was also active as a church composer (see page 163 below). In October 1864 the attendance of one countertenor, tenor and bass (to be decided amongst themselves) was required at weekday matins at which the full complement of twelve choirboys (i.e. including boys on the foundation and supernumeraries) usually sang, as they did on Sunday mornings and now also in the evenings. Weekday evening services were held daily except on Saturdays but the boys were seldom present.[26] In July 1864 the dean had announced his intention no longer to allow daily services to be discontinued during the choirboys' school holidays. Their holidays do however appear to have been respected to the extent that during much of July and August the only boys present were about seven or eight on Sunday mornings and evenings.[27]

[23] C6/1/22/1; C6/1/23/5–7.

[24] William Glover, author of *The Memoirs of a Cambridge Chorister*, cited after Bumpus, 'Irish Church Composers', p. 148.

[25] Vignoles, *Memoir*, p. 189. Born in Dublin in 1825, Stewart was highly regarded in his day as a musician, organist, and composer. Bumpus, who knew him well, reported that 'even when he was quite a young man crowds flocked to the Dublin cathedrals, as they did to the day of his death, to hear Stewart play' ('Irish Church Composers', p. 139). A precocious child, he became a choirboy at Christ Church in 1833 and later, aged eleven, presented John Crosthwaite, then dean's vicar and master of the boys, with a *Te Deum* (Vignoles, *Memoir*, p. 7). See further note 65 below.

[26] C6/1/7/13, pp. 195, 223; C6/1/23/9.

[27] C6/1/7/13, p. 192; C6/1/23/9. Following the reopening of Christ Church in May 1878 a fuller

A revised set of regulations for the choir was promulgated at the end of 1865.[28] While some of these do no more than outline existing or purely practical concerns including attendance, punctuality, and ensuring that music should be provided in a portable form when processional anthems were sung (a reminder that music was still most often sung from the leather-bound manuscript part-books),[29] there is now a clear emphasis on choral standards. The weekly tables of anthems and services should take due regard for the available strengths of the choir and not be changed without urgent cause; if a member of the chapter desire a particular service or anthem that this should be requested in good time; that rehearsals of music to be sung on Sundays or any special occasions should be held as necessary and that no new service or anthem be performed without rehearsal, at least by the choristers; that the senior chorister should place the relevant music in order on the desks (a practice which had first been tried in 1848 and formally instituted in 1850);[30] that three choirmen (an alto, a tenor and a bass) be present on all weekdays (reiterating the order of 1864); that verse anthems on Sundays should be sung 'as nearly as possible on alternate sides of the choir' and that this arrangement should not be changed during the service (a practice which must on occasion have led to a hiatus in performance); and that the organist should give the note of preparation before the anthem and also before the commandments and the Nicene creed 'whether the officiating minister intone or not'.

Before the 1860s Sunday evening services at St Patrick's had been enormously popular because of the performance of solo anthems which led to the service being nick-named 'Paddy's opera'. Stanford later recalled that

> As soon as the anthem began . . . the bulk of the congregation walked out of their seats and stood under the desks and noses of the singers, with all the air of a concert audience, only stopping short at applause. I remember wondering if they would clap after a well-sung solo, and why my mother had not brought her opera-glasses so that we might see better from our stage box. After the anthem there was a general stampede out of the church.[31]

Following the closure of St Patrick's for restoration in 1862 Sunday choral evensong was reinstated at Christ Church, but when St Patrick's re-opened in February 1865 the dean and chapter understandably wanted to resume this popular Sunday afternoon service (which had been the only regular service in the cathedral to be celebrated chorally), not least because they regarded the restored St Patrick's to be 'now more than ever before, the church best fitted for the grandest musical effect'. Furthermore, they argued that public expectations of the resumption of the Sunday afternoon service in their now magnificently restored cathedral would reflect most unfavourably on Christ Church should they not

choir of usually thirteen to fifteen boys sang both morning and evening services seven days a week.
28 C6/1/7/13, pp. 230f.
29 Choir music continued to be copied by hand, there being considerable activity recorded in the accounts, in particular during the period 1842–54 when the copyists were most often choirboys (C6/1/15/3, 1842–3, 1846–8; C6/1/15/4, 1848–54).
30 C6/1/15/4, 1848–9; C6/1/7/12, p. 275.
31 Stanford, *Pages*, p. 37.

agree to the return of this service to St Patrick's. With two more generously minded voices dissenting, the chapter of Christ Church grudgingly allowed just the three Robinson brothers and three other choir members to attend St Patrick's while still maintaining their own Sunday afternoon service.[32] A few months later, doubtless feeling the absence of some of their best voices, Christ Church agreed to move their Sunday evensong to 7pm, 'this hour to be tried only so long as it appears to succeed and not be injurious to adjoining parochial churches'.[33] Now with three full services on Sundays (matins at Christ Church and evensong at both St Patrick's and Christ Church) plus attendance for some at Trinity College and the Castle chapel in the mornings, the vicars choral and stipendiaries sought unsuccessfully in 1869 to be released from the Sunday evening service in Christ Church.[34] But for all the difficulties which the effective sharing of the one choir by the two Dublin cathedrals sometimes occasioned, benefits could also accrue when a threat to the choir at the one cathedral was counterbalanced by its essential role at the other. During the periods when St Patrick's was closed for rebuilding in the 1860s and Christ Church in the 1870s the continuation of services in the other cathedral provided continuity for the choirmen, while the threat to the existence of St Patrick's choir may have contributed to the dropping of the 1868 proposal to suppress the choir of Christ Church and reduce the cathedral to the status of a parish church.[35]

The choirboys and their education

While the choirmen belonged for the most part to both cathedral choirs, the boys had become attached only to one or other of the cathedrals at some stage prior to 1830. In response to the reduced financial climate a proposal was adopted in 1832 'for the future management of the Choir Boys on a Scale which may not diminish either their efficiency or respectability'.[36] Instead of their being provided with board and lodging by the cathedral, the boys' parents would receive an allowance of £15 per annum for their clothes and upkeep. At the same time, in order to have 'an efficient body of singing choir boys equal to the required duty', two supernumeraries would be added so that there would be six choristers on the 'old system' (i.e. as on the foundation). From this date therefore the core of choirboys apprenticed to the cathedral numbered six. In 1847 the additional choirboys were also increased to six 'for the more certain supply of well qualified choristers', these additional boys attending the choir on a daily basis and being educated at the school like the six 'foundation' choirboys.[37] The full complement of boys thus stood at twelve, divided into two groups of six as is reflected in the earliest of the school attendance books which date from 1863–8. In addition there were usually

---

[32] C6/1/7/13, pp. 200, 202–3. John Robinson, the second youngest of the four brothers, had died in 1844 in his mid-thirties.

[33] *Ibid.*, p. 208.

[34] *Ibid.*, p. 278.

[35] Seymour, *Christ Church*, pp. 74f.

[36] C6/1/7/11, pp. 248–9.

[37] C6/1/7/12, p. 255.

between five and seven other boys in the school who might be selected by audition or examination for apprenticeships as full choirboys as vacancies arose.[38]

Richard Beatty was the music master throughout the period of this chapter. In 1850 the chapter had recorded 'the extreme satisfaction with which the dean and chapter regard his care and attention and the great proficiency which the choir boys have made under his instruction' and, notwithstanding his advancing years, the high standards of the choir reported in the late 1860s must have owed much to his training of the boys.[39] It may well be this favourable perception of choir standards, including those of the boys, which prevented the adoption in 1852 of a fairly drastic proposal which would in effect have returned the boys' education and training to the situation that had pertained up to the late eighteenth century: a committee appointed to examine ways of making economies in the running of the cathedral had recommended that the duties of music master and organist might be combined in the one person at a salary of £120 and also that the office of schoolmaster to the boys (known in the eighteenth century as the 'writing master') might be abolished on the next vacancy.[40]

Following the resignation of Charles Osborne as schoolmaster in 1833 the post, most often referred to by then as that of 'classical master', was held by a succession of senior clergy, some but not all of whom were clerical vicars choral who were no longer regular members of the choir.[41] It is not clear where the schoolroom had previously been located (in 1814 the proctor had been asked to look for a 'proper place' for the education of the boys), but in 1832 the former St Mary's chapel (the medieval Lady chapel) to the north of the long choir was altered for use by the dean and as school rooms for the boys.[42] With the boys no longer living with their parents regular school hours were appointed, choir training occupying the first part of the morning before matins. Their curriculum included reading, writing and grammar, mathematics, geography, history, Greek, and Latin.[43] Pianos were bought in the mid-nineteenth century specifically for the 'use of the boys of the choir' or for the school and in 1845 William Telford was asked to quote for a two-manual organ for the use of the boys, although no corresponding payment appears in the accounts.[44]

The educational debate which led to the creation of state-funded national schools in 1833 and the establishment in 1839 of schools run by the Church Education Society is reflected in a growing concern for educational standards within the choir school. In 1845 both Richard Beatty and Revd John Finlayson, the 'classical' master, were examined to see how they were managing their duties, and rules for the better regulation of the school were drawn up with particular

[38]   C6/1/23/8; C6/1/7/12, pp. 1–2.

[39]   *Ibid.*, p. 279.

[40]   *Ibid.*, p. 296.

[41]   The Revd W.J. Lefanu (1833–4); the Revd John Crosthwaite (1834–7); the Revd John Finlayson (1837–52); the Revd James Monaghan (1852–5); the Revd George Barton (1855–61); the Revd Henry de C. Collier (1861–73).

[42]   C6/1/7/9, p. 274; C6/1/7/11, p. 223.

[43]   C6/1/7/11, p. 274; C6/1/7/12, pp. 300–1. On the curriculum see orders for schoolbooks between 1820 and 1845 in C/6/1/21/1 and Vignoles, *Memoir*, pp. 6–7.

[44]   C6/1/7/12, pp. 137 ('a grand piano forte' in 1843), 225 (organ in 1845); C6/1/7/13, pp. 174, 184 ('a grand square Collard pianoforte' in 1864).

attention to the boys' attendance.[45] During the 1840s boys were sometimes given a book prize as a reward for good conduct and in 1846 Dean Henry Pakenham introduced silver medals for those who had satisfactorily completed their term of service, a practice which was however discontinued in 1852 (apparently for economic reasons) although certificates on vellum were later introduced.[46] Half-yearly examinations were introduced in 1850 (but appear to have lapsed since they were reintroduced in 1868), and in January 1852 an examination of the musical abilities of the choirboys was held by the precentor and two of the prebendaries, assisted by the music master, with the threat of removing any who were thought not to be of service to the choir.[47] This resulted in a satisfactory report on all the boys both vocally and instrumentally and must have influenced the decision two months later not to implement a recommendation to discontinue the boys' gratuity on completion of their service.[48] The provision of free education by Trinity College offered in 1864 to choirboys who had served well in the choir provided a way for the university to repay the contribution given by the choirboys to its own chapel services, this offer being welcomed by the chapter as a means of attracting boys of 'a superior class' to enter the choir.[49]

Boys could only practise on the cathedral organ in the presence of the music master but even before the installation of the new Telford cathedral organ in 1856 (see below) the amount of practice by the boys had meant that the organ blower had had to be engaged every day instead of only twice a week, and following the installation of the new instrument requests to play it came in from former choirboys who were now working as church organists.[50] Under Robert Prescott Stewart senior choirboys often acted as temporary assistant organists during weekday services and prizes were instituted in 1867 for the two best choirboys at sight-reading on the organ and also for the two best players of an appointed fugue.[51]

Organs and organists

The alterations made to the long choir in 1830–33 included changes to the arch between the choir and crossing and the organ loft at this point was replaced with what Jebb later described as 'the present clumsy organ loft', adding that 'the organ ought never in any instance to stand over the choir screen'. Some alterations were also made to the back of the organ case to improve visibility within the cathedral (*Plate 10*).[52] In 1832 William Telford, who was appointed organ and piano tuner when the cathedral reopened in 1833, repaired the organ, providing new bellows, keys and actions, and adding open and stopped diapasons to the

---

[45] *Ibid.*, pp. 216, 217, 225.
[46] C6/1/21/1, 3 Aug. 1841, 9 July 1843, 18 Nov. 1846; C6/1/7/12, pp. 244, 299; C6/1/7/13, p. 87.
[47] C6/1/7/12, p. 292.
[48] *Ibid.*, pp. 276, 296; C6/1/7/13, p. 260.
[49] C6/1/7/13, p. 175.
[50] C6/1/7/12, p. 247; C6/1/7/13, pp. 36, 90, 99.
[51] *Ibid.*, p. 253.
[52] C6/1/7/11, pp. 217, 227; Jebb, *Choral Service*, pp. 197, 202.

Plate 10. The interior of the nave in 1835 as illustrated in the *Dublin Penny Journal*, with Byfield's organ of 1752. Services were held entirely within the 'long choir' beyond the chancel screen. The southern side of the nave had been hastily rebuilt following the collapse of the vaults in 1562.

great organ and double open diapason and principal to the pedals at a cost of £277 plus £16 for gilding the pipes.[53] Following the appointment of Robert Prescott Stewart as organist in 1844 Telford substituted a new swell organ of twelve stops and wider compass at a cost of £236, which Stewart subsequently described as having 'in point of fact renovated the whole instrument, which never in its best days could have been compared with St Patrick's organ even as it is at present'.[54] Many years later he described it as having been a 'very feeble instrument . . . without one single redeeming feature'.[55] The decision to build an entirely new organ was reached in 1856 when Telford provided full details of an instrument costing £500 which was to be finished by the end of November.[56] In the event it took longer to install and a number of changes were made before it was ready at the end of 1857, being the first organ in Ireland in which pneumatic action was extensively used. The former Byfield organ was sold to the church of St Nicholas

[53] C6/1/7/11, p. 250; C6/1/7/12, pp. 24–5; C6/1/15/3, 1832–3, 1833–4. The full specification of the organ as improved by Telford was given in the chapter acts for 11 April 1836:
'Three benches of keys from GG to F in alt':
Great ('to Bass C'): Great open diapason, Great stopped diapason, Open diapason, Stopped diapason, Principal, Flute, Twelfth, Fifteenth, Sesquialtra, Cornet, Trumpet, Double open diapason.
Choir ('GG to F in alt'): Stopped diapason, Dulciana, Flute, Principal, Bassoon, Open diapason to middle C.
Swell ('fiddle G to F in alt'): Open diapason, Dulciana, Stopped diapason, Principal, Flute, Hautboy, Trumpet.
Pedals (one and a half octaves): Double open diapason, Great unison diapason, Principal.
'The organ contains 1593 pipes the longest of which (the Double GG open diapason pedals) is twenty feet long by two feet ten inches, diagonal, diameter, the shortest ¾ of an inch long. The wind is supplied by two horizontal bellows the largest is ten feet long by five feet wide loaded with 4½ cwt. of metal.'
[54] C6/1/7/12, p. 190; C6/1/15/3, 1845–6; letter from R.P. Stewart to Dr Marks, 4 July 1853, PRONI, Pakenham papers, TD 5777, Y/11/6 (temporary shelf mark); see also Seymour, *Christ Church*, p. 84. Prior to the installation of a new organ by Bevington and Sons of London in 1860 the organ of St Patrick's cathedral in the 1850s was a mongrel instrument dating back originally to Renatus Harris's 1697 organ but subsequently added to or rebuilt by Byfield in 1730, by Gray of London in 1815–16 and by Bewscher and Fleetwood of Liverpool in 1831 (Grindle, *Cathedral Music*, pp. 134–7).
[55] Bumpus, *Sir John Stevenson*, p. 71. Bumpus states that the new swell was added in 1850 but this is not born out by the accounts.
[56] C6/1/7/13, pp. 26–9. Telford's proposed specification was as follows:
Great ('CC to G. 56 notes'): Double open diapason, Great open diapason, Second open diapason, Flute harmonique, Stopped diapason, Principal, Gomohorn [*sic*, Gemshorn], Twelfth, Fifteenth, Sesquialtera of 4 and 5 ranks, Trumpet, Clarion.
Choir ('CC to G. 56 notes'): Bourdon (stopped), Small open diapason, Stopped diapason, Viol de Gambo Tenor C, Principal, Flute (open) Tenor C, Fifteenth, Cor Anglaise.
Swell ('CC to G. 56 notes'): Bourdon (stopped), Open diapason, Dulciana Tenor C, Stopped diapason, Flute harmonique (Octave), Principal, Fifteenth, Flageolet, Mixture of 3 ranks, Contra Fagotto, Trumpet or Cornopean, Oboe, Clarion, Vox Humana (Tenor C). Tremolo in the Swell organ.
Pedal ('CCC to F. 30 notes'): Double open diapason, Double stopped diapason, Open diapason.
Coupling actions: Great manuals to pedals; Swell Manuals to pedals; Swell to Great; Unison, Swell to Great; Octave above, Swell to Great; Octave below, Swell to Choir manuals.
Movements: Pneumatic action in Great Manuals acting in Couples, 4 Composition pedals in the Great Organ, 3 Composition pedals in Swell organ.

in Cork.[57] When Robert Prescott Stewart was asked to report on Telford's organ he described it as 'notoriously defective in the bass', a fault which was not helped by the absence of lower octaves in the flute stops in the great and choir (referred to at earlier periods as 'chair') organs and a 'doubtful' lower octave in the great open diapason.[58] The lower notes of the trumpet stops in the great and swell were coarse and unequal in tone, the pedal stopped diapason weak, almost all stops of the great were rough, and Telford had altered or added a number of stops. Telford made the necessary modifications in response to Stewart's criticisms and the additional stops were paid for.[59] In 1870 agreement was reached for Telford to add four further stops (a 'clarionet' in the choir, a contra fagotto in the swell, and a violone and a trombone in the pedal organ) which would complete the instrument and the organ screen was also to be removed and the organ re-sited in the north transept in accordance with contemporary thinking.[60] However, before this work was completed Telford advised the removal of the organ to St Bride's church for safe keeping during Street's rebuilding of the cathedral and the outstanding improvements to the instrument were not completed until 1878 after the cathedral had reopened.[61] Seymour had commented in 1869 that Telford's organ had not received justice both because of its being sited in the arch separating the choir and transept, effectively dividing the instrument in two and 'shutting out the pedal organ in to the nave of the church and thus depriving the instrument of bass' (*Plate 9*).[62]

John Robinson (younger brother of Francis who had been assistant organist between 1815 and 1833) acted as organist at Christ Church after William Warren was obliged to step down in 1833, but on his stipendiary's fee since Warren continued to receive his full salary.[63] Robinson was assisted by a deputy organist who usually played the weekday services (which enabled Robinson to sing in the choir), suitably competent choristers also being allowed to play on weekday afternoons and occasionally on Sundays.[64] Following Robinson's death in May 1844 Robert Prescott Stewart (who had been assistant organist since the previous year) was appointed cathedral organist, a position he was to hold for no less than fifty years until his death in 1894.[65] Stewart does not appear to have had a formal assistant during his first seventeen years as organist, weekday services being played after 1855 by one of four senior choirboys in rotation, week by week,[66] but from

57 Following the closure of St Nicholas's in February 1998 the (somewhat mutilated) case of the Byfield organ (all that remains of the original instrument) was re-acquired by Christ Church.
58 C6/1/7/13, pp. 50–1, 58–61.
59 *Ibid.*, pp. 68f (various dates between 13 Jan. and 15 Dec. 1859); cf. C6/1/15/4, 1857–60.
60 C6/1/7/13, pp. 299, 302, 307, 309, 310; the 'clarionet' stop was first proposed in 1866 (*ibid.*, p. 237).
61 *Ibid.*, p. 328; see also pp. 179–80 below.
62 Seymour, *Christ Church*, pp. 86f.
63 C6/1/7/12, p 118. John Robinson had been organist at St Patrick's since 1830.
64 C6/1/7/12, pp. 12, 15, 118–19.
65 *Ibid.*, pp. 152, 186. Despite his appointment as organist in 1844 being subject to the 'daily attendance to his duties' and his not accepting 'any situation incompatible with such duties', Stewart was also organist at Trinity College chapel during the same fifty-year period and at St Patrick's between 1852 and 1861, conductor of the University Choral Society from 1846 and later of the Dublin Philharmonic Society, professor of music at Trinity College from 1861, and a professor of theory at the Royal Irish Academy of Music from 1869.
66 C6/1/7/12, p. 354.

1861 to 1873 William Haughton (a former choirboy) served as his deputy.[67] While probably more actively involved in the cathedral's music during his earlier years as organist, Sunday services later became his only regular duty, the training of the choirboys being left in the hands of the music master Richard Beatty and choir rehearsals deputed to Francis Robinson following Stewart's appointment to Trinity College Dublin in 1861. Even then Stanford recalled rehearsals being 'seldom and scanty, more often than not confined to a haphazard ten minutes at the piano while the surplices were being put on'.[68]

Christ Church composers

Christ Church cathedral musicians continued to contribute music to the repertoire during the mid-nineteenth century, although to a lesser degree than previously. The Revd John Crosthwaite was a composer of some church music including a Service in G, two anthems (*Out of the deep*, and *Praise the Lord, O my soul* which is based on Haydn), a set of responses and a litany, and seven double chants printed in a collection published by Sir Robert Prescott Stewart in 1883.[69] The Revd John Finlayson, described by Bumpus as 'a well-informed musician', composed a setting of the responses and made an adaption of Tallis's English litany which Jebb regarded as 'admirable'.[70] John Horan (1831–1907), a choirboy from 1843–6, was organist of Tuam cathedral before moving to Derry cathedral in 1864, returning to Christ Church in 1873 as assistant organist under Stewart (whom he later succeeded). Although not directly associated with Christ Church for much of his professional career, he can be noted here as composer of seven anthems and two services.[71] Also a choirboy at Christ Church before becoming organist at a number of Dublin churches and then entering the priesthood in 1865 was William Torrance (1835–1907), composer of at least four anthems *I will magnify thee*; *And the Lord said; Blessed art Thou, Lord*; and *Thou wilt keep him*.[72] Torrance was also musical editor of *Hymns for Public Worship* ([Dublin], 1856), its enlarged reissue *Church Hymnal* (Dublin, 1864), and joint editor with Thomas Jozé of *Chants and Responses* (Dublin, 1907) which includes a number of his own settings.

The most prominent composers of this period were Joseph Robinson and Robert Prescott Stewart. Robinson's output of sacred music is however small, comprising only three anthems and two evening services at least some of which were composed specifically for St Patrick's cathedral.[73] His anthem *Bow down*

---

[67] C6/1/7/13, p. 104; C6/1/15/4, 1861–2, 1867–8.

[68] C6/1/7/13, p. 121; Stanford, *Pages*, p. 42.

[69] Bumpus, 'Irish Church Composers', p. 133. Neither of Crosthwaite's two anthems (both in score book C6/1/24/1/34) features in the lists of music sung at Christ Church during 1846 and 1849–50 although his responses were sung once during the six months covered by the 1846 listing.

[70] Bumpus, 'Irish Church Composers', p. 134; Jebb, *Choral Service*, p. 453.

[71] Gillen & Johnstone, *Anthology*, p. 25. See also p. 183 below.

[72] *Ibid.*, p. 25; *Novello's Collection of Words and Anthems* (London, 1898), p. lv. For a biography of Torrance, including reference to his musical training in Leipzig, see Leslie, *Clergy*, p. 1116.

[73] Robinson's editions of three of Stevenson's anthems were referred to in ch. 4.

thine ear, O Lord, composed for St Patrick's in 1853 (although no special event at the cathedral can be identified which might warrant such an ambitious work), is unusual in its scale. As Gillen and Johnstone note, its accompaniment is 'considerably more complex and colourful than is usual in church music of the period' and the influences of Samuel Sebastian Wesley and the multi-voiced *a capella* Lutheran works of Mendelssohn (whom Robinson knew) are also evident.[74] In contrast, and despite claiming to have destroyed a large portion of the music he had written, Stewart is probably the most prolific Irish composer of sacred music of his time. His surviving sacred works comprise four complete services, one incomplete service, various settings of the *Creed* and *Sanctus* to complete services by composers including Aldrich, Boyce, Child, Farrant and King contained in the Dublin cathedral choir books, nineteen anthems (including settings for double choir of Psalm 107 and the *Veni Creator*), a sacred cantata *The Breastplate of St Patrick*, a number of sacred songs, chants, and over thirty hymn tunes (he was editor of the *Irish Church Hymnal* (Dublin, 1876)).[75] Stewart's music enjoyed considerable popularity in the Dublin cathedrals into the early twentieth century: his Service in E flat for double choir composed in 1850 (but not published until 1879), for example, was the most frequently performed service at St Patrick's cathedral during the period 1865–1915 and his Service in G dating from 1866 the most frequently performed at Christ Church between 1878 and 1880.[76] Two of his anthems, both dating from 1863, demonstrate the new, 'dignified' choral style urged by reformers like Jebb existing alongside the more expansive style with extended solos popular since earlier in the century. *If ye love me keep my commandments* is a full anthem for four voices in a restrained, predominantly homophonic style. Clearly inspired by Renaissance models such as those anthems of Farrant and Tallis with which Stewart would have been familiar since his days as a choirboy, it initially maintains a simple, diatonic harmonic range before expanding midway through into richer, more chromatic harmonies (*Ex. 5.1*).[77] In marked contrast, *Thou O God art praised in Zion* is a considerably longer and more elaborate anthem in three contrasting movements. The outer sections for full choir (the first of which can be sung on its own as a full anthem) flank a Mendelssohnian recitative and lyrical solo for tenor (with brief choral interjections) (*Ex. 5.2*). As with Stevenson half a century earlier, Stewart was clearly writing here with a particular singer in mind, in this case most probably Francis Robinson who was regarded as the natural successor to John Spray. The concluding section, a well-crafted choral fugue, again displays Stewart's debt to Mendelssohn. *In the Lord I put my trust*, like *Thou O God art praised in Zion* and dating from the following year, is another fine,

74 Gillen & Johnstone, *Anthology*, pp. 178–9; music edited in *ibid.*, pp. 147–76.

75 Full list of works in Parker, 'Stewart', pp. 189–201. For contrasting discussions of Stewart's sacred music see Bumpus, 'Irish Church Composers', pp. 140f; Grindle, *Cathedral Music*, pp. 199–202 and Parker, 'Stewart', pp. 149–79. See also Vignoles, *Memoir*; Culwick, *Sir Robert Stewart* and Culwick, *Works*.

76 McHugh, 'St Patrick's', p. 186; Seymour, *Choral Services*.

77 Tallis's setting of the same text does not however appear in the contemporary repertoire of Christ Church represented in Finlayson, *Anthems* or the surviving service lists from 1846 and 1849–50 (see note 85 below).

Ex. 5.1 Robert Prescott Stewart, *If ye love me, keep my commandments*: (a) bars 1–5, (b) bars 21–32

expansive anthem also falling into three sections, the central one scored for solo treble (or soprano) accompanied by a solo quartet of voices, and the concluding section being a double fugue for full choir.[78] Stewart's music, secular as well as sacred, suffered from that neglect in the twentieth century to which so much music of the Victorian era was condemned. It is not so long since Grindle

[78] The above three anthems were published during Stewart's lifetime by Novello.

Ex. 5.1 *cont.*

dismissed it as 'generally a model of rectitude, but the absence of that creative spark which, after all, belongs only to a select few in any generation has doomed it to an almost total oblivion from which it is unlikely to emerge'.[79] Grindle has been proved wrong, the above anthems having deservedly found a place in recent years in the repertoire of Christ Church cathedral. Stewart is beginning to be acknowledged as a talented composer who made an important contribution not only to music in nineteenth-century Ireland but also within the wider context of nineteenth-century cathedral music.[80]

The repertoire and the nineteenth-century choral revival

John Jebb reported in 1843 that, despite what he considered 'a most secular taste' having formerly prevailed within the musical repertoire at Christ Church, 'by the most laudable influence of many of its present members . . . it is now recovering, and it is to be hoped, will eventually be rescued altogether'.[81] In his desire to reform cathedral music and services along lines influenced by the Oxford

---

[79] Grindle, *Cathedral Music*, p. 202.

[80] The three anthems cited above entered the repertoires of some English cathedrals. *In the Lord I put my trust* and *Thou O God art praised in Zion* were sung at St Paul's cathedral in 1878 and in 1889–90 (W. Sparrow Simpson, *A Year's Music in S. Paul's Cathedral, Easter, 1878–Easter, 1879: Second Report to the Dean and Chapter* (London, 1879), p. 26; W. Russell, *Musical Services in S. Paul's Cathedral: A Report to the Dean and Chapter of the Music and Other Matters Connected with the Choir and Choral Services, Chiefly from Easter, 1889, to Easter, 1890* (London, 1890)).

[81] Jebb, *Choral Service*, pp. 104, 392.

Ex. 5.2 Robert Prescott Stewart, *Thou O God art praised in Zion*, bars 103–26

movement Jebb was an outspoken critic of the secular, 'operatic' style of music represented by the solo anthems of composers like Stevenson, which he described as 'an abominable perversion of sacred things'.[82] He was, however, thankful that the former practice at Christ Church (and St Patrick's) of the verse singers of the anthem singing from the organ loft had gone out of use:

> It was most indecent, not only operatic in appearance, and contrary to all the properties of the choral system, but as making an interruption in the service: since the singers left their places after the Creed to move up to the organ loft . . .

[82] Jebb, *Three Lectures*, pp. 115–16.

In consequence the Responses were sung in a most meagre manner, being delegated to secondary singers and boys.[83]

Jebb had reiterated in 1843 the proposal first made in 1839 by John Peace that the circulation before services of lists of the music to be sung would avoid the 'indecency of the boys roving about with messages' during the services, a practice which at Christ Church (not specifically by the boys) had called for comment by the dean and chapter as early as 1789.[84] This proposal was adopted at Christ Church in 1846 when a ledger was compiled of music sung between April and October 1846, a period during which a total of seventy-five different anthems were performed. Three further volumes cover successive full years, the last from 7 January 1849 to 6 January 1850 during which 135 different anthems were sung.[85] In 1852 John Finlayson published a book of anthem texts sung in Christ Church, St Patrick's and the chapels of Trinity College and Dublin Castle which maintains the tradition of the earlier volumes from 1662, 1745 and 1821.[86] In this case, however, the co-existence of contemporary music lists presents a more accurate picture of what anthems were actually sung than is provided by the 'potential' repertoires represented by the printed collections.[87]

Jebb's hopes of reform were beginning to be reflected in terms of the overall repertoire. Finlayson divided the 234 anthems in his collection into four distinct classes or categories: 'verse', 'full, with long verses', 'full, with short verses', and 'full, without verses'. The two anthems most frequently sung in the six months of 1846, each being heard nine times, were the full anthem *O how amiable* by Vaughan Richardson (c.1670–1729) and Shenton's 'full, with short verses' *O give thanks*. In the full year 1849–50 *I will arise*, a full anthem by Robert Creighton (1636/7–1734), headed the list with ten performances followed by Richardson's *O how amiable* with eight. Only one of the remaining seventeen anthems sung five or more times during the six months of 1846, *Hear my prayer* by Charles Stroud (d.1720), falls into Finlayson's category of 'full, with long verses' and none can be classified as solo verse anthems. In 1849–50 twenty-three anthems were sung five or more times, all of which were full or full-with-verse. Perhaps most tellingly, the most popular of the six anthems by Stevenson sung

---

83 Jebb, *Choral Service*, p. 374.
84 John Peace, *Apology for Cathedral Service* (London, 1839), p. 60 cited after Rainbow, *Choral Revival*, pp. 250–1; Jebb, *Choral Service*, p. 375; Barra Boydell, ed., *Music: Documents*, p. 126.
85 'Christ Church Cathedral. Course of Services and Anthems . . . 26 April 1846 [to] 24 Oct. 1846' and successive volumes (uncatalogued handwritten ledgers held in Christ Church; the volumes for 1847 and 1848 came to light too late to be analysed in detail here). The presence of some entries which are crossed out and replaced with alternative anthems or service settings confirms that these lists were drawn up in advance. With isolated exceptions, most often in the form of service leaflets relating to commemorative and other special services (and see also Seymour, *Cathedral Services*), there appear to be no surviving service lists between 1850 and 1915, since when a more or less complete (printed) run survives.
86 Finlayson, *Anthems*.
87 This point should also be born in mind concerning the repertoires in earlier anthem books referred to previously. Although slightly over half of the anthems in Finlayson (123 out of 234) fall into his categories of 'verse' or 'full, with long verses', the music lists of 1846 and 1849–50 show an overall predominance of full anthems (or 'full with short verses'). In the absence of the music lists one might reasonably but incorrectly assume that solo anthems still dominated the repertoire.

during this period was his only full anthem *Grant to us, Lord* which was sung eight times in 1846 and four in 1849–50. These figures must however be qualified by the fact that, athough they constituted only a small minority of all the anthems sung during this period and were for the most sung each only once or twice, verse anthems nevertheless remained the preferred type of anthem for Sundays.[88] Referring specifically to Christ Church, an anonymous writer expressed the regret in 1851 that 'the true cathedral style (that is the choral) has made way for the exhibition of solo singing in some half-dozen anthems repeated Sunday after Sunday':[89] with only rare exceptions full or full-with-verse anthems were performed on weekdays and Saturdays, while on Sundays when the largest congregations attended the repertoire consisted almost exclusively of verse anthems. The increasing frequency with which full anthems appeared in the overall repertoire can thus be explained at least partially by the selection of anthems suitable for weekday services sung by a small choir and without the large Sunday congregation present.

Overall the anthem repertoire at Christ Church during the mid-nineteenth century remained very conservative. The most frequently heard composers (i.e. the sum of performances of all anthems by a given composer) were of the eighteenth century: somewhat unexpectedly since his music had previously fallen out of the repertoire, Ralph Roseingrave headed the list in 1849–50 with twenty-seven performances (significantly of his full or full-with-verse anthems rather than any of his solo anthems),[90] followed by Hayes, Ebdon, Greene and Croft in that order (Shenton was ninth equal with Batten). Contemporary composers scarcely featured at all: after the main alphabetical listing of fifty composers, Finalyson's collection separately lists 'composers still living, A.D. 1852', a category containing only four names of whom two, John Smith (with six anthems) and Robert Prescott Stewart (with three), were attached to Christ Church. The only other contemporary composers were George Elvey and Thomas A. Walmisley, each represented by a single anthem.[91] Mendelssohn, who died in 1847, was heard just once in 1846 (his anthem *O Lord thou hast searched me out*) but he is not represented at all in Finlayson. This reluctance to introduce contemporary composers into the repertoire reflects both the growing artistic isolation of Dublin and the conservatism of the Church of Ireland as it underwent a period of retrenchment following the Church Temporalities Act of 1833. Although Robert Prescott Stewart would later prove himself an ardent champion of contemporary choral music in his role as conductor of the University of Dublin

---

[88] Purcell's *Thy word is a lantern* sung three times was the most popular Sunday anthem in the six months of 1846; in 1849–50 Blake's *I have set God always*, Greene's *O God thou art my God*, Travers' *Ascribe unto the Lord* (all verse anthems) and a selection from Handel's *Messiah* including *I know that my Redeemer* with *Worthy is the Lamb* were each sung three times (other selections from *Messiah* were also popular).

[89] *Dublin University Magazine* xxxvii (April 1851), p. 500.

[90] Anthems by Roseingrave performed in 1849–50 were *O come hither* (six times), *I will magnifie thee* (five times), *Blessed is he* and *Bow down thine ear* (four times each), *I will cry unto God* and *Praise the Lord O ye servants* (three times each), and *Rejoice in the Lord O ye Righteous* (twice).

[91] Elvey's full anthem *O Lord from whom all good things come* which was sung six times in April–October 1846 and five times in 1849–50, and Walmisley's verse anthem *Remember, O Lord* which was not sung in either of the above years.

Choral Society,[92] in the later 1840s he was only in his early twenties and, brought up within this musically conservative environment of Christ Church, was perhaps as yet unfamiliar with contemporary developments in English church music.

On the other hand there was a growing interest in composers of the sixteenth and early seventeenth centuries, models for what church music reformers regarded in the words of the anonymous writer cited above as 'the true cathedral style (that is the choral)'. While the most popular of forty-seven morning or evening services sung during 1849–50 dated from the late seventeenth or eighteenth centuries (Aldrich in G, King in F and Travers in F, each with eighteen performances), Richard Farrant's Service in G minor was sung fifteen times (making it the eighth-equal most popular service) and Tallis's Short ('Dorian') Service thirteen times (twelfth equal). Byrd's Short Service in D (seven performances) and Gibbon's Short Service in F (six performances) were also in the repertoire. Anthems by sixteenth- and early seventeenth-century composers including Batten, Gibbons and Farrant (and to a lesser extent Tye, Byrd and others) were sung on a number of occasions, Batten's *Hear my prayer* being the equal-third most popular anthem in 1849–50 with six performances and Farrant's *Call to remembrance* (which had been in the repertoire at least since the 1740s) equal-tenth with five performances. The interest in earlier composers was catered for by existing rather than by new editions of the music: with only isolated exceptions, this repertoire is contained in Boyce's *Cathedral Music*, copies of which the cathedral had owned since its publication and which were now being supplemented by the 1849 editions of Vincent Novello and Joseph Warren.[93] Some earlier music, including that of the previous century, came down in altered or 'improved' versions: Robert Prescott Stewart attempted to 'restore' the 'improved' score and parts copied in the 1790s by John Mathews of a *Jubilate* by the eighteenth-century organist George Walsh to which he had added a whole extra voice besides, in Bumpus's words, 'disfiguring and tinkering the composition generally'.[94]

By the 1840s Tallis's responses or those of Winchester (often harmonised) were most frequently sung on Sundays, without the organ, these having replaced Stevenson's setting which had formerly prevailed.[95] A voluntary or 'soft symphony' was played while the preacher ascended the pulpit for the sermon, after which the anthem was sung. Jebb criticised the singing of a lengthy verse anthem at this point, preferring that there should be a short full anthem which would allow time for the singing of the *Sanctus* and *Gloria* 'which are now but rarely performed as they ought to be'.[96] Despite the continued use of verse anthems on Sundays, the musical reforms taking place within cathedral music

---

[92]   See FitzGibbon, 'College Choral'.

[93]   Copies in the cathedral archive.

[94]   Bumpus, 'Irish Church Composers', p. 122. On Stewart's annotations and alterations to Mathews' score of Walshe's *Jubilate* see ch. 4, note 190 above.

[95]   Jebb, *Choral Service*, pp. 261, 355, 446; 'Christ Church Cathedral. Course of Services and Anthems . . .' (as in note 85). Five hundred copies of the Winchester chant were lithographed in 1862 (C6/1/15/4, 1862–3). Jebb's own *Choral Responses and Litanies* were purchased by Christ Church some years later (C6/1/7/12, p. 354; C6/1/15/4, 1857–8).

[96]   While settings of the *Gloria* are rare in Irish cathedral sources, including those from Dublin, the *Sanctus* is usually present. Jebb's comment seems to refer specifically to St Patrick's where (in

during the mid-nineteenth century were beginning to make their mark at Christ Church before 1850 even though the more 'efficient' regulation of choral services through the week urged by the reformers would not make itself apparent much before the 1860s.

The mid-nineteenth century witnessed significant challenges to both the cathedral and its music, the continued existence of the cathedral and its choir even being brought into question in 1868. These challenges would be overshadowed by the more radical changes brought about by Disestablishment. As the provisions of the Irish Church Act came into effect on 1 January 1871 the prospects for maintaining full cathedral services on a drastically reduced budget must have seemed bleak. However, the decision to proceed with Street's plan for a complete restoration of the building which resulted in the closure of the cathedral between 1872 and 1878 would allow for something of a breathing space and few can have anticipated that within a few years the choir would find itself re-established on what, initially at any rate, appeared to be a secure financial foundation, though in a very different climate to that of earlier times.

contrast to Christ Church) settings of the *Sanctus* are indeed rare (on the emergence of a locally composed repertoire of communion settings at Cashel cathedral see Barra Boydell, 'Manuscript Sources').

SIX

Decline and Revival: Disestablishment and the Twentieth Century

The century after the disestablishment of the Church of Ireland in 1871 would witness social and political changes arguably more challenging than any that had previously affected Christ Church, changes which would alter the relationships between the cathedral, the city of Dublin and the country as a whole and which would at times call into question the very survival of the cathedral, not to mention the continuation of its musical traditions. The Land Acts of the late nineteenth century, the establishment of democratically elected county councils in 1898 and the vigorous growth of Ireland as a Catholic nation had contributed to the reduction in the wealth and influence of the Protestant landed gentry whom Grindle characterised as 'those pillars of the Church of Ireland'.[1] This process came to a head during the period of 'the Troubles' immediately preceding independence when the houses of many Protestant landowners were burnt down, their owners often moving to England or Northern Ireland. After 1922 when (with the exception of the six counties of Northern Ireland in which Protestants constituted a majority of the population) Ireland gained its independence from British rule, the Church of Ireland represented no more than 5 per cent of the population of a new, independent nation whose religious ethos was overtly, even triumphantly Catholic. Christ Church cathedral, which had maintained its tradition of loyalty to the British crown during the decades leading up to independence, holding memorial services for Queen Victoria in 1901 and presenting an address of welcome to the king and queen on their visit to Ireland in 1903,[2] now found itself very much an outsider within its own city and state. With diminishing congregations and finances but inheriting the country's historic church buildings, the Church of Ireland struggled to maintain both its buildings and its traditions. In this climate it is little wonder that Christ Church cathedral entered one of the darkest periods of its existence, an inward-looking period during which its musical tradition largely stagnated, reaching a nadir with the closure of the choir school in 1972 after nearly five hundred years of existence. But by then change was already in the air. Dean Salmon, appointed in 1967, encouraged a more forward-looking, inclusive relationship with the city and with Irish society as a whole which was itself beginning to emerge from the narrow conservatism which had prevailed since

---

[1] Grindle, *Cathedral Music*, p. 117.
[2] Milne, 'Stripping of the Assets', p. 334.

independence. President Eamonn de Valera personally supported the dean's hopes for the regeneration of the cathedral and friendly relationships were established with the Roman Catholic diocese of Dublin. The appointment of Peter Sweeney as organist and choirmaster in 1980, replacing Arnold McKiernan who had retired after twenty-four years in the post, initiated a regeneration of the cathedral's music through the building of a new organ which would be (and remains) one of the finest in the city and through the development of a choir of mixed voices which is now recognised as one of Ireland's leading choirs. The increasing wealth and confidence of the country and Dublin's growing popularity as a tourist destination have also played their parts in the regeneration of both the cathedral and its music in recent years, the thousands who visit Christ Church each year and attend its services contributing significantly to the maintenance of the cathedral and its many activities, not least its choir and music.

The Roe endowment and the re-establishment of the choir

Under the terms of the Irish Church Act which came into effect on 1 January 1871 the choral establishment of Christ Church as it had been since the New Foundation in 1539 and James I's charter of 1604 formally ceased to exist. The vicars choral, stipendiaries and organist were, like the clergy, guaranteed their positions and incomes as an annuity during their working lifetimes, the capital from the sale of church property (including the former vicars' estates) being vested for this purpose in the Commissioners of Church Temporalities in Ireland. The former choirmen, or annuitants, were encouraged to commute their interest for a lump sum estimated on the basis of their current income and life expectancy and this was entrusted to the Representative Church Body. The capital thus realised was invested and the annuitants' salaries paid out of the interest incurred. As the annuitants retired or died their places were filled by new appointees who would be paid directly by the cathedral. One of the more significant outcomes was that, as the annuitants (who had most often been members of both cathedral choirs) declined in number, the choirs of each cathedral came to be entirely separate, no longer sharing any of their singers as had so long been the case. While this arrangement provided in principle for the continuation of Christ Church cathedral's choral establishment along secure lines, had it not been for the generosity of Henry Roe the future of music in the cathedral might have been very different. In January 1873, in addition to his funding of the restoration of the cathedral buildings, and out of concern that its services should match the splendour of the new building when it reopened, Roe further endowed £20,000 to be added to the fund held by the Representative Church Body out of which the annuities to the organist, vicars and choirmen were paid, provided that the balance of that fund remained at or in excess of £20,000. At least £40,000, to be known as the Endowment Fund, was thus available for the provision of choral worship, the terms of which included the choral celebration of morning and evening prayer every Sunday and weekday in the year, of holy communion every Sunday and on Christmas and Ascension days, and the establishment of the choir of twelve choirmen and at least twelve choirboys, in addition to the organist (in 1885 a reduction to ten choirmen was permitted due to the difficulties in finding twelve 'efficient' choirmen, but at one stage in the same year the number grew to fifteen).[3] The full choir was to attend all services on Sundays, Christmas Day, Good Friday and the greater holy days, with a lesser number on weekdays (typically six choirmen, or half that number during July and August)[4] and the organist or his deputy was to be present every day. The fund also provided for the salaries of sub-dean (a post which was not retained), precentor and three residentiary canons, the latter of whom oversaw the education of the choirboys and looked after the cathedral library and music library. Fulfilment of the terms of the endowment were to be certified each year by the archbishop. Bearing in mind the threat as recently as 1868 to reduce Christ Church to the status of a parish church, Roe's principal of £20,000 was to revert to him and his successors should Christ Church cease to be a cathedral church. Roe's endowment ensured a greater frequency of choral services, twice daily every day of the year, than the cathedral had enjoyed for certainly more than a century. As the twentieth century progressed, however, the diminishing real value of the endowment would prove insufficient to maintain services as originally intended, but without it the severe difficulties which the cathedral was to experience would unquestionably have arisen even earlier on, to the extent that recovery might not have been possible.

The re-opening of the cathedral on 1 May 1878 following its restoration was marked by an impressive service which started with a procession of about four hundred clergy with the choir singing Child's anthem *Praise the Lord, O my soul*. Robert Prescott Stewart's *Te Deum* and *Jubilate* in E flat for double choir and his setting of the communion service were sung, the anthem being Boyce's *I have surely built thee an house*. The service ended with Benjamin Rogers' recessional anthem *Behold now, praise the Lord*. The elaborate nature and high standard of the choral music was described as

> a subject of astonishment to strangers, who were ignorant of the high level attained in the Dublin cathedrals, while even those who were familiar with the excellence of the cathedral services acknowledged that their execution . . . surpassed anything they had ever heard.[5]

While the choir was re-established at full strength, including four supplementary choir members being appointed to sing services on Sunday afternoons and weekdays for which Henry Roe provided £250 a year during his life,[6] the increase in choral services led to problems with the annuitants who challenged the authority of the dean and chapter to require them to attend services other than had been their duty prior to Disestablishment. Legal advice was sought and rules for their attendance were drawn up, but offence had been taken on both sides and disagreement rumbled on. In 1882 legal opinion eventually ruled that the dean and chapter could not successfully take any action provided the annuitants performed their duties 'reasonably well'.[7] But these difficulties were resolved by

---

3   *Christ Church Cathedral Endowment* (Dublin 1885), p. 13; C6/1/13/1, p. 407.
4   C6/1/22/2.
5   Vignoles, *Memoir*, p. 124.
6   C6/1/13/1, p. 104.
7   C6/1/7/13, pp. 396, 406–7, 410, 413, 424, 430, 434, 441; C61/7/14; pp. 38–44, 47–50, 55–8.

time as the former vicars choral and stipendiaries retired or died. A contributory superannuation fund for non-annuitant choirmen was established in 1889, the fund being substantially increased in 1903 by the Winstanley bequest.[8]

Declining resources

By the 1890s provision from the Roe endowment for the income of choir members was already beginning to decline in real terms. Citing the extent of their duties, the cost of living and comparison with English cathedrals, the choirmen in 1891 sought a pay increase with a return from the current system of 'payment by service' to a regular salary. The board found that the salaries of Christ Church singers were in fact higher than the English average, although modifications were made in the numbers of days off allowed in the year.[9] Further requests for salary increases in 1898 and 1900 which the board felt unable to meet mark the beginning of what was to become a regular pattern which only deteriorated as the new century progressed.[10] In 1902, however, it was agreed to allow the choirmen one day off in the week and from then Monday matins and evensong were sung by the boys.[11] In 1905 a reduction in the number of supernumerary choirmen or their salaries was proposed, but such moves threatened the terms of the endowment and required recourse to legal opinion.[12] One acceptable way of reducing costs was to celebrate weekday services with either choirmen or choirboys but not both, but the cathedral was otherwise legally bound to pay the full quota of choirmen and maintain choral services twice every day. The cessation of the last annuities paid under the Irish Church Act released additional capital for the running of the cathedral which provided some relief from 1909, but the cathedral board was reminded by the Representative Church Body that, lacking any wealthy supporters, it was entirely dependant on its own resources which were described as adequate if 'prudently and energetically fostered'.[13]

Although salary increases had in the meantime again been refused, bonuses to each choirman were paid on occasion between 1916 and 1919 and the board recognised the choirmen's need to supplement their earnings outside the cathedral. The appointment of a competent deputy was agreed to in 1919 should any lay clerk have a definite offer of employment which would interfere with his weekday morning duties in the cathedral, but a request to abandon choral weekday matins could not be granted.[14] A similar request by the lay vicars four years later was referred to the archbishop who now saw no problem under the terms of the endowment, weekday matins thenceforth being sung by the choristers alone with the organist.[15] A choir fund established in 1932 provided additional small-scale

8   *Ibid.*, p. 504; C6/1/13/2, pp. 64, 72, 75–6.
9   C6/1/13/1, pp. 525, 527.
10 C6/1/13/2, pp. 25, 36.
11 *Ibid.*, p. 46.
12 *Ibid.*, pp. 93, 94, 104f.
13 *Ibid.*, p. 155.
14 *Ibid.*, p. 244.
15 *Ibid.*, pp. 280, 281; C6/1/22/5.

funding for the choir beyond what was available from the endowment and the superannuation funds.[16] The superannuation scheme was however insufficient to encourage retirement of older singers: in 1942 John Horan, then approaching fifty-nine years as a member of the cathedral choir, wished to resign but relied on his lay vicar's income. In view of his exceptional service the board agreed to supplement his superannuation to ensure him a pension equivalent to his former salary (in gratitude Horan was subsequently to bequeath £250 to the choir super-annuation fund).[17] With the value of their salaries continuing to fall in the late 1940s the choirmen unsuccessfully questioned the use of income from the Winstanley trust to provide pocket money for the choirboys rather than for their own benefit, manifested their lack of morale through poor attendance and, with the support of the precentor, by making repeated but unsuccessful attempts to be exempted from attendance at Saturday evensong or, failing that, for only three lay vicars to be required for that service.[18] In an increasingly tight financial climate the board had to choose between the legal terms of the Roe endowment which provided for most of what little was available for maintaining the choir and its music, their desire to preserve what they could of choral services, and the real needs of the choir members. One solution agreed on was not to replace the two alto lay vicars when their places became vacant but to use boys to sing their parts or make use of the part-time members of the Sunday choir.[19] In 1951 the attendance of only three lay vicars at Saturday evensong (which had in fact been the practice for two years) was approved, together with small increases in choir pay.[20]

By the mid-1950s the regular weekday choral services comprised matins sung daily by the choirboys and evensong sung on Mondays by the boys, on Tuesdays, Thursdays and Fridays by the boys with six gentlemen (on Friday there was no organ), and on Wednesdays by the gentlemen only.[21] The fundamental problem for the choir was that it was becoming more and more difficult to attract new singers as salaries became less attractive and weekday evensong at 3pm conflicted with most jobs outside the cathedral. The position was exacerbated by comparison with St Patrick's (with which the choir and organist at this time had little or no contact) which was wealthy enough to attract singers from English cathedrals while at Christ Church most of the singers struggled to hold other jobs, in some cases putting in deputies on weekdays as a matter of course. Choir members not infrequently resigned in favour of better-paid positions at St Patrick's, but a suggestion made in 1954 that the choirs of both cathedrals might be amalgamated fell on deaf ears.[22] The repeatedly unsuccessful attempts to fill vacancies in the choir during 1957, especially that of an alto lay vicar, prompted the organist Arnold McKiernan to propose a committee to consider these difficul-ties. Recommendations that Friday evensong be sung by the boys only and that

16   C6/1/13/2, pp. 336, 337.
17   *Ibid.*, 29 Jan. 1943, 28 Apr. 1950; see also *ibid.*, p. 345.
18   *Ibid.*, 19 Dec. 1947; 30 Apr., 24 Sept., 29 Oct. 1948; 25 Feb., 27 May, 30 Sept. 1949; 24 Feb. 1950.
19   *Ibid.*, 30 Sept. 1949.
20   *Ibid.*, 30 Sept. 1949, 1950; C6/1/13/3, pp. 5, 7, 9, 11; C6/1/22/8, *passim.*
21   C6/1/13/3, p. 46.
22   *Ibid.*, p. 31.

evensong be changed from 3pm to 5.30pm on Wednesdays and Thursdays when the men sang were tried out during May and June and became permanent thereafter until 1963 when evensong was changed to 6pm, initially to allow more time for the choristers' schooling, and Saturday evensong abandoned.[23]

Choirboys and the closure of the choir school

If the problems for the choirmen became increasingly difficult, those of the boys and their schooling proved in the long run to be terminal, despite a growth in the numbers attending the school up to the early 1960s. Difficulties arising out of the cathedral's declining finances were compounded by social and educational developments demanding more fundamental change and investment in the school which the cathedral was simply unable to afford. During the closure of the cathedral for rebuilding between 1872 and 1878 the choirboys had continued to be provided with an education, the governors of the Erasmus Smith schools agreeing to accept six choristers free at their Brunswick Street school, the other six becoming paying pupils at the Harcourt Street school (the High School).[24] In the light of the Roe endowment new parameters were drawn up in 1873 for the master of the choristers and for the cathedral school which now came to be known as the 'cathedral grammar school'.[25] All current choristers were to be examined and replaced if unsuitable. New choirboys, to be selected by competition 'with due regard to the social position of parents or relations before being admitted', were to be divided into six 'stipendiaries' each receiving between £5 and £15 a year based on merit regardless of seniority, six 'probationers', and additional good singers as available referred to as 'supernumeraries'. They would attend daily from 9am to 4pm, the school day consisting of two hours of musical instruction followed by matins at 11am, and three hours of general education followed by evensong at 3pm, in addition to their singing at both Sunday services. Later in 1878 it was decided to adjust the service times so that the boys, who had no playground, would be kept occupied during their time at the cathedral, and by 1882 a gymnasium had been provided. Schooling on Saturdays was discontinued in 1885.[26] The 'master of the choristers', a position now linked to that of assistant organist, was to teach vocal and instrumental music including organ and at least two pupils would be articled to him to play the organ on weekdays in his absence. The overall number of boys in the choir would vary over the years according to how many supernumeraries were available: at the re-opening of the cathedral in 1878 there were fifteen, dropping to thirteen by the end of 1879, but the number would rise to sixteen in the mid 1880s.[27]

Until the end of the nineteenth century the average number of pupils in the school seldom exceeded twenty. They were divided into three classes (all of which were taught by one teacher in one room), the emphasis in the lowest class

---

[23] *Ibid.*, pp. 73, 74, 75, 77, 78, 114, 115.
[24] C6/1/7/13, p. 324.
[25] C6/1/13/1, pp. 20–3.
[26] *Ibid.*, pp. 296–7, 399.
[27] C6/1/23/8, *passim*; C6/1/13/1, p. 407.

(third) being on tables and English, though Latin, French, and English history were also taught. The boys in the first class (seniors) also learnt algebra, geometry, Irish history and German.[28] The small size of the school was beginning to be recognised as a limiting factor both in the boys' education and in attracting new choristers to the cathedral since with its larger grammar school St Patrick's cathedral remained likely to attract the best potential choristers and pupils. Although a proposed merger with the Merchant Tailors' School came to nothing, the decision in principle in 1879 to take in private, fee-paying pupils would lay the grounds for a gradual development of the school.[29] In 1898 the dean and chapter decided to hold an enquiry with the view of improving the running of the school, but no less than three changes of headmaster over a period of six years between 1903 and 1909 reflect the difficulties which they continued to experience.[30] There were now two teachers (and a part-time teacher for what were known as 'commercial' classes) and about forty or so pupils including both choirboys and fee-paying pupils up to 1936 when the appointment of Revd Robert J. Ross, who had been assistant organist prior to his ordination in 1934 and was committed to the cathedral and its music, ushered in a period of growth and development.[31] The school had moved in the 1920s to the adjacent Fishamble Street Mission building but by 1938 this was deemed unsafe and the school was transferred to the upper floor of the chapter house where it would remain until its closure in 1972. Recognition in 1939 from the department of education as a secondary school (teaching up to Intermediate Certificate) suggests an improvement in standards and made the school eligible for capitation grants, and by 1946 applicants were being turned away.[32] A number of scholarships were available to the choristers.[33] From 1949 ten non-chorister pupils paying a fee of 4 guineas per term were admitted but, while these fees from non-choristers were essential for the running of the school, the board was unwilling to charge the twelve choristers since the provision of free education provided an important incentive for attracting suitable candidates. A voluntary contribution by parents was however agreed in 1950.[34]

Numbers increased during the 1950s, reaching fifty-seven in 1959, and the syllabus was expanded to include science and French (experimental science was introduced in 1964 when Guinness & Co. presented laboratory equipment), Greek having been dropped in favour of drawing and commerce in 1951.[35] However, by 1963 the future of the school was increasingly being questioned. Rumours of closure led to two pupils being withdrawn, fees had to be raised and a number of meetings were held to discuss possible options but, although the possibility of closure was aired, the school was to continue for the time being.[36] It was

28 C6/1/25/1–3.
29 C6/1/13/1, pp. 120, 171; C6/1/7/14, pp. 71–2.
30 C6/1/7/14, p. 227; C6/1/13/2, pp. 97, 122, 153.
31 C6/1/13/2, p. 357.
32 Ibid., pp. 411, 424; 27 Sept. 1946.
33 The Winstanley scholarship (1901), the Ross Browne (1930) and the Dungan (1938). The Zerubbabel medal for proficiency in scripture was instituted in 1938 (C6/5/4/1; C6/1/13/2, pp. 378, 399).
34 C6/1/13/2, 30 Sept. 1949; 24 Nov. 1950.
35 C6/1/13/3, pp. 6, 123, 124.
36 Ibid., pp. 114, 115, 116, 117, 118.

soon realised that the closure of the junior school (for boys aged under eleven) in the summer of 1963 inevitably cut off the supply of potential choristers so it was reopened the following January.[37] A proposed merger with St Patrick's grammar school was rejected in 1970 and in December 1971, by which time numbers in the school had shrunk to twenty-eight with no more boys being available for the choir by 1973, the board recommended that the school be closed as from September 1972.[38] And so the cathedral choir school, which had existed effectively since 1480, ceased to exist. An arrangement was made for the cathedral's choristers to be educated at St Patrick's but to receive their musical training at Christ Church. Despite the provision under this scheme of free schooling, quarterly payments, and free organ tuition for selected pupils, the numbers of choirboys continued to drop. Advertisements failed to attract sufficient (or at times even any) applicants, the commitment to weekend services, the general availability of free secondary education which had been introduced by the government in 1967, and the feeling by parents that if their boys were attending St Patrick's school they might just as well sing in St Patrick's choir, all combining to remove motivation for joining what must have been only too evidently a choir in sharp decline.[39] By 1975 the number of boys was too small to sing the choral services adequately and the resulting lack of musical interest was causing the choirmen to leave, four in as many weeks. It could be argued that the cathedral choir, in the traditional sense, was in terminal decline. The decision, radical at the time, was taken to introduce younger female singers, the first two girls joining in October 1975 although attempts to attract boys continued until 1977.[40] As the number of boys declined weekday choral matins was discontinued in 1976, choral evensong having dropped to two days in the week the previous year.[41] By 1980 when Peter Sweeney was appointed organist and director of music there was only one boy left in the choir, and from March 1981 weekday choral evensong was only celebrated on Thursdays.

Organs and organists

Telford had won the contract in 1875 to re-erect the organ using a new case designed by Street to suit the new building, the cost once more being met by Henry Roe. He also added a fourth (solo) manual as well as dulciana and cornetto di basso stops, thus completing the work which had been interrupted by the rebuilding of the cathedral.[42] The organ was situated on a gallery in the north transept, a position which was acoustically and visually poor: for the next hundred years (until it was replaced in 1984), the choir was overwhelmed when the full organ was playing while the congregation at the west end could hardly hear the instrument. Furthermore, the organist was out of sight of the choir. The eminent

---

[37] *Ibid.*, pp. 117, 118, 120.
[38] *Ibid.*, pp. 174, 176, 177, 191, 194.
[39] *Ibid.*, pp. 201, 226, 233, 239.
[40] *Ibid.*, pp. 246, 275, 284, 287.
[41] *Ibid.*, pp. 260, 273.
[42] C6/1/13/1, pp. 58, 60, 74, 82, 90.

English organist and composer Henry Smart was asked to report on the rebuilt instrument. Smart's report was mixed: he agreed that Telford had fulfilled the terms of his contract but considered that, despite many good points, the organ was 'not on the whole a first-class or even very good instrument' and that it was unworthy as an organ for the newly rebuilt cathedral. The main problems lay in its being the result of three periods of construction: the original instrument of 1857 whose character was considered dated by the late 1870s, the additions made in 1870, and the more recent work including the new solo organ.[43] Telford responded by offering to add a new diapason at his own expense if the board paid for other additional stops to remedy Smart's criticisms, but the board declined to spend any more money on the instrument.[44]

Robert Prescott Stewart was an unrelenting critic of Telford's organ which he described in 1881 as a 'saw-sharpener' which would 'stagger at every full chord . . . for lack of wind' and which he detested 'daily more and more'.[45] He urged both board and chapter to replace the organ, but the financial implications meant that his suggestion was ignored.[46] Instead, estimates for less expensive alterations were discussed, Telford carrying out some work on the pedals in 1883. While a proposal for a new organ was agreed to in principle, this was not considered practicable.[47] Eventually, after much further debate, some money was raised but Telford's plan to lower the organ gallery in the north transept in an attempt to improve the sound was not approved by the Representative Church Body and the money was put towards an earlier contract agreed with Telford which included provision of hydraulic power for the blower.[48] Stewart reported his approval of these improvements in January 1888.[49] Apart from minor alterations and repairs there were no significant complaints by Stewart's successors John Horan and James Fitzgerald, who formally succeeded as organist in 1907, a role he had been filling for some years after Horan's final years were clouded by mental illness.

Following his appointment as organist in 1913 Charles Kitson reactivated moves for a new organ, an appeal was launched and an estimate agreed with Harrison and Harrison of Durham in 1916.[50] The changed circumstances of the war prevented the carrying out of the work, however, and when Thomas Weaving became organist in 1920 £450 of the £500 deposit paid to Harrisons was retrieved and Telford was asked to rebuild the organ using all existing pipes since 'we cannot get anything as good for £5000 to £8000 now'.[51] At a cost of £1635 trumpet and Zauberflöte stops were added to the great organ, with a tremulant to the swell, the action was made entirely pneumatic, an electric blower installed,

[43] Smart, *Report*.
[44] C6/1/13/1, p. 140.
[45] Letter to Canon Seymour, 26 Sept. 1881, quoted in Vignoles, *Memoir*, p. 130.
[46] C6/1/13/1, p. 280; C6/1/7/14, p. 16.
[47] C6/1/13/1, pp. 312–13, 315, 317, 318, 334, 344, 385; C6/1/7/14, pp. 85–6.
[48] C6/1/13/1, pp. 402, 439, 440–1, 442, 456.
[49] *Ibid.*, p. 468.
[50] C6/1/13/2, pp. 194, 197, 198, 218. Charles Kitson was professor of music at University College Dublin from 1915 to 1920 when he returned to England to join the staff of the Royal College of Music. In the same year he was also appointed professor of music at Trinity College Dublin, a position which did not at that time require residency.
[51] *Ibid.*, pp. 260, 262, 267, 268.

the whole instrument thoroughly cleaned and retuned, the choir organ transferred from behind the player and incorporated into the main case, and the console set at right angles so that the organist could better see and hear the choir. The rebuilt organ was formally opened at a service on 22 March 1923 followed by a recital by Thomas Weaving who expressed satisfaction with the rebuilt instrument.[52]

Telford's rebuilt 1857 organ with its later additions continued in service until renovation began to be discussed again in the early 1950s. Lack of funds prevented any progress until 1956 when the organ of the church of St Mathias in Adelaide Road, which was to be demolished, was offered to Christ Church provided they organised and paid for its removal.[53] Once safely stored in the cathedral attention turned to how best to incorporate the St Mathias organ into the existing instrument. The decision was made to raise the estimated £5000 that would be needed for a first-class rebuild before making further plans but it was 1960, by which time the organ fund was approaching £2500, before a contract costing nearly £6000 was agreed with the London organ builders Willis & Co.[54] The rebuilt organ was dedicated on 26 October 1961 with a recital by John Dykes Bower, organist of St Paul's cathedral, and the outstanding balance of £3000 was eventually to be cleared in 1965.[55]

In addition to the main organ there were a number of smaller organs in the cathedral: the purchase for the choir school of an organ belonging to the late Dr Morgan was discussed in 1876, this possibly being the instrument presented by Henry Roe in 1879 which, doubtless due to the heavy use it received, needed frequent repair for which the choirboys were on one occasion given permission to hold concerts to raise funds.[56] A small organ was presented by Mrs Ellis and Precentor Hogan in 1916 which may be the same as the small chancel organ by Telford used during the eight months while the cathedral organ was being rebuilt in 1922–3 and which Telford repaired the following year.[57] The sale of 'the small organ in the south transept' to the Royal Irish Academy of Music was agreed in 1948. The organ presented in 1916 was advertised for sale in 1955 but there is no reference to its having been sold, suggesting that this is the single-manual Telford organ now in the south transept.[58]

On his appointment as organist in 1980 it was Peter Sweeney's conviction that the replacement of the old organ, by this stage only partially usable, would act as the catalyst for transforming the cathedral into a recognised centre of music, attracting good singers for the choir, and redefining the public's perception of cathedral music. The board responded positively and a new organ by Kenneth Jones was opened in 1984 with a recital by the Japanese organist Kei Koito as part of the (now triennial) Dublin International Organ and Choral Festival for which Christ Church, now with the finest organ in Dublin, became the centre. The new organ was situated no longer in the north transept but free-standing below the

52 Programme and service sheet, 22 Mar. 1923, C6/4/2/8; C6/1/13/2, p. 281.
53 C6/1/13/3, pp. 4, 21, 22, 56, 57.
54 *Ibid.*, p. 68.
55 *Ibid.*, pp. 68, 97, 108, 136.
56 C6/1/13/1, p. 72; C6/1/7/13, p. 410; C6/1/7/14, p. 44.
57 C6/1/13/2, p. 287. See also C6/4/2/8.
58 *Ibid.*, 27 Feb. 1948, 25 Mar., 27 May, 24 June 1955; C6/1/13/3, pp. 43, 45, 46.

north arch of the crossing, immediately behind and above the *cantoris* side of the choir. Suitable to accompany a much wider choral repertoire than the old instrument and situated closer to the choir with the organist in visual contact, the new organ undoubtedly played a major role in reanimating the choir and contributing to the subsequent renaissance of music at Christ Church. A Guinness organ scholarship was established in 1995 which not only provides valuable experience for younger organists but also helps in spreading the burden of the assistant organist's duties as the number of choral services has increased.

The late nineteenth-century repertoire

Edward Seymour, appointed precentor in 1876, had previously demonstrated his interest in and support for the musical tradition of the cathedral.[59] He is credited with first introducing choral communion into the Irish church and was largely responsible for the first Irish church hymnal tune book.[60] By 1880 however the dean and chapter were accusing him of poor attendance and of having neglected his duties, to which Seymour responded by publishing a booklet containing letters solicited from leading churchmen, musicians and others praising the high standard of music and including a list of anthems and services sung on Sundays and festivals during that period.[61] While negative remarks would not be expected in such public testimonials, those of respected musicians including Robert Prescott Stewart (a close friend of Seymour), Joseph Robinson and John Stanford (father of the composer Charles Villiers Stanford) are uniformly positive and speak in particular of the high quality of the boys. Despite his high praise in 1880 Stewart described the choirboys in 1885 as 'not generally good' and in 1890 he wrote that they had 'squalling bad voices' and that 'the slow tempi spoil the whole service'.[62]

Seymour's list of anthems sung since 1878 is revealing: out of 236 performances of eighty anthems by thirty composers there were only four of music from before 1660 (one anthem by Farrant and one by Gibbons, each sung twice), composers of the later seventeenth and eighteenth centuries (up to c.1775) accounting for 68 per cent of the music sung. The single most popular composer was Stevenson with six anthems sung a total of forty times. In marked contrast with the mid-nineteenth century, however, contemporary composers were beginning to make a significant impact on the repertoire. Compared with Finlayson's list of anthems in the repertoire of the Dublin cathedrals in 1852 in which there were only four living composers out of fifty-four names, six out of the thirty composers listed by Seymour were contemporary. The most frequently heard of these were John Goss (two anthems performed nine times, making him the eighth most popular composer overall), Robert Prescott Stewart (two anthems heard five

---

59 Seymour, *Christ Church*, especially pp. 71, 83; Seymour, *Cathedral System*, pp. 21–2.
60 Vignoles, *Stewart*, p. 190.
61 C6/1/7/13, pp. 443, 445–6, 447, 449; Seymour, *Choral Services*. Although Seymour's booklet appears to have silenced his critics, he resigned as precentor three years later (C6/1/7/14, pp. 60–1).
62 Letters to Seymour quoted after Vignoles, *Memoir*, pp. 132, 190.

times), John Horan (two anthems heard three times), and Arthur Sullivan (one anthem heard three times).[63] The most popular service settings in 1878–80 were Stewart in G (thirty performances) followed by Aldrich in G (twenty-nine) which had topped the list in 1849–50. Gibbons in F (fourteen performances) and Tallis's Dorian (ten) were the only services by Tudor and Stuart composers sung in 1878–80 although Farrant, Tallis, Byrd and Gibbons (in that order, with fifteen performances of Farrant) had all featured in 1848–50.

While maintaining an emphasis on the core repertoire of the late seventeenth and earlier eighteenth centuries, this growing inclusion of anthems by contemporary or recent composers is also reflected in a book of anthem texts sung at the Dublin cathedrals and published in 1880, which includes a total of 793 anthems by 167 composers.[64] Mendelssohn (with forty-five) is the only nineteenth-century composer amongst the top five, the others being, as ever, Greene (forty-seven), Croft, Handel and Boyce. Thereafter, however, more recent or living composers are well represented: Goss is the sixth most-represented composer with twenty-two anthems, Ouseley with sixteen shares twelfth place with Alcock, Blow and Purcell, while Gounod (thirteen), Elvey (twelve), Barnby and Sullivan (eleven each) and Stainer are amongst the twenty-two composers represented by ten or more anthems. Other prominent nineteenth-century composers represented by five or more anthems include Vincent Novello, R.P. Stewart, Sterndale Bennett, S.S. Wesley, Thomas Walmisley, John Bridge and Michael Costa.[65] No less than 94 of the 167 composers in this 1880 collection are only represented by one or two anthems. This large group reflects the wide availability from the second half of the nineteenth century of cheap octavo editions of anthems composed by often minor composers and published by Novello and others: nearly half of this group (forty-one) are contemporary or had only died within the previous decade. Alongside many others who are now forgotten, we find the first recorded appearance in the Christ Church repertoire of Charles Villiers Stanford (his anthem *God is our hope and strength*). In addition to R.P. Stewart noted above, Joseph Robinson (with four anthems) and John Horan (with three anthems) are amongst the more prominent contemporary musicians associated with Christ Church.[66] In contrast to this growing proportion of contemporary music in the repertoire, Tudor and Stuart composers are, overall, poorly represented. Gibbons has seven anthems, Tallis six, Farrant and Batten five, and about eight others are each represented by between one and four anthems (in the case of Byrd), these composers only accounting for between 4 and 5 per cent of the total.

A revised edition of the 1880 anthem word book, retaining the contents of the earlier volume but with 131 new anthems added in an appendix, was published in

[63] Goss, *Praise the Lord O my soul*, *The wilderness*; Stewart, *In the Lord I put my trust*, *Plead thou my cause*; Horan (then assistant organist), *And it shall come to pass*, *Ponder my words*; Sullivan, *Sing O Heavens*. Elvey's *In that day* and Smart's *O be joyful* were each heard once.

[64] *Cathedral Anthems* (1880).

[65] George Allen, a member of Armagh cathedral choir 1843–62, has seven anthems and John Smith (d.1861) of Christ Church has five.

[66] Horan composed seven anthems (two for eight voices) and two services which were in the repertoire of Christ Church (see also *Cathedral Anthems* (1895) and bound choir book Volume 'D' in the cathedral archive); Gillen & Johnstone, *Anthology*, p. 25 cite six anthems by Horan.

1895.[67] Forty of the composers included in the 1880 edition have benefitted from the inclusion of additional anthems, most notably Stainer with an additional nine, Barnby with seven and John Horan with five. Only fourteen of these forty composers are not contemporary or relatively recently deceased, these fourteen including Mozart, J.S. Bach and Schubert alongside additional composers representative of the more traditional cathedral repertoire (no additional anthems by Stanford are included). George Clement Martin, with six anthems, tops the list of composers represented for the first time, followed by the English-born organist and composer James Culwick who had moved to Dublin in 1866 and was amongst the foremost musicians in Dublin at the time. As in 1880, most of the names appearing for the first time, however, are only represented by a single anthem and are for the most part forgotten names, although Fauré and Ebenezer Prout, appointed professor of music at Trinity College Dublin in 1894, are present.

The growing interest in contemporary or recent composers revealed in the above lists of anthems is also reflected in the multiple volumes now in the cathedral archives which comprise the regular repertoire used by the choir in the late nineteenth and early twentieth centuries. These volumes consist of individual services and anthems published by Novello's, Cramer and others which were bound together with a dated titlepage (which only survives in isolated volumes) and which, as indicated by the presence of signatures of certain of the cathedral's organists and choirmen, continued in use in at least some cases into the later twentieth century. The earliest of these, a collection of services dated 1886, includes one service each by seventeen composers of whom only three (Boyce, Arnold and Attwood) are not contemporary or recently deceased (these include Parry in D, Stainer in A, Stanford in B flat and Culwick's morning service in D).[68] The next dated volume was assembled in 1895 and contains services by nineteen composers, all contemporary (including Stanford in F).[69] Subsequent volumes of this type, each containing both services and anthems and assembled in 1903, 1906 and 1910 respectively, do however reflect a broader range of repertoire from the sixteenth century through to contemporary composers.[70]

With the exception of occasional service sheets which survive for special occasions, music listings for regular services do not survive before autumn 1915, after which a more or less complete run of printed service lists exists. The repertoire at this period very much reflects the contents of the music books described above, with nineteenth-century composers predominating, but also with occasional anthems and services by musicians attached to the cathedral including Charles Kitson, who had been appointed organist in 1913. In the light of the increasing retrenchment and difficulties experienced not only by the choir but by the cathedral as a whole during the mid-twentieth century, it is perhaps not surprising to

---

[67] *Cathedral Anthems* (1895).

[68] Volumes 'C' in the cathedral archive.

[69] Volumes 'D' in the cathedral archive.

[70] Volume 'A', 'B' and 'E' in the cathedral archive. The inclusion of Bateson's *Holy Lord God Almighty* in Volume 'A' marks the revival of this anthem for the first time in the cathedral repertoire since the seventeenth century.

find that the repertoire had changed little if at all by the 1950s: it would only be in the later part of the twentieth century that Barnby, Harwood, Stainer and the other Victorian composers who had so dominated the repertoire would go out of favour.[71]

During the rebuilding of the cathedral its books and music had been stored in Marsh's library but in 1904 James Fitzgerald, the assistant organist, drew attention to the need for suitable presses for the music.[72] Costings and proposals were to be drawn up but in 1906 temporary arrangements had to be made for the collection of Boyce's *Cathedral Music* which was stored on chairs in the transept and three volumes of which had been lost.[73] Further presses were purchased in 1949 when the music was also catalogued and partially rebound.[74] Attention was focused on the music collection in 1954 when Nigel Fortune enquired about an anthem thought at the time to be by Purcell, the only known copy of which lay in the cathedral library.[75] The value of the cathedral's collection of manuscript choir books was beginning to be recognised in 1957 when a strong leather-covered chest was purchased for the collection to be stored in within the strong room.[76]

With income from the collection plates contributing to an ever more significant proportion of the cathedral's finances, the role of music in attracting congregations became more important, an increasing emphasis on more recent music being blamed in 1909 for a decrease in the numbers attending the cathedral.[77] Almost fifty years later, by which time the choir was run on a shoe-string, the dean suggested that there was too much repetition of repertoire and insufficient practice.[78] The responsibility for selecting the music had passed in 1946 from the precentor to the organist, since 1913 officially designated 'organist and choirmaster, and instructor of the choristers in music'.[79] Undoubtedly, musical standards had sunk very low in the course of the century. As well as conducting musical societies in Dublin, in order to earn an adequate living Thomas Weaving, who was organist in the 1940s, was also on the staff of the Royal Irish Academy of Music and examined for the department of education, entailing prolonged absences including Sundays. The music was left largely in the hands of the assistant organist Edgar (Billy) Boucher who was only being paid for teaching the junior boys twice a week, playing two afternoon services, and taking over during the organist's annual four weeks leave. Dr Boucher recalled that

> Given that [Mr Weaving] was trying to do two jobs which were incompatible, and that the Board were trying the impossible – running the school and daily

[71] Cf. below, p. 186.
[72] C6/1/13/1, pp. 61, 62–3; C6/1/13/2, p. 78.
[73] C6/1/13/2, pp. 107–8, 109.
[74] *Ibid.*, 25 Feb. 1949.
[75] C6/1/13/3, pp. 38, 39, 40. The anthem *Christ is risen* was subsequently found not to be by Purcell; however, ironically, incomplete parts of another previously unidentified anthem by Purcell, *Praise the Lord ye servants*, have since been found in the libraries of St Patrick's and Christ Church cathedrals. See Houston, 'Music Manuscripts'.
[76] C6/1/13/3, p. 69.
[77] C6/1/13/2, pp. 157, 158, 161–2, 163.
[78] C6/1/13/3, pp. 44, 45.
[79] C6/1/13/2, p. 187, 26 July 1946.

services with insufficient money, with male singers not all of top class, with a loud but poor organ – it was inevitable that the standard was low.[80]

If anything, standards were to decline even further during the following decades. Around 1960, one former lay vicar recalls, musical standards were 'pretty awful', choir morale was low, there was a feeling that the dean had no time for music, and the choir sometimes even found themselves on their own at Thursday evensong with no clerics present, having to read the prayers and conduct the service themselves. The musical repertoire was bound by tradition, certain anthems and services of little musical value being repeated 'because they had always been done'.[81] The use of the cathedral for a series of organ recitals given by Fred Tulan (USA), Nicolas Kynaston (Westminster cathedral), Kamiel D'Hooghe (Bruges) and Gerard Gillen (Dublin) in 1965 and the affiliation in the same year of the choir to the Royal School of Church Music suggest the beginnings of a more positive outlook for the cathedral and its music, an outlook encouraged by the use of the cathedral as a venue for a number of very successful performances by outside musicians.[82] But with low standards, the decreasing numbers of boys, the demise of the choir school and considerable resentment amongst some of the older choirmen towards the introduction of women to the choir after 1975 choir morale remained low and it would be the 1980s before a significant turnaround would take place towards the flourishing musical life that has distinguished Christ Church cathedral since the final years of the twentieth century.

The phoenix rises

By 1980 there was only one boy left in the choir. As older lay vicars resigned or retired, the choir had gradually been re-formed as a mixed chamber choir, independent of the traditional structures which were considered inappropriate to the new choir as a mixed ensemble. The growing acceptance of female choristers and the introduction of new, younger singers contributed to a significant rise in musical standards. Peter Sweeney resigned as organist and choir master in 1991 being succeeded by Mark Duley in 1992, and the 1990s witnessing a further dynamic expansion in the choir, most notably in the founding in 1995 of a girl's choir who sing evensong on Wednesdays. With three weekday choral evensongs in addition to the two sung services on Sundays, the number of choral services in the cathedral is greater than had been the case since 1976 when sung matins was abandoned and choral evensong reduced to twice, subsequently once a week. The choir made its first tour to England in 1993, including short residencies at Westminster abbey and Canterbury cathedral, the first time it had sung outside Ireland. Week-long residencies at English cathedrals have since become a regular part of

[80] Private communication, 28 June 1998.
[81] Information from George Bannister, tenor lay clerk, 1958–63.
[82] C6/1/13/3, pp. 135, 137; notable performances at this time included Monteverdi's *L'Orfeo* and John Blow's *Venus and Adonis* directed by Eric Sweeney in 1974 and 1975, and concerts of medieval and renaissance music by the Consort of St Sepulchre in 1976.

the choir's activities, with tours to France (1998), New Zealand (1999) and Croatia (2002) amongst more recent foreign visits. The choir's repertoire, which includes recent commissions from Irish composers, is now the largest of any cathedral in the country and it broadcasts regularly and has made a number of commercial recordings. Mark Daley resigned as organist and choirmaster in February 2003. His successor, Judy Martin, is thought to be the first woman to be appointed to such a position in an English or Irish Anglican cathedral. Christ Church cathedral's reputation as a centre for musical excellence has been further enhanced by its continuing use as the central location for the Dublin International Organ and Choral Festival and by the establishment in 1998 of Christ Church Baroque (now the Irish Baroque Orchestra), Ireland's first professional, period-instrument chamber orchestra which has given regular public concerts in the cathedral and elsewhere as well as combining with the cathedral choir both for concerts and in concerted liturgical performances.

As it approaches the celebration of the millennium of its foundation c.1030 Christ Church cathedral can look back at what is one of the longest institutional histories in Ireland. The history of music at Christ Church is likewise exceptional within the Irish context for the time span it covers, and of note within the wider context of English and Irish cathedrals for the range and extent of its documentary sources. This history has not only given emphasis to the continuing existence of a cathedral and its music after nearly a thousand years, but has also highlighted the often complex relationships between cathedral, city and state which have shaped both the cathedral's history and the conditions and nature of its music. The complex web of religion and politics which has marked so much of Irish history has played a determining role in this musical history of a cathedral, Anglican since the Reformation but which has so often occupied an ambiguous position, regarded by many in Ireland as English within the Irish context, and by the English as Irish within the Anglican context.

Appendix One

Succession Lists of Organists and Assistant Organists

An asterisk before a name indicates that that person was also organist (or assistant organist) at St Patrick's cathedral during part or all of the same period.

Organists

Robert Heyward	1546.
Walter Kennedy	1586(?); resigned 19 November 1595. Named as organist in 1586 by Finlayson (*Anthems*) whose source is not known. Otherwise first confirmed as organist and master of the boys (as distinct from just vicar choral) in 1594.
George Goshan	November 1595 to February 1596.
John Farmer	2 February (confirmed 16 February) 1596 to 1599(?).
Richard Myles(?)	Appointed master of the boys, 30 January 1600. Before 1647 the duties of organist and master of the boys were most often carried out by the one person, suggesting that Myles may also have been organist.
John Fido(?)	Appointed master of the boys, 30 May 1600 and thus likely also to have been organist.
Thomas Bateson	Appointed 5 April 1609; died March 1630.
*Randall Jewett	March 1630 to June(?) 1638. Organist at St Patrick's, 1631–43.
Benjamin Rogers	June/July 1638 (appointment confirmed 9 September 1639) to 1641(?).
*Randall Jewett(?)	July 1646(?) to 1647(?). Jewett returned to Christ Church as a vicar choral in July 1646 but is not mentioned as organist although he may have acted in that capacity. He is listed as a vicar choral at St Patrick's in January 1645 and specifically as organist in March 1650.
John Hawkshaw(?)	1646(?) to 1647(?). Cotton (*Fasti*, ii, p. 84) stated that Hawkshaw was appointed organist in 1646, but his source is not known.
*John Hawkshaw	1660(?); died before 9 January 1689. Appointed organist at St Patrick's on 24 October 1660, Hawkshaw is first cited at Christ Church in the context of organist in 1661 but his presence is recorded since November 1660.
*Thomas Godfrey	Appointed 9 January 1689, to March(?) 1689. Godfrey was paid as organist for the half year from March to Michaelmas 1689, but see next entry. Organist at St Patrick's, 1685 to 1689 (see also Thomas Finell, below).

[*]Thomas Finell	March 1689 (retrospective payment ordered on 31 October 1689) to 25 December 1690. See also below, 1691–2, 1694–9. May have been organist at St Patrick's, 1688/9–1691.
Thomas Morgan	Appointed from 25 December 1690 but by 17 February 1691 he was absent, training as an organist in England.
Thomas Finell	Re-appointed 17 February 1691 to 31 March 1692.
*Peter Isaack	Appointed 31 March 1692; died August 1694. Also organist at St Patrick's during the same period.
Thomas Finell	Re-appointed (initially on probation) on 10 October 1694 with pay retrospective from Michaelmas 1694, to November 1698 but paid to March (Lady Day) 1699.
*Daniel Roseingrave	Appointed 11 November 1698 (to receive payment from Michaelmas 1698, although the proctor's accounts only record payment from March (Lady Day) 1699); died May 1727. Organist at St Patrick's, 1698 to 1719.
*Ralph Roseingrave	Appointed 30 October 1727; died December 1747. Organist at St Patrick's, 1719–1747.
*George Walsh	Appointed 24 December 1747; died March(?) 1765. Organist at St Patrick's, 1760–5.
Richard Woodward (junior)	Appointed 7 March 1765; died 22 November 1777.
*Samuel Murphy	Appointed 29 November 1777; died 7 November 1780. Organist at St Patrick's, 1769–80.
Langrishe Doyle	Appointed 14 November 1780; duties taken from February 1813 by William Warren (assistant organist) who received equal full salary. Doyle died in 1814.
*William Warren	Succeeded in 1814 having acted as cathedral organist since 1813 (see previous entry); unsuccessful attempts in 1833 by the dean and chapter to persuade him to retire due to old age culminated in his enforced retirement on full salary on 6 November 1833; died June 1841. Served briefly as organist at St Patrick's, 1827–8.
*John Robinson	Acting organist (on his stipendiary's salary) following Warren's retirement in November 1833; continued as organist following Warren's death in June 1841; died May 1844. Organist at St Patrick's, 1830–43.
*Robert Prescott Stewart	Appointed 15 May 1844; died 31 March 1894. Organist at St Patrick's, 1852–61.
John Horan	Appointed 31 March 1894; effectively organist until January 1905 when James Fitzgerald was appointed joint organist (see below); Horan's position as organist was declared vacant 19 April 1907, his 'having become mentally incapable of fulfilling his duties with no prospect of recovery'; he died in 1908.[1]
James Fitzgerald	Appointed joint organist (with John Horan) and master of the

---

[1] The memorial to John Horan in the cathedral states that he was organist to 1906 and that he died on 31 January 1907 (cf. Shaw, *Organists*, p. 415). However the board minutes for 19 April 1907 (when Fitzgerald was named to succeed him as organist) note him as still alive (C6/1/13/2, p. 119) and his death is recorded in the board minutes of 13 Feb. 1908 (*ibid.*, p. 130). John E. West, *Cathedral Organists Past and Present*, 2nd ed. (London, 1921), p. 32 stated that he died on 1 February 1908.

	boys in January 1905; appointed organist 3 May 1907; resigned 28 March 1913.
Charles Kitson	Appointed 23 May 1913 to position now designated as 'organist and choirmaster, and instructor of the choristers in music'; resigned 23 February 1920.
Thomas Henry Weaving	Appointed 4 June 1920; resigned with effect from 31 August 1950.
Leslie Reed	Appointed 30 June 1950; resigned 24 June 1955 with effect from 30 September.
Arnold McKiernan	Appointed 16 September 1955 (approved by chapter, 30 November); resigned 31 December 1979.
Peter Sweeney	Appointed 15 January 1980; resigned December 1990.
[Trevor Crowe	Acting organist, January to December 1991.]
Mark Duley	Appointed March 1991, taking up duties in January 1992; resigned February 2003.
[Andrew Johnstone	Acting organist, February 2003.]
Judy Martin	Appointed May 2003, taking up duties in September 2003.

Assistant organists
(also referred to as 'deputy organist', 'sub-organist')

During the eighteenth century choirboys (and sometimes the organist's son or daughter) are known to have substituted for the organist on some occasions, and there are earlier references to the organist using a deputy,[2] but with rare exceptions (see Richard Galvan, below) the position of assistant organist was not formally recognised before 1805. Occasional temporary assistants and honorary appointments are not otherwise listed here.

Richard Galvan	Paid 10 May 1631 'uppon necessitie or otherwise as occasion shall serve to supplie the Organist place'.
William Warren	Appointed 25 November 1805 at request of Langrish Doyle, organist; paid same full salary as Doyle from February 1813; succeeded as organist, 1814.
*Francis Robinson	Paid as assistant organist from January 1815; following his appointment as a stipendiary choirman on 17 July 1829 he requested a substitute but continued to receive his salary as deputy organist until 29 September 1833. Organist at St Patrick's, 1828–30.
*John Robinson	Became assistant organist sometime between January 1832 and mid-1833; became acting organist following Warren's enforced retirement on 6 November 1833 (see above).
James Hill	Named as assistant organist on 2 April 1835 having probably succeeded John Robinson in November 1833.
[J. Mosse]	[Appointment to position as assistant organist recorded on 2 April 1835 but rescinded at following chapter meeting, 27 April 1835]

2 See for example Barra Boydell, ed., *Music: Documents*, pp. 62, 169.

Mattias Crowley	Paid as assistant organist from 24 June 1841 to 24 September 1842; formally resigned 26 April 1843.
Robert Prescott Stewart	Paid as assistant organist from 29 September 1842, formally appointed 26 April 1843; succeeded as organist 15 May 1844.
William Haughton	Paid as assistant organist from 14 February 1861 to early 1873 (Thomas Jozé, a senior choirboy, deputized for Haughton during his six months of illness in 1869 and was subsequently allowed to play at evening service whenever Stewart approved).
John Horan	Appointed 8 April 1873 as music master and assistant organist; succeeded as organist, 31 March 1894, after which no payments to assistant organists are recorded before October 1898 when Horan was paid an 'allowance for deputy'.
James Fitzgerald	Appointed 27 September 1901 but possibly acting since 1898 (see previous entry); promoted to joint organist, 1 January 1905.
Sterling.F. Johnstone	A supernumerary choirman, appointed 3 November 1913 following recommendation by Charles Kitson, but had received payment as assistant organist since July 1913; remained as a choirman until April 1915 but not subsequently specified as assistant organist.
Sydney Lovett	A supernumerary choirman, appointment as deputy organist noted (without date) in 1916; paid as '[holiday] deputy for organist' in September 1918 and 1919.
*Turner Huggard	Appointed 1 October 1920 following recommendation by Thomas Weaving, organist; appointed assistant organist at St Patrick's in June 1928, resigning at Christ Church 31 July 1929.
Robert J. Ross	Appointed 19 September 1929 with effect from 1 October, but had received payment as assistant organist since August 1929; resigned 26 June 1934 due to his forthcoming ordination.
William Sydney Greig	Appointed 26 June 1934; resigned 29 January 1943.
Edgar Boucher	Appointed 29 January 1943; resigned 30 May 1947.
William Watson	Appointed 1 June 1947; resigned 1955.
Julian Dawson	Appointed 27 January 1956; resigned January 1959 (resignation noted in board minutes as subsequently being withdrawn at request of dean).
Kathleen Louden	Appointed 29 September 1961 (had served on a temporary basis since the previous July); resigned December 1979.
Patrick Devine	Appointed 29 April 1980; resigned 19 March 1981. Between 1981 and 1986 the position of assistant organist was replaced by that of an organ scholar appointed annually.
Trevor Crowe	June 1986 to March 1992 (served as acting cathedral organist between the resignation of Peter Sweeney in December 1990 and the arrival of Mark Duley in January 1992).
Barbara Dagg	September 1992 to August 1995.
Andrew Johnstone	September 1995 – (served as acting cathedral organist between the resignation of Mark Daley in February 2003 and the arrival of Judy Martin in September 2003).

Appendix Two

Succession List of Masters of the Boys/ Music Masters/Choir Masters

Before 1647 the organist was most often also master of the boys: where the organist is known but without any reference to his acting as master of the boys, that name or the period of such activity is given in square brackets. After 1807 the duties of music master were separated from the overall responsibility for the boys' general education and accommodation. The duties of what was now referred to as the choirmaster were combined in 1873 with that of assistant organist and after 1894 with that of organist.

An asterisk before a name indicates that that person was also master of the boys (or music master) at St Patrick's cathedral during part or all of the same period.

Robert Heyward	1546.
Walter Kennedy	1586(?); resigned as organist 19 November 1595. See Organists in appendix one.
[George Goshan]	1595 to 1596. See Organists.
[John Farmer]	1596 to 1599(?). See Organists.
Richard Myles	Appointed master of the boys, 30 January 1600.
John Fido	Appointed master of the boys, 30 May 1600.
Thomas Bateson	Appointed 5 April 1609; died March 1630.
Randall Jewett	[March 1630 to June(?) 1638, see Organists]. Paid for teaching the boys, June 1638 to December 1639. [For 1646(?) to 1647(?) see Organists.]
*Richard Hosier	1661 (but first cited in context of master of the boys in December 1662); died 1677.
*Nicholas Sanderson	Appointed 1677; died 1698.
Robert Hodge	Appointed 11 November 1698; died 1709.
Henry Swords	Appointed 2 June 1709; Swords disappears from the records when Worrall was appointed in 1714. It is not clear what became of him.
John Worrall	Appointed 9 January 1714; resigned Michaelmas 1746.
William Lamb	Appointed 30 August 1746 to take office at Michaelmas; died September 1758.
*Samuel Murphy	Appointed 27 September 1758; resigned December 1768.
Richard Woodward (senior)	Appointed 5 December 1768; resigned 8 October 1776.
Richard Woodward (junior)	Appointed 8 October 1776; died November 1777.

(*?)Samuel Murphy	Re-appointed 29 November 1777; died November(?) 1780.
*Langrishe Doyle	Appointed 14 November 1780; resigned 18 December 1797 but looked after the boys for a further six months.
*John Clarke	Appointed 18 December 1797 (but see above); resigned (in his absence) 26 December 1798.
*John Spray	Appointed 31 December 1798; resigned 21 June 1800.
*Charles Osborne	Appointed (initially on a temporary basis), 27 June 1800; resigned 6 April 1807 (not to be confused with his namesake (his son?) who was writing master to the boys, 1821–33).
Robert Tuke	Appointed April 1807; resigned November 1809 (not to be confused with the choirboy/stipendiary of the same name, d.1797). After 1807 the boys' subsistence was entrusted separately to James Hewitt (junior).
John Elliot	Appointed November 1809; resigned December 1814 because of his wife's ill health.
William Hamerton	Appointed December 1814; sacked in February 1830 having 'absented himself so many months longer than his leave of absence as granted by the dean and chapter'.
Richard Beatty	Appointed February 1830, having already discharged Hamerton's duties during the latter's absence; resigned February 1873, by which time he must have been in his seventies (he had concluded his apprenticeship as a choirboy in 1814–15 when he would have been in his early to mid teens).
John Horan	Appointed 'music master' (and assistant organist) April 1873; remained as music master following his appointment as organist in 1894; duties assumed by James Fitzgerald in 1905.
James Fitzgerald	Appointed joint organist (with John Horan) and master of the boys in January 1905; resigned 28 March 1913.
Charles Kitson	Appointed 23 May 1913 to position now designated as 'organist and choirmaster, and instructor of the choristers in music'; thereafter the position of choir master (and music master up until the closure of the choir school in 1973) have been combined with that of organist (see Organists in appendix one).

Abbreviations and Bibliography

Abbreviations

Library sigla

D-W	Wolfenbüttel, Herzog August Bibliothek
GB-Ccc	Cambridge, Corpus Christi College library
GB-Cu	Cambridge, University Library
GB-DRc	Durham, Dean and Chapter library
GB-GLr	Gloucester, Record Office
GB-Lbl	London, British Library
GB-Ob	Oxford, Bodelian library
GB-PB	Peterborough, Dean and Chapter library
GB-WRch	Windsor, St George's Chapel library
IRL-CAb	Cashel, Bolton (Diocesan) library
IRL-Da	Dublin, Royal Irish Academy
IRL-Dtc	Dublin, Trinity College library
IRL-Dm	Dublin, Marsh's library
US-NYp	New York, Public Library

Other abbreviations

BCMIC	*The Blackwell Companion to Modern Irish Culture*, ed. W.J. McCormack (Oxford, 1999)
BIOS	*Journal of the British Institute of Organ Studies*
EECM	Early English Church Music
EM	*Early Music*
HCCDD	A History of Christ Church, Dublin: Documents
IMS	Irish Musical Studies
JRMA	*Journal of the Royal Musical Association*
JRSAI	*Journal of the Royal Society of Antiquaries of Ireland*
LR	*Long Room*
MB	Musica Britannica
MD	*Musica Disciplina*
ML	*Music and Letters*
NCBMS	*Nineteenth-Century British Music Studies*
NG2	*The New Grove Dictionary of Music and Musicians*, 2nd ed., ed. Stanley Sadie, 29 vols (London, 2001)
NHI	*A New History of Ireland*, ed. T.W. Moody, F.X. Martin, F.J. Byrne *et al.*, 9 vols (Oxford, 1976–)
NMI	National Museum of Ireland
NUI	National University of Ireland
OCIH	*The Oxford Companion to Irish History*, 2nd ed., ed. S.J. Connolly (Oxford, 2002)

PRIA   *Proceedings of the Royal Irish Academy*
PRONI   Public Record Office of Northern Ireland
RMA   Royal Musical Association
RN   *Reportorium Novum*
TCD   Trinity College Dublin
UCD   University College Dublin

Bibliography

Anthems to be Sung at the Celebration of Divine Service in the Cathedrall Church of the Holy and Undivided Trinity in Dublin ([Dublin], 1662).

Aylmer, Gerald and Tiller, John, eds, *Hereford Cathedral, A History* (London, 2000).

Baldwin, Elizabeth, *Paying the Piper: Music in Pre-1642 Cheshire* (Kalamazoo, 2002).

Ball, F. Elrington, 'Extracts from the Journal of Thomas Dineley, or Dingley Esquire, Giving some Account of his Visit to Ireland in the Reign of Charles II', *JRSAI* Part 4, xliii (1913), pp. 275–309.

Barnard, John, *The First Book of Selected Church Musick* (London, 1641).

Barnard, Toby, 'Church of Ireland 1660–1760', *BCMIC*, pp. 112–13.

Barrett, Philip, *Barchester: English Cathedral Life in the Nineteenth Century* (London, 1993).

Bent, Margaret, 'Rota Versitilis: Towards a Reconstruction', *Source Materials and the Interpretation of Music. A Memorial Volume to Thurston Dart*, ed. Ian Bent (London, 1981), pp. 65–98.

Bernard, J.H., ed., *The Registers of Baptisms, Marriages and Burials in the Collegiate and Cathedral Church of St Patrick, Dublin, 1677–1800* (Dublin, 1907).

Berry, H.F., ed., *Register of Wills and Inventories of the Diocese of Dublin 1457–1483* (Dublin, 1898).

Berry, Mary, 'Augustinian Canons', *NG2* ii, pp. 174–5.

Berry, Mary and Gellnick, Franklyn, 'Cistercian Monks', *NG2* v, pp. 869–70.

Blezzard, Judith, *Borrowings in English Church Music 1550–1950* (London, 1990).

Bliss, A.J., 'The Inscribed Slates at Smarmore', *PRIA* 64 (1965), pp. 33–60.

Bowers, Roger, 'The Almonry Schools of the English Monasteries, c.1265–1540', *Monasteries and Society in Medieval Britain. Proceedings of the 1994 Harlaxton Symposium*, ed. Benjamin Thompson (Stamford, 1999), pp. 177–222.

———, 'Canterbury Cathedral: The Liturgy of the Cathedral and its Music, c.1075–1642', *A History of Canterbury Cathedral*, ed. P. Collinson, N. Ramsey and M. Sparks (Oxford, 1995), pp. 408–50. Repr. in Bowers, *English Church Polyphony*.

———, *English Church Polyphony. Singers and Sources from the 14th to the 17th Century* (Aldershot, 1999).

———, 'The Musicians of the Lady Chapel of Winchester Cathedral Priory, 1402–1539', *Journal of Ecclesiastical History* xlv (April 1994), pp. 210–37. Repr. in Bowers, *English Church Polyphony*.

———, 'Obligation, Agency, and *Laissez-faire*: The Promotion of Polyphonic Composition for the Church in Fifteenth-Century England', *Music in Medieval and Early Modern Europe*, ed. I.A. Fenlon (Cambridge, 1981), pp. 1–19. Repr. in Bowers, *English Church Polyphony*.

———, 'The Performing Ensemble for English Church Polyphony, c.1320–c.1390', *Studies in the Performance of Late Medieval Music*, ed. Stanley Boorman (Cambridge, 1983), pp. 161–92. Repr. in Bowers, *English Church Polyphony*.

———, 'To Chorus from Quartet: The Performing Resource for English Church

Polyphony, c.1390–1559', *English Choral Practice, 1400–1650*, ed. John Morehen (Cambridge, 1995), pp. 1–47. Repr. in Bowers, *English Church Polyphony*.

———, 'The Vocal Scoring, Choral Balance and Performing Pitch of Latin Church Polyphony in England, c.1500–58', *JRMA* cxii (1987), pp. 38–76. Repr. in Bowers, *English Church Polyphony*.

Boydell, Barra, 'The Archives of Christ Church, Dublin, as a Source for the History of Music in Ireland', *Irish Archives* v/2 (1998), pp. 12–18.

———, ' "A Bright Exception to the General Rule"? Musical Standards at Christ Church Cathedral Dublin in the Early Nineteenth Century', *NCBMS ii*, ed. Jeremy Dibble and Bennett Zon (Aldershot, 2002), pp. 46–58.

———, 'Cathedral Music, City and State: Music in Reformation and Political Change at Christ Church Cathedral, Dublin', *Music and Musicians in Renaissance Cities and Towns*, ed. Fiona Kisby (Cambridge, 2001), pp. 131–42.

———, 'The Development of the Dublin Music Print Trade to 1800', *LR* xli (1996), pp. 25–33.

———, 'John Baptiste Cuvillie, Ferdinand Weber, and the Organ of Trinity College Chapel, Dublin', *The Organ* lxxii no. 283 (1992), pp. 15–26.

———, 'Manuscript Sources from Irish Cathedrals: the Cashel Cathedral Choir-Books, a Preliminary report', *Brio* xxxix/2 (Autumn/Winter 2002), pp. 21–31.

———, ed., *Music at Christ Church before 1800: Documents and Selected Anthems*, HCCDD V (Dublin, 1999).

———, *Music in Christ Church Cathedral from the Late Fifteenth Century to 1647* (Dublin, [1997]).

———, 'Music in the Medieval Cathedral Priory', 'The Establishment of the Choral Tradition, 1480–1647', 'The Flourishing of Music, 1660–1800', 'Music in the Nineteenth-Century Cathedral, 1800–1870', 'Optimism and Decline: Music, 1870–c.1970', *Christ Church Cathedral Dublin: A History*, ed. Kenneth Milne (Dublin, 2000), chs 7, 12, 14, 16, 18.

———, ' "Now that the Lord hath Readvanc'd the Crown": Richard Hosier, Durham MS B.1 and the Early Restoration Anthem Repertoire at the Dublin Cathedrals', *EM* xxviii (2000), pp. 238–51.

———, 'Prickers and Printers: The Copying and Purchase of Music at Christ Church Cathedral, Dublin, in the 17th and 18th Centuries', *LR* xliii (1998), pp. 20–28.

———, 'St Michan's Church, Dublin: The Installation of the Organ in 1725 and the Duties of the Organist', *BIOS* xix (1995), pp. 74–97.

——— and Klein, Axel, 'Carter', *Die Musik in Geschichte und Gegenwart: Personenteil* IV, ed. Ludwig Finscher, rev. ed. (Kassel, 2000), cc. 1175–8.

Boydell, Brian, *A Dublin Musical Calendar 1700–1760* (Blackrock, 1988).

———, 'Music up to 1850', *A New History of Ireland IV: Eighteenth-Century Ireland, 1691–1800*, ed. T.W. Moody and W.E. Vaughan (Oxford, 1986), pp. 542–628.

———, 'Organs Associated with Handel's Visit to Dublin', *BIOS* xix (1995), pp. 54–72.

———, *Rotunda Music in Eighteenth Century Dublin* (Blackrock, 1992).

———, 'Thomas Bateson and the Earliest Degrees in Music Awarded by the University of Dublin', *Hermathena* cxlvi (1989), pp. 53–60.

Boyse, Joseph, *Remarks on a Late Discourse Concerning the Inventions of Men in the Worship of God* (Dublin, 1694).

Brannon, Patrick, 'Medieval Ireland: Music in Cathedral, Church and Cloister', *EM* xxviii (2000), pp. 193–202.

———, 'The Search for the Celtic Rite: The TCD Sarum Divine Office MSS Reassessed', *Music and the Church*, IMS II, ed. Gerard Gillen and Harry White (Blackrock, 1993), pp. 13–40.

Bridge, Joseph C., 'The Organists of Chester Cathedral. Parts 1 & 2', *Journal of the Architectural, Archaeological and Historic Society for the County and the City of Chester, and North Wales, New Series* xix/2 (1913), pp. 63–124.

Brown, David, 'Bateson, Thomas', *NG2* ii, pp. 903–4.

Buckley, Ann, 'Celtic Chant', *NG2* v, pp. 341–9.

———, 'Music and Musicians in Medieval Irish Society', *EM* xxviii (2000), pp. 165–90.

———, 'Music-Related Imagery on Early Christian Insular Sculpture: Identification, Context, Function', *Imago Musicae/International Yearbook of Musical Iconography* viii (1991), pp. 135–99.

Bumpus, John S., *A History of English Cathedral Music, 1549–1889*, 2 vols (London, 1908; repr. Farnborough, 1972).

———, 'Irish Church Composers and the Irish Cathedrals', *Proceedings of the Musical Association*, twenty-sixth session (1899–1900), pp. 79–159.

———, *Sir John Stevenson: A Biographical Sketch* (London, 1893).

Burrows, Donald, 'Handel's Dublin Performances', *The Maynooth International Musicological Conference 1995. Selected Proceedings: Part One*, IMS IV, ed. Patrick Devine and Harry White (Blackrock, 1996), pp. 46–70.

———, *Handel: Messiah*, Cambridge Music Handbooks (Cambridge, 1991).

Caldwell, John, *The Oxford History of English Music, i: From the Beginnings to c.1715* (Oxford, 1991).

Calendar of the Christ Church Deeds, 20th, 23rd, 24th, and 27th Reports of the Deputy Keeper of the Public Records, Ireland (Dublin, 1888, 1891, 1892, 1895).

Calendar of the State Papers Relating to Ireland, of the Reign of Elizabeth, 1600, March–October (London, 1903).

Cathedral Anthems Published for the Cathedrals of Christ Church and S. Patrick, Dublin (London, 1880; [second impression], 1881).

Cathedral Anthems (new edition, Dublin, 1895).

Clark, J. Bunker, 'Adrian Batten and John Barnard: Colleagues and Collaborators', *MD* xxii (1968), pp. 207–99.

Clark, Mary and Refaussé, Raymond, eds, *Directory of the Historic Dublin Guilds* (Dublin, 1993).

Clarke, Howard, ed., *Dublin. Part 1, to 1610*. Irish Historic Towns Atlas XI (Dublin, 2002).

———, ed., *Medieval Dublin: the Making of a Metropolis* (Dublin, 1990).

Clifford, James, *The Divine Services and Anthems* (London, 1663; 2nd ed. 1664).

Clutton, Cecil and Niland, Austin, *The British Organ* (London, 1963; repr. Wakefield, 1976).

Collins, Derek, 'Music in Dublin, 1800–1848', *To Talent Alone: The Royal Irish Academy of Music 1848–1998*, ed. Richard Pine and Charles Acton (Dublin, 1998), pp. 12–27.

Collinson, P., Ramsey, N., and Sparks, M., eds, *A History of Canterbury Cathedral* (Oxford, 1995).

Connolly, Sean, 'Catholics and Catholicism', *BCMIC*, p. 100.

Cotton, Henry, *Fasti Ecclesiae Hibernicae*, 6 vols (Dublin, 1848–78).

Cressy, D., *Bonfires and Bells: National Memory and the Protestant Calendar in Elizabethan and Stuart England* (Cambridge, 1989).

Croker, Richard L., Caldwell, John and Planchart, Alejandro E., 'Sequence', *NG2* xxiii, pp. 91–107.

Crosby, Brian, *A Catalogue of Durham Cathedral Music Manuscripts* (Durham, 1986).

———, 'An Early Restoration Liturgical Music Manuscript', *ML* lv (1974), pp. 458–464.

———, 'The Musical Scene at Durham Cathedral', *NCBMS* ii, ed. Jeremy Dibble and Bennett Zon (Aldershot, 2002), pp. 70–9.

Culwick, James C., *Sir Robert Stewart, with Reminiscences of his Life and Works* (Dublin, 1900).

———, *The Works of Sir Robert Stewart* (Dublin, 1902).

Cunningham, Carol, 'Selected Eighteenth Century Anthems by Composers at Christ Church Cathedral Dublin' (unpubl. MA thesis, NUI Maynooth, 1997).

Daniel, Ralph and Le Huray, Peter, *The Sources of English Church Music, 1549–1660*, EECM, Suppl. 1, 2 vols (London, 1976).

Dearnley, Christopher, *English Church Music 1650–1750 in Royal Chapel, Cathedral and Parish Church* (London, 1970).

Dennison, Peter, *Pelham Humfrey* (Oxford, 1986).

Dobson, E.J. and Harrison, F.Ll., *Medieval English Songs* (London, 1979).

Donnelly, Eithne, 'Richard Woodward: A Study of his Life and Music' (unpubl. MA thesis, NUI Maynooth, 1998).

Doran, Caitriona, 'The Robinsons: a Nineteenth-Century Dublin Family of Musicians, and their Contribution Towards the Musical Life in Dublin' (unpubl. MA thesis, NUI Maynooth, 1998).

Egan-Buffet, Maire, and Fletcher, Alan J., 'The Dublin *Visitatio Sepulcri* Play', *PRIA* 90 (1990), pp. 159–241.

Erck, John, *An Account of the Ecclesiastical Establishment Subsisting in Ireland, as also an Ecclesiastical Register . . .* (Dublin, 1830).

Fassler, Margot E., 'Adam of St Victor', *NG2* i, pp. 142–3.

Fellowes, Edmund H., *English Cathedral Music from Edward VI to Edward VII* (London, 1941; 5th ed. rev. Westrup, London, 1969).

———, *The English Madrigal Composers* (Oxford, 1921).

Fenlon, Iain, *Cambridge Music Manuscripts 900–1700* (Cambridge, 1982).

Finlayson, John, *A Collection of Anthems as Sung in the Cathedral of the Holy Trinity, Commonly Called Christ Church (Her Majesty's Chapel Royal), in the Collegiate and Cathedral Church of St. Patrick, in the Chapel Royal, Dublin Castle, and in the Chapel of Trinity College, Dublin* (Dublin, 1852).

FitzGibbon, Gerald, ' "College Choral", 1837–1987', *Hermathena* cxliv (Summer 1988), pp. 35–68.

Fletcher, Alan J., *Drama, Performance and Polity in Pre-Cromwellian Ireland* (Cork and Toronto, 2000).

———, 'Liturgy in the Late Medieval Cathedral Priory', *Christ Church Cathedral Dublin: A History*, ed. Kenneth Milne (Dublin, 2000), pp. 129–41.

Flood, W.H. Grattan, 'Irish Organ-Builders from the Eighth to the Close of the Eighteenth Century', *JRSAI* xl (1910), pp. 229–34.

———, 'The Organs of Christ Church Cathedral, Dublin' [newspaper cutting, n. d., source not known].

Flynn, Jane, 'The Education of Choristers in England during the Sixteenth Century', *English Choral Practice, 1400–1650* ed. John Morehen (Cambridge, 1995), pp. 180–99.

Ford, Alan, *The Protestant Reformation in Ireland 1590–1640*, 2nd ed. (Dublin, 1997).

Gatens, William J., *Victorian Cathedral Music in Theory and Practice* (Cambridge, 1986).

Gifford, Gerald and Platt, Richard, 'Roseingrave: (2) Thomas Roseingrave' *NG2* xxi, pp. 687–90.

Gilbert, J.T., *Facsimiles of National MSS of Ireland* iv (Dublin, 1882).

Gillen, Gerard and Johnstone, Andrew, *A Historical Anthology of Irish Church Music*, IMS VI (Dublin, 2001).

Gillespie, Raymond, 'The Archives of Christ Church Cathedral, Dublin', *Irish Archives* v/2 (1998), pp. 3–12.

——, 'Borrowing Books from Christ Church Cathedral, Dublin, 1607', *LR* xliii (1998), pp. 15–19.

——, 'The Coming of Reform, 1500–58', *Christ Church Cathedral Dublin: A History*, ed. Kenneth Milne (Dublin, 2000), pp. 151–73.

——, 'The Crisis of Reform, 1625–60', *Christ Church Cathedral Dublin: A History*, ed. Kenneth Milne (Dublin, 2000), pp. 195–217.

——, ed., *The First Chapter Act Book of Christ Church Cathedral, Dublin, 1574–1634*, HCCDD III (Dublin, 1997).

——, ed., *The Proctor's Accounts of Peter Lewis 1564–1565*, HCCDD I (Dublin, 1996).

——, 'The Shaping of Reform, 1558–1625', *Christ Church Cathedral Dublin: A History*, ed. Kenneth Milne (Dublin, 2000), pp. 174–94.

Grindle, H.W., *Irish Cathedral Music: A History of Music at the Cathedrals of the Church of Ireland* (Belfast, 1989).

Gushee, Marion S., 'The Polyphonic Music of the Medieval Monastery, Cathedral and University', *Music and Society: Antiquity and the Middle Ages*, ed. James McKinnon (London, 1990), pp. 143–69.

Gwynn, Aubrey, 'The First Bishops of Dublin', *RN* i (1955–6), pp. 1–26. Repr. in *Medieval Dublin: the Living City*, ed. Howard Clarke (Blackrock, 1990), pp. 37–61.

—— and Hadcock, R. Neville, *Medieval Religious Houses: Ireland* (Blackrock, 1970; repr. 1988).

Hand, Geoffrey J., 'Cambridge University Additional MS 710', *RN* ii (1957–60), pp. 17–23.

——, 'The Medieval Chapter of St Patrick's Cathedral, Dublin: The Early Period (c.1219–c.1270)', *RN* iii (1963–4), pp. 229–48.

—— 'The Psalter of Christ Church, Dublin (Bodleian MS Rawlinson G. 185)', *RN* i (1956), pp. 311–22.

——, 'Rivalry of the Cathedral Chapters in Medieval Dublin', *JRSAI* xcii (1962), pp. 193–206; repr. in *Medieval Dublin: the Living City*, ed. Howard Clarke (Blackrock, 1990), pp. 100–111.

—— 'The Two Cathedrals of Dublin: Internal Organisation and Mutual Relations, to the Middle of the Fourteenth Century' (unpubl. MA thesis, NUI, 1954).

Harper, John, 'The British Church Organ and the Liturgy: A Historical Review 1480–1680', *The Organ Yearbook* xxviii (1998/9), pp. 91–8.

——, *The Forms and Orders of Western Liturgy from the Tenth to the Eighteenth Century* (Oxford, 1991).

—— and le Huray, Peter, 'Anthem §I: England', *NG2* i, pp. 719–26, 728.

Harrison, Frank Ll., *Music in Medieval Britain*, 4th ed. (Buren, 1980).

——, 'Polyphony in Medieval Ireland', *Festschrift Bruno Stäblein zum siebzigsten Geburtstag*, ed. M. Ruhnke (Kassel, 1967), pp. 74–8.

—— and Wibberly, R. eds, *Manuscripts of Fourteenth Century English Polyphony*, EECM 26 (London, 1981).

Hawkes, W., 'The Liturgy in Dublin 1200–1500: Manuscript Sources', *RN* ii (1958), pp. 33–67.

Hemmens, Sue, 'Christ Church Dublin Music: Title Index, Composer Index', 2 vols (typescript, Representative Church Body library, Dublin).

Henry, F. and Marsh-Micheli, G.L., 'A Century of Irish Illumination (1070–1170)', *PRIA* 62 (1962), pp. 101–64.

Hesbert, Dom R.J., ed., *Le Tropaire-Prosaire de Dublin* (Rouen, 1966).

Hickman, E. Peter, *A History of the Renatus Harris Organ in St John's Church Wolverhampton* (rev. ed., [Wolverhampton: St John's Church], 2003).

Hoeg, Michael E., *The Music of St Columb's Cathedral, Londonderry* (Londonderry, 1979).

Hogan, Ita, *Anglo-Irish Music 1780–1830* (Cork, 1966).

Holman, Peter, 'Bartholomew Isaack and "Mr Isaack" of Eton', *The Musical Times* cxxviii (1987), pp. 381–5.

———, *Four and Twenty Fiddlers: The Violin at the English Court 1540–1690* (Oxford, 1993).

———, 'Rogers, Benjamin', *NG2* xxi, pp. 517–18.

———, 'Tollett, Thomas', *NG2* xxv, pp. 553–4.

Houston, Kerry, 'The Eighteenth-Century Music Manuscripts at Saint Patrick's Cathedral, Dublin: Sources, Lineage, and Relationship to Other Collections' (unpubl. PhD thesis, TCD, 2002).

Humfrey, Pelham, *Complete Church Music*, ii, ed. Peter Dennison, MB 25, 2nd ed. (London, 1985).

Jebb, John, *The Choral Service of the United Church of England and Ireland* (London, 1843).

———, *A Few Observations Respecting Christ Church Cathedral and its Precinct* (Dublin, 1855).

———, *Three Lectures on the Cathedral Service*, 2nd ed. (Leeds and London, 1845).

Jefferies, H.A., 'The Irish Parliament of 1560: The Anglican Reforms Authorised', *Irish Historical Studies* xxvi (1988), pp. 128–41.

Jellett, Revd Morgan, *A Collection of Anthems Sung in His Majesty's Chapels Royal, and in the Cathedral Churches of England and Ireland* (Dublin, 1821).

Johnston, Roy, *Bunting's 'Messiah'* (Belfast, 2003).

Johnstone, Andrew, 'Incongruous Organ Music in an Irish Cathedral', *Music and the Church*, ed. Gerard Gillen and Harry White, IMS 2 (Blackrock, 1993), pp. 149–63.

Kinsella, Stuart, ed., *Augustinians at Christ Church: The Canons Regular of the Cathedral Priory of Holy Trinity, Dublin* (Dublin, 2000).

———, 'From Hiberno-Norse to Anglo-Norman, c.1030–1300', *Christ Church Cathedral: A History*, ed. Kenneth Milne (Dublin, 2000), pp. 25–52.

Knight, David, 'Nineteenth-Century Repertoire and Performance Practice at Westminster Abbey', *NCBMS* ii, ed. Jeremy Dibble and Bennett Zon (Aldershot, 2002), pp. 80–98.

Lawlor, Hugh Jackson, 'A Calendar of the Liber Niger and Liber Albus of Christ Church, Dublin', *PRIA* 27 (1908), pp. 1–93.

———, *The Fasti of St. Patrick's, Dublin* (Dundalk, 1930).

le Huray, Peter, 'Jewett, Randolph', *NG2* xiii, pp. 23–4.

———, 'Towards a Definitive Study of Pre-Restoration Anglican Service Music', *MD* xiv (1960), pp. 167–95.

——— and Morehen, John, 'Holmes, John', *NG2* xi, pp. 644–5.

Lefferts, Peter M., 'Medieval England, 950–1450', *Music and Society: Antiquity and the Middle Ages*, ed. James McKinnon (London, 1990), pp. 170–96.

Lehmberg, Stanford E., *The Reformation of Cathedrals* (Princeton, 1988).

Lennon, Colm, 'The Chantries in the Irish Reformation: The Case of St Anne's Guild, Dublin, 1550–1630', *Religion, Conflict and Coexistence in Ireland. Essays Presented to Mgr Patrick J. Corish*, ed. R.V. Comerford, M. Cullen, J.R. Hill and C. Lennon (Dublin, 1990), pp. 6–25.

———, *The Lords of Dublin in the Age of Reformation* (Dublin, 1989).

———, 'The Survival of the Confraternities in Post-Reformation Dublin', *Confraternitas* vi (1995), pp. 5–12.

Leslie, Canon J.B., *Clergy of Dublin and Glendalough: Biographical Succession Lists*, rev. ed. W.J.R. Wallace (Ulster Historical Foundation and Diocesan Councils of Dublin and Glendalough, 2001).

Lewis, Anthony, 'English Church Music', *Opera and Church Music 1630–1750*, ed. Anthony Lewis and Nigel Fortune, New Oxford History of Music V, rev. ed. (Oxford, 1986), pp. 493–556.

Little, Patrick, 'Discord in Drogheda: A Window on Irish Church-State Relations in the 1640s', *Historical Research* lxxv (2002), pp. 355–62.

Llanover, Lady, ed., *Autobiography and Correspondence of Mary Granville, Mrs Delaney*, 5 vols (London, 1861–2).

Lydon, James, 'Christ Church in the Later Medieval Irish World, 1300–1500', *Christ Church Cathedral: A History*, ed. Kenneth Milne (Dublin, 2000), pp. 75–94.

Malcomson, A.P.W., *Archbishop Charles Agar. Churchmanship and Politics in Ireland, 1760–1810* (Dublin, 2002).

Martin, F.X., 'The Crowning of a King at Dublin, 24 May 1487', *Hermathena* cxliv (1988), pp. 7–34.

Mason, William Monck, *The History and Antiquities of the Collegiate and Cathedral Church of St. Patrick, near Dublin, from its Foundation in 1190, to the Year 1819* (Dublin, 1820).

McCartney, Alistair G., *The Organs and Organists of the Cathedral Church of St Patrick, Armagh, 1482–1998* (Armagh, 1999).

McCurtain, M., *Tudor and Stuart Ireland* (Dublin, 1972).

McEnery, M.J. and Refaussé, Raymond, *Christ Church Deeds*, HCCDD VIII (Dublin, 2001).

McHugh, Barbara, 'Music in St Patrick's Cathedral, Dublin 1865–1915' (unpubl. MA thesis, UCD, 1980).

McKee, Joseph, 'The Choral Foundation of Armagh Cathedral 1600–1870' (unpubl. MA thesis, Queen's University, Belfast, 1982).

Meech, S.B., 'Three Musical Treatises in English in a Fifteenth-Century Manuscript', *Speculum* x (1935), pp. 242–58.

Mills, David, 'Music in the City', in Elizabeth Baldwin, *Paying the Piper: Music in Pre-1642 Cheshire* (Kalamazoo, 2002), pp. 54–78.

Mills, James, ed., *Account Roll of the Priory of the Holy Trinity, Dublin 1337–1346*, repr. introduced by James Lydon and Alan J. Fletcher, HCCDD II (Dublin, 1996).

Milne, Kenneth, ed., *Christ Church Cathedral: A History* (Dublin, 2000).

——, 'Restoration and Reorganisation, 1660–1830', *Christ Church Cathedral: A History*, ed. Kenneth Milne (Dublin, 2000), pp. 255–97.

——, 'The Stripping of the Assets, 1830–1960', *Christ Church Cathedral: A History*, ed. Kenneth Milne (Dublin, 2000), pp. 315–38.

Moran, Andrea, 'Three Eighteenth Century Anthems from Christ Church Cathedral, Dublin' (unpubl. MA thesis, UCD, 1994).

Morash, Christopher, *A History of Irish Theatre, 1601–2000* (Cambridge, 2002).

Morehen, John, ed., *English Choral Practice, 1400–1650* (Cambridge, 1995).

——, 'Fido, John', *NG2* viii, p. 776.

Neal, John and William, *A Collection of the Most Celebrated Irish Tunes . . . Dublin 1724*, ed. Nicholas Carolan (Dublin, 1986).

Neary, Denise, 'Music in Late Seventeenth- and Eighteenth Century Dublin Churches' (unpubl. MA thesis, St Patrick's College, Maynooth, 1995).

——, 'Music in Late Seventeenth- and Eighteenth-Century Dublin Churches', *The Maynooth International Musicological Conference 1995. Selected Proceedings: Part One*, IMS IV, ed. Patrick Devine and Harry White (Blackrock, 1996), pp. 103–10.

————, 'Cuvillie', *NG2* vi, p. 793.

Nestor, Emer, 'Post-Restoration Attitudes to the Place of Music in Protestant Worship in Late Seventeenth-Century Ireland' (unpubl. MA thesis, NUI Maynooth, 2001).

Nicholson, E.W.B., *Introduction to the Study of Some of the Oldest Latin Musical Manuscripts in the Bodleian Library, Oxford. Early Bodleian Music*, iii (London, 1913).

O'Keeffe, Eamonn, 'The Score-Books of Christ Church Cathedral Dublin. A Catalogue', *Fontes Artis Musicae* xliv/1 (1997), pp. 43–104.

————, 'Sources of Church Music in Ireland in the 18th Century', *The Maynooth International Musicological Conference 1995. Selected Proceedings: Part One*, IMS IV, ed. Patrick Devine and Harry White (Blackrock, 1996), pp. 111–18.

————, 'The Study of Irish Musical Sources: The Case of Christ Church Cathedral' (unpubl. MA thesis, UCD, 1993).

Owen, Dorothy, ed., *A History of Lincoln Minster* (Cambridge, 1994).

Pächt, Otto, 'A Giottoesque Episode in English Medieval Art', *Journal of the Warburg and Courtauld Institutes* vi (1943), pp. 51–71.

Page, Christopher, 'An English Motet of the 14th Century in Performance: Two Contemporary Images', *EM* xxv (1997), pp. 7–34.

Parker, Lisa, 'Robert Prescott Stewart (1825–1894): an Assessment of his Compositions and Contribution to Musical Life in Dublin' (unpubl. MA thesis, NUI Maynooth, 2000).

Payne, Iain, *The Provision and Practice of Sacred Music at Cambridge Colleges and Selected Cathedrals, c.1547–c.1646* (New York and London, 1993).

Plummer, Charles, ed., 'Vie et Miracles de S. Laurent, Archévêque de Dublin', *Analecta Bollandiana* xxxiii (1914), pp. 137–8.

Pollard, M., *A Dictionary of Members of the Dublin Book Trade 1550–1800* (London, 2000).

Preston, Sarah, 'The Canons Regular of St Augustine: The Twelfth-Century Reform in Action', *Augustinians at Christ Church*, ed. Stuart Kinsella (Dublin, 2000), pp. 23–40.

Rainbow, Bernarr, *The Choral Revival in the Anglican Church* (London, 1970).

Refaussé, Raymond and Lennon, Colm, eds, *The Registers of Christ Church Cathedral, Dublin*, HCCDD IV (Dublin, 1998).

Robinson-Hammerstein, Helga, 'With Great Solemnity: Celebrating the First Centenary of the Foundation of Trinity College, Dublin, 9 January 1694', *LR* xxxvii (1992), pp. 27–38.

Sayce, Linda, 'Continuo Lutes in 17th and 18th Century England', *EM* xxiii (1995), pp. 666–84.

Seymour, Edward, *The Cathedral System* (Dublin, 1870).

————, *The Choral Services of Christ Church Cathedral Dublin and their Efficiency, during the First Two Years after the Restoration of the Cathedral from its Re-Opening on the 1st of May, 1878* (Dublin, 1880).

————, *Christ Church Cathedral, Dublin* (Dublin, 1869).

Shaw, Watkins, *The Succession of Organists of the Chapel Royal and the Cathedrals of England and Wales from c.1538* (Oxford, 1991).

Sherwin, Elaine, 'An Edition of Selected Anthems by Sir John Stevenson, with Critical Commentary' (unpubl. MA thesis, NUI Maynooth, 2000).

Sing O Ye Heavens. Historic Anthems from Christ Church Cathedral, ed. Barra Boydell, HCCDD VI (CD recording, CCCD 001, 1999).

Smart, Henry, *Report to the Dean and Chapter of Christ Church Cathedral, Dublin, on the Organ of the Cathedral Church* (Dublin, 1878).

Spink, Ian, *Restoration Cathedral Music 1660–1714* (Oxford, 1995).

Stalley, Roger, 'The Architecture of the Cathedral and Priory Buildings, 1250–1530', *Christ Church Cathedral: A History*, ed. Kenneth Milne (Dublin, 2000), pp. 95–128.

———, 'The Construction of the Medieval Cathedral, c.1030–1250', *Christ Church Cathedral: A History*, ed. Kenneth Milne (Dublin, 2000), pp. 53–74.

———, 'George Edmund Street and the Restoration of the Cathedral, 1868–78', *Christ Church Cathedral: A History*, ed. Kenneth Milne (Dublin, 2000), pp. 353–73.

———, ed., *George Edmund Street and the Restoration of Christ Church Cathedral, Dublin*, HCCDD VII (Dublin, 2000).

———, 'The Medieval Sculpture of Christ Church Cathedral, Dublin', *Archaeologia* cvi (1979), pp. 107–22. Repr. with minor revisions, *Medieval Dublin: The Making of a Metropolis*, ed. Howard Clarke (Blackrock, 1990), pp. 202–26.

Stanford, Charles Villiers, *Pages from an Unwritten Diary* (London, 1914).

State Papers. King Henry the Eighth, 11 vols (London, 1830–52), vol. ii, part iii: *Correspondence between the Governments of England and Ireland, 1515–1538*.

Stuckburgh, E.S., ed., *Two Biographies of William Bedell, Bishop of Kilmore* (Cambridge, 1902).

Temperley, Nicholas, 'Music in Church', *The Eighteenth Century*, ed. H. Diack Johnstone and Roger Fiske, The Blackwell History of Music in Britain IV (Oxford, 1990), pp. 357–96.

Thompson, Robert, 'Manuscript Music in Purcell's London', *EM* xxiii (1995), pp. 605–18.

Vignoles, Olinthus J., *Memoir of Sir Robert P. Stewart* (London and Dublin, [1899]).

Walsh, T.J., *Opera in Dublin, 1705–1797. The Social Scene* (Dublin, 1973).

———, *Opera in Dublin, 1798–1820* (Oxford, 1993).

Warburton, J., Whitelaw, Revd J., and Walsh, Revd Robert, *History of the City of Dublin*, 2 vols (London, 1818).

Ware, Robert, *The Hunting of the Romish Fox and the Quenching of Sectarian Fire-Brands* (Dublin, 1683).

Weber, William, *The Rise of Musical Classics in Eighteenth-Century England: A Study in Canon, Ritual, and Ideology* (Oxford, 1992).

Wetenhall, Edward, *Of Gifts and Offices in the Publick Worship of God*, 2nd ed. (Dublin, 1678).

Whiteside, Lesley, *The Chapel of Trinity College Dublin* (Dublin, 1998).

Young, Percy M., *Lichfield Cathedral Library. A Catalogue of Music. Vol. 1: Manuscripts* (Birmingham, 1993).

Index

Page numbers in *italics* refer to musical examples; page numbers in **bold** refer to plates.